Everything you Need for an NVQ in Management

2nd edition

Julie Lewthwaite

ЈOOD

Published by Thorogood Publishing Ltd
10-12 Rivington Street
London EC2A 3DU
Telephone: 020 7749 4748
Fax: 020 7729 6110
Email: info@thorogoodpublishing.co.uk
Web: www.thorogoodpublishing.co.uk

A CIP catalogue record for this book is
available from the British Library.

ISBN 1 85418 704 X
     978 185418704 8

Designed and typeset by Driftdesign

Printed in the UK by Ashford Colour Press Ltd

Acknowledgements

Whilst anything that is unclear, ambiguous or incorrect is my sole responsibility, I owe a debt of thanks to a number of people for their help in ensuring that this book was completed.

First and foremost a huge thank you to Steven Miscandlon for invaluable research assistance, insightful suggestions, eagle-eyed proofreading skills and boundless encouragement, for all of which this is a much better book.

My sincere appreciation also goes to Angela Spall and the team at Thorogood for their continuing hard work and support.

I gratefully acknowledge the permission granted to reproduce the copyright material in this book.

I have made every effort to contact copyright holders and to obtain their permission for the use of copyright material. Should any have been inadvertently omitted please accept my most sincere apologies; I would be grateful to be notified of any corrections that should be incorporated in future reprints or editions of this book.

Contents

Part 2
Managing the business 89

Part 3
Managing change   **147**

Part 5

Managing resources 285

Part 6
Managing progress   341

Introduction

Running a profitable business is easy, isn't it? Say you sell widgets: you buy 100 widgets for £1 each then sell them for £2 each. Money for jam!

Except that doesn't take into account how you find manufacturers of widgets and select the one you will buy from, and you need to be sure people are not only still buying widgets, but are buying the type of widget that you are selling. And what about price? Making 100 per cent profit sounds great, doesn't it? Double your money!

Except that doesn't take into account the cost of office and storage space, advertising your widgets so that people know they can buy them from you and at what price, and delivering the widgets to your customers. This all eats into the £1 per widget you stand to make. And what if it should cost more? If all those costs added up come to £1.10 per widget, then for every one you sell, you lose more money.

You'll need people to help you, too: people to answer the telephone, take customer orders, deal with queries, process payments, pay the widget supplier, even clean the windows... and what if those people aren't very good at what they do? What do you do then? You can't just sack them... can you...?

Suddenly it's not quite so easy.

As managers, we need to be able to call upon a range of skills, some that we will use every day and others that we will call upon less frequently. Management theorist Henri Fayol identified five functions of management: planning, organising, commanding, co-ordinating and controlling. Henry Mintzberg identified three main roles, which he termed interpersonal (dealing with people), informational (gathering and disseminating information) and decisional (making decisions).

The work of management theorists and experts provides us with a framework that helps us to understand the function of management and the role of the manager. Once something has been analysed and broken down, it can be understood and learned.

Management training and qualifications

A wide range of management and leadership training and qualifications are available to people within the UK. They range from academic through professional to vocational, although that is in no way an order of relevance or importance. Even group learning and conferences very often result in participants being issued with a certificate.

The Management Standards

In amongst these opportunities for learning and development are three types that relate to the National Occupational Standards for Management and Leadership, as defined by The Management Standards Centre (MSC). (The MSC is the Government recognised standards setting body for the management and leadership areas. Other bodies exist for other areas of development.) These are National Vocational Qualifications (NVQs), Scottish Vocational Qualifications (SVQs) and Vocationally Related Qualifications (VRQs).

The Standards are statements of best practice that describe the activities and functions of management and leadership at various levels. The Standards cover the core functions of management, breaking each down into areas of competence that are then described in detail as units of competence. Units are similarly broken down into the required outcomes, behaviours, knowledge and understanding that must be demonstrated to illustrate mastery.

The Standards cover the following qualifications:

- Level 2 NVQ/SVQ in Team Leading; and,

- Levels 3, 4 and 5 NVQ/SVQ in Management.

Arguably the real strength of the Standards is that they aren't simply a range of statements compiled by people who only know management in theory. Their development is based on extensive consultation with actual managers who are facing, on a daily basis, exactly the same challenges as you face in your job. In other words, they analyse and break down the function of 'management' so that we can understand it and, more importantly, learn how to do it effectively.

Just because your job title may be 'team leader' or 'supervisor', don't think you aren't a manager. Broadly speaking, managers control three things: people, things and tasks. If you control any or all of these things, then you are a manager. Similarly, it makes no difference whether you work in the corporate, not-for-profit or health sector; the role of the manager and the function of management is the same.

If you are interested in NVQ/SVQs in management you can download the full suite of Management Standards and the qualifications structure for all levels from the MSC website (www.management-standards.org).

About the book

Title notwithstanding, it is hard to imagine a single resource that could, in itself, cover absolutely everything you could wish to know about a subject like management. However, what the book does aim to do is to give an introduction to and a broad understanding of a topic and then offer suggestions for places you can go to find more information on any subject that you need or wish to know in more depth. Taken in that context it lives up to its title wholeheartedly.

Throughout the book you will find frameworks to help you to get to grips with different topics. You will be encouraged to take a step-by-step approach, both to build confidence in your ability and to maximise your chances of success. You will also find that the basic approach is always the same: assess what should be done, make a plan, implement and monitor the plan, then review the experience.

We will be looking very much at an ideal world within the pages of this book. Much management theory and writing revolves around what should happen. Let us not forget, however, that managers deal with what does happen, and very often our best intentions to plan, implement, and monitor progress are foiled by things outside of our control. However, just as learning any skill thoroughly and by the book enables you to know what you must do and what you can omit when necessary, so it is with management. That knowledge also gives you a pretty good idea of what the outcome will be when you try something new. Yes, you may find yourself taking a risk, but it will be a calculated risk.

I have, in the layout of the book, kept in mind the structure of the standards as developed by the MSC.

The book	The standards
Section 1: Managing yourself	A: Managing self and personal skills
Section 2: Managing the business	B: Providing direction
Section 3: Managing change	C: Facilitating change
Section 4: Managing people	D: Working with people
Section 5: Managing resources	E: Using resources
Section 6: Managing progress	F: Achieving results

There is inevitably some crossover between sections but as far as is practical I have kept information within these boundaries. You will find at the start of each chapter a list of the units to which the information in it relates along with a list of other chapters that contain complementary information. The appendices also show how the chapters relate to the Standards, and vice versa.

How to use this book

I love books. They are wonderful things to own and to spend time with and some become very dear companions over the years. They can see us through hard times, impart wisdom, make us think and make us laugh. Some books, like this one, are also tools to be used.

A friend of mine recently made me a gift of some books. He apologised for having marked up the text in one of them, which he tells me does habitually. Far from spoiling the book for me, it made the experience of reading it so much richer. I loved seeing the points he had pulled out to emphasise and comparing his reading to mine – I was also impressed by just how neatly he had marked up the pages. (Both that and his handwriting put me to shame!)

With this book, you will very likely not start at the beginning and read all the way through to the end. Whilst you can if that suits your needs best, I think it is more likely that you will dip in to find whatever is useful to you at the time. To support that approach, each chapter has been written, as far as possible, to stand alone. Whichever approach you take, I would encourage you to write notes in the margin, highlight and underline sentences and paragraphs, dog-ear pages – whatever will help you to quickly find the information that is most useful to you when you want it.

Each chapter also contains a case study, exercise or quiz that is intended to provoke thought about the subject matter and to aid the process of review and consolidation of learning. It is, of course, up to you whether you choose to complete any of these; you should do whatever best suits your needs.

Whilst this book is aimed primarily at those who will study for Management NVQ/SVQs at levels 3, 4 and 5, it will also prove useful for anyone starting at level 2 with the team leader qualification. Not only that, but for anyone who wishes to progress having achieved level 2; the book will be a useful companion as they forge ahead in their career.

It should be noted that there is something here also for those people who are managers but who do not wish, for whatever reason, to pursue a qualification. The book can be used as a companion to a formal training course, to support pursuit of an NVQ/SVQ, or equally to aid those who prefer to work on their own to steadily develop their skills.

However you choose to use it, I wish you the best of luck with your development goals.

You don't have development goals? Read on and you soon will!

Part 1
Managing yourself

Chapter 1.1
Planning and managing your own professional development

NVQ Application:

This chapter is relevant to the following NVQ in Management Units:

- A1 Manage your own resources

- A2 Manage your own resources and professional development

Linked chapters:

The information in this chapter is related to information in the following chapters:

- 1.2 Clear communication

- 1.3 Managing your time

- 1.4 Managing information and developing networks

Introduction

A series of events brought you to the role you currently fulfil: decisions, opportunities, instinct and just plain luck, for good or ill. Think back to when you were at school or college and imagining your working life and career: did it look like the reality you are now experiencing? More importantly, what are your thoughts on the job you now have? Is it:

- fulfilling?

- satisfying?

- sufficiently well paid?

- offering enough opportunities, for development and advancement?

Now look to the future: what do you see yourself doing in one year, three years, five years? And how will you get there?

Objectives

The aim of this chapter is to encourage you to take positive action to shape your future. It will help you to:

- take a planned, proactive approach to your professional development;

- look at your future holistically;

- make the most of the development opportunities that come your way; and,

- manage your stress.

Your amazing brain

We are each of us born with some 100 billion brain cells, or neurons. Each neuron has three basic parts: the cell body, the axon, and the dendrite. Dendrites make connections with other neurons, and that's the important bit. Each neuron has the astonishing ability to grow up to twenty thousand dendrites. That makes the capacity of the human brain absolutely incredible.

How is it, when we have such breathtaking potential, we aren't a planet of superhuman beings?

A quick trip inside your head

What we think of as 'the brain' is made up of three distinct parts.

The first is the brain stem, also known as the reptilian brain, which controls basic functions and instincts, such as heart rate, breathing and 'fight or flight'.

The brain stem is a stalk and at the top (but slightly behind) is the cerebellum. This takes responsibility for balance and movement, and has some duties with regard to memory.

Put your arms together from elbows to wrists. If the area to the wrist is the brain stem, then the area from wrist to the base of your thumb is the cerebellum. Now make two fists: they represent the cerebrum or thinking brain. This is the 'wrinkly' brain that we are used to seeing in pictures: the neocortex is folded. If it were opened out it would cover the surface of a desk. The neocortex is the seat of our intelligence and is, in effect, what makes us human. It controls such things as sight, thought, speech – all those things that we need to grow both as a species and as individuals.

In addition to comprising three separate elements, our brain is also divided into two hemispheres, left and right. Your two fists represent these clearly and are even about the same size. The left and right hemispheres are joined by a network of brain cells known as the 'corpus callosum', which transmits information as required between the two. As a general rule, the left hemisphere looks after logical matters (language, numbers, sequences, analysis) and the right hemisphere takes care of artistic things (rhyme and rhythm, colour and images, and concepts such as beauty and loyalty).

We often show a preference in learning. 'Left brain learners' are said to prefer a step-by-step linear approach to learning, whereas 'right brain learners' like to see the big picture and take a global approach. It is important to remember, however, that when you are engaged in an activity your whole brain is involved. In a training session your left-brain might attend to the words spoken and the meaning inherent in them, but the right brain will be picking up on tone and inflection.

Maximise your memory

We have an incredible capacity for memory and we can use our knowledge of how the brain works to develop little tricks and techniques to boost this to our advantage.

Mnemonics

A mnemonic is a device that is used to aid the memory. One I have used for years comes from *'Have Space Suit: Will Travel'* by Robert A. Heinlein (Ballantine Books Inc., reissue edition [1994]) and it helps me to remember the order of the planets from the sun. The mnemonic is 'Mother Very Thoughtfully Made A Jelly Sandwich Under No Protest' and the first letter of each word relates to a planet. It translates as follows:

- Mercury
- Venus
- Terra
- Mars
- Asteroids
- Jupiter
- Saturn
- Uranus
- Neptune
- Pluto

It not only refers to Earth as 'Terra' but also includes the asteroid belt, vitally important for a geeky kid, and it's served me well for over thirty years now. You can make up your own mnemonics or you may well come across tried and tested ones that appeal to you and that you can use to your advantage.

Acronyms

Another similar trick is to use an acronym, where every letter of a word stands for a word beginning with the same initial letter. For example: SWOT analysis looks at Strengths, Weaknesses, Opportunities and Threats, and ASAP is widely used for 'as soon as possible'. Names and brands are routinely reduced to acronyms: ACAS, SAAB and NATO being just a few examples.

Memory joggers

People have all sorts of little memory joggers to keep them on the right track. Some we learn as children in school, such as: 'Thirty days hath September, April, June and November, All the rest have 31, Except February alone which has 28 days clear and 29 each leap year'. Whilst that one loses something in the latter stages, rhymes like this appeal to both sides of the brain and so are especially useful. Other 'joggers' can be very simple indeed: for example, if you get 'stationery' and 'stationary' mixed up, just remember that you get your paper from the stationer and you'll be fine!

Notation maps

Notation maps are a powerful way to take notes, to represent ideas or to recap learning. Research by Dr Robert Ornstein and Tony Buzan (amongst others) shows that not only are they are a fun, visual and yet logical way of showing the various strands that make up a topic, they are also very effective. With notation maps, unlike traditional linear note taking, you start at the centre of the page. Ideas then branch out from the central premise or topic, with related thoughts and facts tied in where relevant. I find them very useful for plotting stories, among other things.

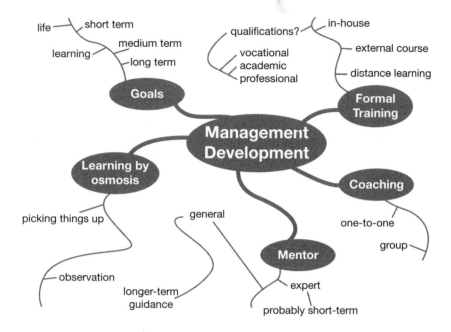

Example notation map

Devices like these are so effective because they appeal to both sides of the brain: they are logical and linear to appease your left-brain and yet quirky and clever, to appeal to your right brain. We use our brains to best effect when we can satisfy both hemispheres.

Learning styles

Whilst many theories on learning styles and types of learning exist, there are in essence four main ways in which people learn:

- By osmosis: an intuitive style that happens without you being conscious of it. We pick up things from what we see, hear, feel and do.

- By accident: an incidental learning style, where an event causes us to spend time thinking about what happened, why it happened, and what it means.

- By reflecting: a retrospective style that involves us actively and systematically reviewing activities and events and analysing what it is that they taught us.

- By design: a prospective style where we plan our learning. We consider what it is that we need to know and take positive steps to undertake training to meet the need, then review and analyse afterwards to consolidate learning. This type of learning is the most efficient and ties in neatly with the learning cycle.

The learning cycle

The learning cycle is derived from the planning cycle with its four stages of 'plan, do, check, act,' with each continually leading onto the next.

- **Plan:** we plan a learning experience, perhaps by booking a course, setting aside some time for study or booking time with a mentor.

- **Do:** we undertake the experience.

- **Check:** we review and analyse what we learned, either using our own notes or perhaps by discussing it with our mentor or manager. This stage is key: if we undertake a learning experience without reinforcing the knowledge or skills gained afterwards by referring back to notes and/or notation maps and recapping the main points, we will lose that information.

- **Act:** we work out how we can incorporate that learning into our way of doing things, and assess what it is that we need to learn next. This may involve developing complementary skills or digging deeper into the current subject.

In fairness, it's more like a continuous spiral, with one 'Plan, Do, Check, Act' cycle leading into the next.

What do you need to learn?

Take a long, hard look at your life and ask yourself this very question. Learning takes commitment, can be difficult and is undertaken at a cost, possibly financial, definitely in terms of time that would otherwise be spent doing other things. Consequently it makes good sense to consider what it is that interests you or that you want or need to learn in order to achieve your life goals. It is a good idea to make a plan, perhaps to record it formally, and to see that it ties in with your job plan and appraisal. That way you can involve your manager, which should help at least with sorting out work-related training.

Exercise: Where do you see yourself?

It is a good idea to take the time to set some personal and professional goals. You might want to think about:

- where you want to live, both geographically and in terms of type of dwelling;

- whether you want to own or rent your home;

- who you want to work for (here you can specify the sector, name a firm, or decide that you would rather work for yourself); and,

- what you want to be doing, and at what level.

For example:

	Now	1 year	3 years	5 years
Place	London	London	Newcastle	Edinburgh
Type	Flat	Flat	House (2 beds)	House (3 beds)
Status	Rent	Rent	Buy	Buy
Work for				
Position	Team leader	Supervisor	Manager	Manager
Earn				
Drive				

We'll return to this a little later. For now, just let some ideas develop.

Once you have your starting point and a series of milestones on the way to your destination, you are in a position to plan your journey. As with all things, break the various goals down into manageable steps.

John Bird, founder of 'The Big Issue', advocates starting with three per cent, because whilst you might aim big, the path to success is travelled via a series of small steps.

Firstly, assess how the requirements and opportunities of your current job will help you to move toward your overall goal. There must be some synergy in order for you to be able to enlist your employer's help: if you work in IT and want to learn some technical skill, chances are you can work that into your job plan. If you work in IT and want to take a creative writing course, chances are you're on your own. (Although some enlightened employers do provide funding for such unrelated pursuits, they tend to be in the minority.)

Ask yourself a series of 'What if...?' questions so that you have a contingency plan. The question 'What if... I am made redundant?' may spark a number of ideas, some of which might surprise you. For example:

- I could take a year out and do a PGCE;
- I could start my own business;
- I could take time out to travel;
- I could buy a new suit, update my CV – and get back out there!

There is no right or wrong answer to any of this, there is only what is right for you at a given point in time.

As an aside, money saving expert Martin Lewis advocates trying to have at least three months' survival money in the bank 'just in case'. I've rarely managed that, but if you can do it, then it is a very good idea. If you have that safety net, then any sudden job loss without any – or immediate – monetary compensation does not also have to constitute a financial crisis.

Working with a mentor

A mentor can offer advice and assistance and help you to keep on track and achieve your goals. Consider someone from your network, your manager or perhaps a specialist. When asking for help, decide if you feel it would be most desirable in the shorter or longer term. A specialist mentor might be useful in the shorter term whereas a generalist might be better to work with for longer. Ultimately it will depend on their availability and willingness to mentor you. As you progress in your career, be prepared to return the favour for more junior colleagues and contacts and to act as a mentor to them in return.

You should make a point of seeking out feedback on your performance and progress. If you have a mentor, then much will come from that source, or if not, then look to your manager or other managers with whom you work, and your peers. Don't be defensive when you get feedback that consists of more than a slap on the back; whilst praise where it is due is always welcome, it is this second, more balanced kind of feedback that we can learn most from.

Shy bairns get nowt!

Ask for chances and opportunities; do not assume they will automatically come your way. You might be the perfect person to take on a department while the existing manager is absent for a period of time, but even the best management have been know to miss what is under their noses. Put yourself forward: 'You have to show willing', as I used to be told time and again when I was growing up.

Under pressure

The cost of workplace stress, it seems, is very high indeed. It was reported by Nick Triggle on the BBC news website in November 2009 that the National Institute for Health and Clinical Excellence (NICE) had estimated the cost of work-related mental illness to be £28bn, or one quarter of the UK's total sick bill. More than 13 million working days a year are lost as a result of work-related stress, anxiety and depression and – according to NICE – the single biggest cause of problems is bad management.

These costs, of course, are purely financial: there is also the toll on individuals to take into account. Stress can cost people their jobs and relationships, and do significant long-term damage to their physical and mental health. Stress is a serious issue.

What is 'stress'?

A simple workplace definition of stress is to have more to do than your time will allow. Stress can also be caused by monotony, boredom and insufficient stimulus. Whichever, the common denominator is a feeling of helplessness, of having little or no control over your life. As organisations increasingly try to achieve more with fewer people, the pressure on each individual increases and whilst one person's nightmare is another person's challenge, everyone has their breaking point. In October 2009, a teacher in a Nottinghamshire school attacked a pupil and is currently awaiting trial on a charge of attempted murder; it seems that stress was a major factor in this experienced teacher's actions.

Causes of stress

There are many causes of stress, but the main ones arguably are as follows:

- **Conflict:** this may be experienced with a spouse or partner, child or other family member, friend or work colleague.

- **Major life events:** marriage, divorce, childbirth, bereavement: both difficult and happy life events come with stress attached.

- **Finances:** not only a lack of money now, but also perhaps the knowledge that a secure future hasn't been planned and provided for whilst the clock is ticking.

- **Holidays:** most of us look forward to our holidays, and yet they can still be stressful; travel arrangements and organising Christmas are just two examples. There are also those who dread their holidays, perhaps because they will mean a period of isolation or they fear their absence from the office will diminish their control over their job.

- **Lifestyle:** constantly burning the candle at both ends can take its toll and also lead to other types of stress, such as financial.

- **Change:** stress is often related to change: in the workplace, this could be a change in job role and/or responsibilities, a reorganisation, a merger, a change in staffing levels or level of output. This change may be perceived as opportunity or threat, and our threat response generally has three stages: shock, which will reduce performance levels; panic, which will increase performance levels dramatically for a period of time; and resignation, when the stressor remains in place for a period of time and wears the individual down, resulting in feelings of exhaustion and helplessness.

- **Work:** the causes of workplace stress may be grouped into four broad categories:

  1 **Environment:** the physical environment in which people work. Stress can be triggered by such factors as temperature (constantly too hot or too cold); lack of natural light and/or fresh air (an unnatural environment); noise; shabby facilities.

  2 **Role requirements:** expectations about job title and grade; inequality of status and remuneration between people on the same grade; relationships between people at work; required output levels; variety and content of work, promotion or demotion.

  3 **Personal needs:** individual's development needs in order to adequately fulfil the job role and develop their career in the short, medium and long-term; job satisfaction; sense of achievement and self-worth; appreciation.

  4 **Role conflict:** we all have a range of roles that we fill in our lives; these are related to work, family and social situations and stress arises when there is conflict between them. For example, missing a friend's birthday party due to work requirements; being unable to work overtime due to attending a parents' evening at school.

Signs of stress

We all have our own stressors, signs of stress and ways of coping with it. In general, however, stress makes us feel:

- overwhelmed – we feel that we cannot cope and cannot think straight;

- overburdened – we are fighting a losing battle, as no matter how hard we work, we simply cannot keep up; and,

- overtired – physically and emotionally, partly due to trying so hard to get on top of things and partly due to the anxiousness and nervous tension we are experiencing.

The signs that we are experiencing undue levels of unhealthy stress may be physical, mental, emotional and behavioural. Let's take a closer look.

Physical signs of stress

- Digestive disorders
- Headaches
- Insomnia
- Racing heart
- Muscular aches and pains
- Nail biting, teeth grinding
- Nervous tics
- Hair pulling

Cognitive signs of stress

- Poor memory
- Inability to concentrate
- Poor judgement
- Constant worry
- Apathy

Emotional signs of stress

- Depression
- Anxiety
- Frustration
- Helplessness
- Hopelessness
- Impatience
- Restlessness
- Irritability

Behavioural signs of stress

- Aggression
- Inactivity in the face of deadlines
- Frantic activity
- Emotional outbursts
- Over-reacting
- Fast and/or loud speech pattern
- Stammering

How stressed are you?

In 1967, Thomas Holmes and Richard Rahe conducted some research into the connection between stress and illness. Their results were published as the 'Social Readjustment Rating Scale' (SCRS), but are more commonly known as the Holmes and Rahe Stress Scale. The scale takes a range of life events, including deaths of family and friends, illness, and changes in circumstance experienced over a period of two years as a predictor of illness. Each event is given a life change unit score or rating, ranging from the highest (death of a spouse, which scores 100 units) to the lowest (minor violation of the law, at 11 units). Scores are tallied and the results are as follows:

- **300+:** serious risk of illness
- **150 – 299:** moderate risk of illness
- **150-:** slight risk of illness

The 'Further reading: Online' section at the end of this chapter has a URL you can use to access an online version of the scale, where you can score your own stress level and judge whether this constitutes a risk to your health. When I completed the test as part of the research for this book, my score was over 500; perhaps unsurprisingly, I was also recovering from illness at the time.

Stress response

Stress is a happening that makes us feel threatened or fearful. The natural reaction is fight or flight. There are times, however, when neither reaction is possible: being scolded by a manager at work or cut up by another motorist, for example. Despite not being able to react in the way we might like, we still experience the same physical stress response as if we were in a life or death situation. Adrenaline and other stress hormones flood the body, the heart rate, blood pressure and breathing rate increase and senses become more acute. The more often this happens, the more threatening it is to a person's health.

Stress busters

We each have our own methods of dealing with stress, and not all of them are necessarily good for us. If we overindulge in alcohol or resort to comfort eating, we can actually add to our stress by trying to work when we feel jaded or unwell, and making ourselves unhappy as we find that increasingly our clothes feel uncomfortably tight. A little of what you fancy is fine – just try not to overindulge. Healthy stress busters include:

- **Visualisation:** a proven technique that can either provide a break (at your desk) from the daily routine or help you to be more effective in your job role: there is evidence that if we 'see' things as we would like them to be, then we can move closer to that reality. *'Human beings can alter their lives by altering their attitudes of mind.'* (William James, philosopher.)

- **Meditation:** in use for over 2,500 years, meditation is a technique that helps you to relax and clear your mind of mental clutter and chatter. It is simple, free, and has been shown to reduce stress, blood pressure and anxiety. See the 'Further reading: Online' section at the end of this chapter for sources of further information.

- **Exercise:** jogging, gym, yoga – whatever you do, exercise has many benefits; just be sure to choose something you enjoy. If your heart sinks at the thought of it, you will add to your stress!

- **Breathing:** stress is often accompanied by hyperventilation (fast or overly-deep breathing). This in turn can cause dizziness, sweating, palpitations and chest pains, which further increases anxiety. Simple breathing exercises, however, can help to alleviate the problem. Try this:

  1. Sit in a chair with your back straight and your hands in your lap.

  2. Breathe in through your nose to a count of five.

  3. Breathe out through your mouth, also to a count of five. Repeat as necessary.

- **Budgeting:** this should be done for both your money and your time. (See Chapters 1.3, Managing your time and 5.2, Setting and working with budgets.)

- **Planning:** for a secure future.

- **Taking a break:** whether it's a five-minute visualisation holiday, a brisk walk at lunchtime, a week in the sun or even tendering your resignation, getting away from it all is a great way to rejuvenate yourself. It may feel like you get more done by staying at your desk all day and grabbing a sandwich for lunch, but you are likely to be more productive if you take even just ten minutes away to clear your head and get a breath of air.

- **Eating healthfully:** it can be easier and more gratifying to snack on fast food and chocolate, but it doesn't nourish and rarely satisfies for very long. Distract yourself from over-eating by reading, cleaning your teeth, going for a walk, whatever works for you, and do be sure that when you do eat, you do so consciously and with relish. *'Let your food be your medicine and your medicine be your food.'* (Hippocrates, ancient Greek physician.)

- **Talking to people:** having a support network of friends and family is a powerful way to cope with life's problems. You must balance that, however, with some time for yourself. We all need time alone to recharge our batteries and do just exactly what we please.

- **Getting enough sleep:** you can't keep up either physically or mentally if you constantly rob yourself of sufficient sleep. Try to get what you need, whether six, seven or eight hours a night.

- **Getting a hobby:** finding something that both distracts you from your stressors and provides satisfaction is a great way to help alleviate stress. My main ones are reading, writing and photography. When the chips are really down I often make soup. I find the simple action of balancing flavours and preparing vegetables almost hypnotic, and those actions and the resulting meal are soothing.

- **Focusing on 'now':** we all spend time going over and over things in our minds, fretting and agonising over details. 'If only I'd said that…' or 'I wish I'd though of this then…'. Then we start to imagine what we will do next: 'Just wait until she does that again!' and 'I won't give him the satisfaction next time.' We drive ourselves mad at times. It can be very hard to do, but letting go what has happened and focusing on the current situation rather than dwelling on the past or trying to second-guess the future is a great skill, especially in a time of crisis.

- **Remember how good you are:** if you are feeling really overwhelmed, either have a read of your CV or make a list of all the things that you can do well. You will very likely surprise yourself and boost your spirits at the same time.

- **Resist the temptation to take on other people's stress:** some folk do their utmost to dump their problems on others, and if you are the sort of person who always tries to help, you are likely to be a target. Empathise or offer advice by all means, but encourage such people to deal with their own problems.

- **Change what you can:** some things we must live with, but if it is in your power to change anything that is causing you undue anxiety or unhappiness, then you owe it to yourself to make that change.

Conclusion

Remember, life is all about balance. Balance between mind and body, what you earn and what you spend, the food you eat and the energy you expend. When things are in balance, we are in control and can cope with life's problems better when they arise. When things are out of balance, issues can quickly spiral out of control.

Also bear in mind the twin issues of rights and responsibilities. You have the right to make mistakes, but you have the responsibility to own up to them and put them right. You have the right to say 'no', but you have the responsibility to only do that when saying 'yes' would be very difficult or impossible. You have the right to be paid a fair wage for what you know and do, but you have the responsibility to provide a fair day's work in exchange.

We cannot avoid stressful situations: the act of living means they are inevitable at some point. We can, however, take steps to both avoid and eliminate unnecessary stress and equip ourselves to deal effectively with unpreventable stress.

Your future is in your hands!

Exercise: Where do you see yourself?

Earlier in the chapter we started to think about where you might like to be in the future. Use the table below to make some notes. Add in extra categories if that would suit you better – and be honest, it's just for you at this stage.

	Now	1 year	3 years	5 years
Place				
Type				
Status				
Work for				
Position				
Earn				
Drive				

Planning and managing your own professional development checklist

- My brain is amazing!

- I use mnemonics, acronyms and other devices to boost my memory.

- I know how to draw a useful notation map.

- I have a plan to help me achieve my personal goals, staged over a number of years.

- I have a plan for my personal development, which supports the achievement of my goals.

- I understand my stressors, signs of stress and stress reactions.

- I take positive steps to manage my stress.

Further reading

In print:

- Accelerated Learning for the Twenty First Century, Colin Rose and Malcolm J. Nicholl, Judy Piatkus (Publishers) Ltd (1999)

- Shaping Your Career, Harvard Business Press Pocket Mentor, Harvard Business School Publishing Corporation (2008)

- How to Change Your Life in Seven Steps, John Bird, Vermilion (2006)

- 10 Minute Guide to Stress Management, Jeff Davidson, Macmillan USA, Inc. (2001)

- The Book of Stress Survival, Alex Kirsta, Thorsons (1992)

Online:

- http://managementhelp.org/mgmnt/prsnlmnt.htm – The Free Management Library – see the section on 'Managing Yourself'.

- http://www.quintcareers.com/SWOT_Analysis.html – Quintessential Careers website.

- http://helpguide.org/mental/stress_signs.htm – website for Helpguide, an organisation that aims to provide information to help people deal effectively with life's challenges.

- http://www.meditationexpert.co.uk/ – website packed with information on meditation techniques, practices and stress relief.

- http://www.harvestenterprises-sra.com/pages/article/TheHolmes-RaheScale.htm – online version of the stress test.

Chapter 1.2
Clear communication

NVQ Application:

This chapter is relevant to all NVQ in Management Units, but especially to the following:

- A1 Manage your own resources
- A2 Manage your own resources and professional development
- A3 Develop your personal networks
- B5 Provide leadership for your team
- B6 Provide leadership in your area of responsibility
- B7 Provide leadership for your organisation
- D1 Develop productive working relationships with colleagues
- D2 Develop productive working relationships with colleagues and stakeholders
- D10 Reduce and manage conflict in your team
- D12 Participate in meetings
- E11 Communicate information and knowledge

Linked chapters:

The information in this chapter is related to all other information in the book, but especially that in the following chapters:

- 1.1 Planning and managing your own professional development
- 1.3 Managing your time
- 1.4 Managing information and developing networks

Introduction

In primitive times, it might be fair to say that both people and animals behaved in much the same way. If they saw something they wanted and no personal threat was involved, they took it. If they had something that was of no use, they discarded it or broke it. If they felt an emotion: anger, happiness, sadness, they expressed it. And if they were threatened, they either fought or ran away.

It might still be possible to observe such behaviour nowadays, in children, the overly powerful or the dysfunctional, for example, but for the majority of us that simply isn't how we are expected – or indeed would choose – to behave. This moderation of behaviour, allowing teamwork, negotiation, compromise and so on, is all made possible because we learned to communicate effectively with one another.

In your home life you must be able to get your message across to your parents, siblings, partner, children, friends, neighbours and many others. At work, you must be able to communicate equally effectively with your manager, your subordinates and your peers. Whether communication is conducted face to face, on the telephone or in writing (informally, as with emails and formally, as with reports) is irrelevant: what matters is that the message is clear, accurate and fully understood.

Objectives

The aim of this chapter is to raise awareness of how improving your communication skills can improve your effectiveness and help you to get the results you want. It will help you to:

- know how to best get your message across to others;

- read non-verbal signals;

- think about how you come across when you meet people, particularly those you meet for the first time;

- use the telephone to best effect; and,

- write clearly and concisely.

Communication in action

Communication makes things happen. Imagine if Joan of Arc, inventor of the World Wide Web Tim Berners-Lee or even film-maker Steven Spielberg had simply kept their dreams and visions to themselves: the world today would be very different. A number of things combined to make those dreams a reality – drive, commitment, hard work – but the catalyst and the fuel that kept the fires burning was communication.

Suppose your CEO wakes up one morning having realised that as well as being the right thing to do, reducing the business's carbon footprint would give competitive advantage. He is passionate about this. He wants to start working towards that end immediately. What do you think his first step will be?

Quite simply, the first step will be to *tell* someone. The idea will have to be discussed and evaluated, accepted as a goal, plans will have to be made to help achieve it, the aim and in time the results will have to be made known… that's a whole lot of communication! Some words will be spoken, on the telephone, in face to face informal chats and in meetings; others will be written, in emails, reports, staff bulletins, press releases; the board and management team will have to be told, then staff, stakeholders, the public – and that's without all the work that needs to be done to make the goal a reality.

Definitions

'Communication' may be defined as 'the act of imparting', whether news, information, gossip, or anything else. 'Clear' may be defined as 'unambiguous; easily understood'. Hence our chapter title of 'clear communication', since this should be our goal at all times.

Politicians are perhaps the last people to spring to mind when we talk of 'clear communication'. They have a reputation for saying what they want to be heard rather than necessarily giving a straight answer to a straight question or telling it like it is. As a consequence, everything they say becomes subject to suspicion.

In business, we cannot afford to have that kind of reputation; we need to be perceived as honest, to have integrity. The easiest way to achieve this is simply to *be* honest and to *act* with integrity; one needs a very good memory to be a liar. So, rather than be 'political', we should perhaps instead choose to be 'politic', which may be defined as 'prudent and sagacious'. I'd rather be thought of as 'careful to avoid undesired consequences' and 'showing wisdom' any day!

There are many benefits of clear communication, including:

- relationships are strengthened;
- goals and objectives are understood by all who are working towards them;
- trust is deepened;
- time is saved;

- understanding is achieved; and,

- problems are avoided.

Case study: Pat's problem

Pat is the Customer Services team leader for a company manufacturing widgets. One of her team has gone on holiday and as a result of a phone call from an irate customer, Pat has found out that a particular customer complaint has gone unresolved for quite some time.

The call itself was very tricky to handle although the subsequent investigation has shown what went wrong and where the fault lies – and that's partly with the customer and partly with the organisation. The situation isn't straightforward; it took Pat a while to get her head around it and now she has to explain it to the customer and gain agreement for the way forward.

How should Pat handle the situation from this point on?

We'll come back to Pat later. Now we are going to move on to consider the three main methods of communication: face to face, on the telephone, and in writing.

Talking face to face

Talking face to face is something people do every day, so you would expect us to be very good at getting our message across. Let's consider what happens when we talk.

What happens when we talk?

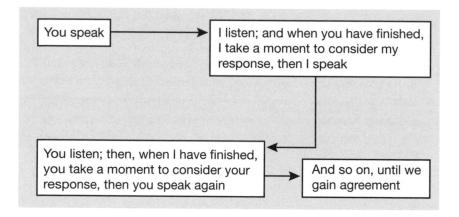

Above is what we would like to think happens when we talk. In reality, it is more like this:

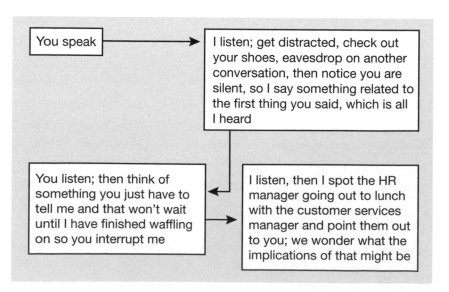

Obviously, this is simplistic and tongue in cheek, and yet there is rather more truth in the process than we might feel comfortable admitting to!

Like so many things in life, whether business or personal, communication is all about managing the relationship. In order to allow clear communication to take place, the following are essential:

- **Respect:** if you do not respect the other person for what and who they are and accept them as an equal, then you will fail to communicate effectively.

- **Empathy:** you may well not agree with what someone is saying, but can you understand why they feel as they do? Perhaps if you were in their position, you would, too. That, in a nutshell, is empathy: understanding another's point of view without necessarily sharing it.

- **Honesty:** being truthful, keeping your promises, making sure the verbal and non-verbal messages you give are congruent.

When you don't agree with the message

There are going to be times when you have to go along with or agree to do things you don't like. That's life, I'm afraid; we all have to compromise from time to time. Suppose you have been given a task by your manager that you feel is a waste of time: you make your feelings clear, but are told that on this occasion you must complete the task anyway. (Known in some quarters as a 'JDI' instruction – just do it!) Your manager may well share your misgivings, but have no more choice in the matter than she is giving to you. How will you convey that to your team?

You could say, 'Look, we all know this is a waste of time, but…'. This will very likely result in your team not trying terribly hard to achieve the goal and, if it gets back to your manager, seriously undermine your relationship and perhaps damage your prospects.

You may order them to do it and not allow discussion, so that you don't fall into the trap mentioned above. This will very likely alienate your team, particularly if at other times you show respect, empathy and honesty.

You could fake enthusiasm and lie to them about what a good idea you think the task is. You may well undermine your credibility, however, as your words will not be in agreement with your body language and may well also contradict opinions you have expressed previously.

Alternatively, you could put the task to them with the reasoning presented to you by your manager, and allow them to discuss the matter. You might be surprised by how many of the team are quite happy to go ahead, and to do so with enthusiasm. You might have to listen to the same objections you raised when your manager delegated the task to you; showing empathy will allow you to accept those concerns. Then, having allowed the team to get things off their chest, you can move on to ask how people feel you can best do what needs to be done, resulting in a jointly-owned plan of action to take things forward.

Body language

It is frequently reported that in face to face communication, around seven per cent of the message received is via the words spoken, 38 per cent via tone, inflection and 'listening noises', and a massive 55 per cent via what we see – non-verbal communication, or body language. I recently discovered that these statistics (derived from research carried out by Albert Mehrabian in the 1970s) have been taken out of context, and that these percentages apply only when we are dealing with a situation that is emotionally charged and we are discussing feelings and attitudes. Hence, if your partner is sitting with arms and legs crossed and is avoiding eye contact and yet, when you ask 'What's the matter?' snaps 'Nothing!', you know without a shred of doubt that something is very wrong indeed. Despite this, there is no doubt that body language is a key component of face to face communication in all circumstances, although the balance in a business context is not as extreme as we have often been led to believe.

Body language may be thought of as the art of learning a person's thoughts, attitudes and emotions by observing their movements, expressions and behaviour. When we meet someone for the first time, the first five minutes are key – during this short time frame, around three-quarters of the overall impression made by you on others and the impression they have on you is made – and it sticks.

The study of body language is a massive area and many books exist to help you learn more and improve your skills; therefore I am going to focus solely on three core elements here, those being hands, face, and personal space.

Hands

When we meet someone, especially when we meet for the first time, the most common greeting ritual involving touch is the handshake. Handshakes can tell you a great deal about another person, provided that information is interpreted in context. You should aim for a firm grip, although not a crushing one, particularly when shaking hands with women or those whose hands are used to earn their living, such as musicians, artists and medical people. Women generally lack the physical size and strength of men and so a 'confident' grip might come across as an attempt at bullying or dominance, and those whose hands are sensitive will try to protect them. (Note that this might make their handshake feel 'weak' to you; but read in context, this may be a false signal.)

When you offer your hand, hold it vertically. Palm down grips are put downs, assertions of dominance (they may be countered by using a two-handed grip and putting your left hand on top of the other person's right hand, giving you 'the upper hand'). Be wary of people who try to put you down with a handshake (provided there are other supporting signals); chances are, they won't stop there.

A word to the wise here: be very careful about pointing a finger at someone. You might intend to emphasise a point, they might take it as an accusation or insult. Be especially careful of finger pointing when saying 'you', particularly when you really mean the more general 'one'. You might trigger a 'fight or flight' response that you had no intention of provoking.

Face

Along with the handshake, the smile is very widely used in greeting rituals. It is a shame that in certain business arenas those who smile may be perceived as 'weak' or 'eager to please': it seems that for some, 'serious' means 'po-faced'. However, smiles are contagious and if you give one, you will almost certainly receive one in return. Personally, unless someone is pre-occupied or the situation is extremely serious, I am very suspicious of those who cannot manage to return something as simple and welcoming as a smile.

Eye contact is also vital, although staring is aggressive. Hold someone's gaze for as long as feels comfortable, and if you have something to say, in a meeting or interview, for example, don't look down at the table in front of you but keep your head up. Even if you are referring to notes, keep raising your head and making eye contact when you can. Another benefit of this is that your voice is more easily heard and understood when you face your audience and you both look and sound more confident.

Overall, we tend to mirror the facial expression that we see, and mirroring is a useful social tactic. Do remember, however, that 'to mirror' is a far more subtle action than 'to mimic'. The aim is to build rapport – to say (non-verbally) to the other person, 'look at how alike we are'.

Personal space

People generally move and act as if they had a bubble of space around them, especially in crowded or new situations. The size of the bubble depends on who is nearby: if we don't know (or don't like) someone, we may 'keep them at arm's length', whereas with our loved ones, we 'hold them close'. Culture plays a great part in how close people will tolerate you standing near them. Remember also that to stand too close is threatening, whilst to stand too far away may appear unfriendly (or 'stand-offish'). If you have dealings with international clients, then please do study some of the basic cultural norms; what is friendly and polite for one may be hugely insulting to another person.

Finally, remember to read things in context. Look for clusters of signals that all point to the same conclusion and seek congruence in both verbal and non-verbal communication. I would also recommend that you read up on the subject; it is fascinating, entertaining, and beneficial in both work and private lives. Allan Pease is the recognised expert in this field and his books (written with his wife, Barbara) are warm, funny, accessible and hugely enlightening.

Nine steps to clear communication

1. **Do your homework:** be as fully prepared as is possible and know your subject inside out. According to Albert Einstein: 'If you can't explain it simply, you don't understand it well enough.'

2. **Have an objective:** as with everything you do, you should know what you want to achieve as a result of opening a dialogue or calling a meeting; as well as a primary objective, have a fall back position.

3. **Let the other person know what you hope to achieve:** then you both know why you're there. Also, be upfront about any inherent advantage to them: people agree far more readily when they can see something in it for themselves.

4. **Ask helpful questions:** use those that will move the dialogue forward and avoid those that will cause problems.

    *   Questions that help: open and probing questions (asking what, when, how, why and who) are likely to be most useful as they get people talking without making assumptions about what it is they have to say;

    *   Questions that hurt: multiple questions are confusing; people will not remember them all and will likely only answer the last one, if any at all, and loaded or undermining questions simply make people feel threatened and foolish. Examples include 'Didn't you know that?' and 'What did you think would happen?'

    *   Closed questions, which elicit either a short, definite response (yes/no/three o'clock/red) can either help or hurt, depending

on how and when they are used. A useful technique is the 'statement-question technique', where you make a statement to give information then ask a related question to control the conversation. For example, 'You could either fly or travel by train to your destination. Do you have a preference?'

5.   **Listen:** don't just tolerate the other person speaking for part of the time – actually focus on what is being said. You never know – they might know something you don't or have a great idea about how to achieve your goal that hadn't occurred to you. Use listening noises and repetition so that they know you are hearing what they are saying. If you don't intend to listen, don't insult people by talking at them.

6.   **Be assertive:** stand up for yourself while still showing respect, empathy and honesty. As was mentioned earlier, you should beware of saying 'you' too often, particularly if you mean the department or organisation the person is from, or really mean 'one' in a more general sense. 'You' may sound accusatory and could provoke a fight or flight response. (The exception to this rule would be in an appraisal or disciplinary meeting, for example, when it is the behaviour of that person that is under the spotlight, for good or ill.)

7.   **Be honest:** but remember that being honest and forthright is never an excuse for simply being rude.

8.   **Be 'politic':** which, as you may remember, is 'prudent' and 'sagacious'.

9.   **Don't forget your mask:** no, not a contradiction of honesty and congruence, merely a necessity at times. Just as you would wear a suit for a business meeting, you may also need to hide personal feelings or a lack of experience. We're not talking about game playing here, just about showing your organisation and yourself in the best possible light.

Telephone tactics

Tone and inflection are of paramount importance in telephone communication, as is the use of listening noises. Silence should only be used if you want to put pressure on the other person to speak. Unless you know the person you are speaking to very well – and they know you – avoid sarcasm on the phone. Without the accompanying wry smile or roll of the eyes, something you intended to be ironic or witty might sound petty or aggressive.

Words should be chosen very carefully. Using too much jargon or language that is complicated will jar badly and might even cost you a sale or a deal. Keep it simple; remember that your aim is to be understood, not to impress with your vocabulary.

A vital tool is 'repeat back'. Confirm key facts, times, dates, prices, whatever may have relevance in your dialogue. It shows you are paying attention to the other person's words.

It is a good idea to match language and pace. With language, avoid jargon and aim to use the same terminology the other person does. Say you work in the banking industry and a customer refers to a returned cheque as 'bounced', it is best if you do the same as they are clearly familiar and comfortable with this term. If you use some other term such as 'dishonoured' they may not understand it, or may feel patronised or insulted. With pace, if the other person speaks much more slowly than you, slow down a little. Similarly, if he or she speaks more quickly, speed up a little. What you are effectively doing here is mirroring, but with voice alone.

Finally, always summarise. 'So, what we have agreed here is…' or 'Let me check I have all the facts…' are useful phrases. If you have misunderstood, you can go over details and correct them and once everything is clearly understood and agreed, you can go on to determine what should happen next.

Writing

We're taught to write at school, aren't we? Well, if we could manage it back then, what's the big deal about it now? After all, if kids can do it, just how hard can it be?

Actually, for a lot of people, it can be pretty difficult. And for all of us, it can be only too easy to get something wrong, either technically, with poor grammar and spelling, or in the meaning, by choosing the wrong words or tone.

Whether rightly or wrongly, we are judged just as much on our writing ability and style as on our accent, dress or grooming. It is an indication of who we are, so whilst it might be acceptable – even desirable – to be casual in our approach when texting or emailing friends, we must be very careful of both the image we present and the clarity of our communication when we write in a business context.

The main types of written communication we use are emails, letters and reports. Before we go on to look at those in more detail, however, let's just spare a moment to think about text messages.

It is more common nowadays to text a client or colleague than perhaps ever before and texting is a very useful tool. However, there are some perils and pitfalls to beware of, including:

- use only the most easily understood and commonly accepted abbreviations in texts; you cannot be sure that the other person is as practised as you are and you wish to be understood;

- do not fall into the trap of becoming overly familiar: texting is a casual type of communication and it can be easy to overstep the mark; and,

- if you have the mobile numbers of business contacts stored in your phone, be very, very careful of sending texts 'to all'. If it's your new phone number, fine, but if it's a 'funny' that one of your friends has sent to you, beware!

Emails

Emails are a fantastic way to communicate with people; not only do they give you a chance to consider what you want to say and how, but they are instant. You can even track when they were delivered and opened, so you know just when your message got through.

Like text messages, however, emails have a tendency to be a casual form of communication and you should beware of how you and your message will come across to the recipient. When in doubt, stick to the formal structure outlined below for letter writing. Alternatively send a brief email introducing the subject with a formal letter added as an attachment. Be aware, however, that some organisations are suspicious of attached files and there are those that go so far as to refuse to open them.

Use the subject field to indicate exactly what your message is about and keep your message concise and to the point; people do not like scrolling down through long, rambling emails. Remember that the standard rules of spelling and grammar apply also to emails. Include contact details – postal address and telephone number(s) – at the bottom. Finally, and this should be obvious, have a 'sensible' email address. It might be amusing for your friends to know you as 'gothgirl27' or 'gangstaman', but do you want to be known like that in business? Your work email address should pose no problem, but for those of you who might email from a personal address from time to time, consider having a separate one just for business. The standard format of 'forename.surname@…' should serve the purpose.

Finally, never forget the Data Protection Act. Emails you send to a colleague about a particular client may be scrutinised by that client or his representatives. Keep it professional and polite!

Letters

Before you so much as set pen to paper, consider why you are writing your letter; you need to clearly understand your objective. Is it to gain information, inform the recipient of a decision, arrange an appointment, sell something? Once you have that clearly in mind, you can go ahead and write.

It is helpful to have a framework, and a good structure to work with is the standard 'beginning, middle and end' used by storytellers. Your beginning is your introduction, your middle is the current situation, and the end is the action or outcome now required. Top and tail this with a salutation and sign-off, and your letter is complete.

Introduction

Tell the recipient why you are writing. 'Your November account is now overdue'; or 'I have completed the investigation into the charges on your account'; or 'I would like to tell you about a new product'. It doesn't have to be long or complex, it is just your lead into the main information.

Situation

Tell the recipient about the current situation. 'If we do not receive payment within seven days, your account will be placed on stop'; or 'I have found that whilst the first charge was correct, the second was added in error'; or 'Party Pizzas are an exciting new taste sensation that kids love!'

The chances are you will need to include more than just one sentence here, but focus on the message you want to give and don't be tempted to add unnecessary detail; that just confuses the issue. For example, if you write: 'I noticed when I checked your account that this isn't the first time payment has been late. Really, I could put you on stop right now, but I'm giving you a chance…' you just dilute the message of this letter, which is clear-cut: November's account is overdue. When you receive payment, by all means send a reminder of the standard terms and conditions, but don't deviate from your objective with this letter.

Action

Tell the recipient what you want to happen next. 'Please either send a cheque by return of post to the above address or telephone me on the number below'; 'I have credited the incorrect charge, you will see it appear on your next statement'; 'To order Party Pizzas at this special promotional rate, call me on… but don't delay – the offer ends 30th September'. Be quite clear about what should happen next, how, and by when. That way, everyone knows what to expect.

Salutation and sign-off

Address the recipient using the title they use themselves, whether Mr, Mrs, Miss, Ms, Doctor, Reverend – whatever is appropriate. I receive letters addressed to Miss, Ms and Mrs and it doesn't bother me in the slightest, but not everyone feels like that: take time to get it right. What does bother me, however, is when people and organisations spell my name incorrectly. Always check. Make a phone call if you must, but do get it right, otherwise you've annoyed someone before they've even opened your letter.

When you sign off, include all necessary details. Obviously your name should appear, but you might also wish to include position, department, direct line, email address and so on. Consider having a standard signature for letters and emails, not just for you, but also for the team.

Incidentally, if you have a group of staff that regularly write letters and emails to customers, you might also consider creating standard letters and paragraphs that they can access readily. Not only will it help them to get their message across in an accepted company style, it will also save time: just think how many times the same situation crops up with different customers.

Reports

A simple but effective structure for reports is as follows:

- contents;
- introduction;
- body of evidence; and,
- conclusion.

Let's look at those in more detail.

Contents

Include main headings, sub headings and page numbers, so people can get to what interests them quickly. Don't forget that if you edit your report, you will have to check that the contents list is still accurate.

Introduction

Keep this brief, but include enough so that people know exactly what the report is about: why the project was undertaken, what you hoped to achieve and how you went about your task. You may also need to include dates and personnel involved. Anyone reading the introduction should understand the nature of the project and the scope of the activity.

Body of evidence

In this section you detail all the work undertaken, in logical – perhaps chronological – order. If your project aimed to engage college students in a particular activity and raise awareness of a related website, then your body of evidence might include the following:

- work undertaken to engage colleges, gain permission to go on campus, arrange a time to conduct a training session;

- on-campus promotional activity;

- details of the training session design and development, stated objectives, sessions delivered, feedback received;

- hits on the website; and,

- etc, etc, as relevant.

Conclusion

The conclusion may be the first thing you write and the only thing some people read; it should be concise and clear and include outcomes and any recommendations for further activity.

Last words

Writing can be a minefield; just think of the opportunities there are to get it wrong! It is also a valuable method of communication; you can take time to phrase things just so and be sure you are putting the right message across. How often have you wished you could go back and say something differently in a meeting or interview? Writing gives you the chance to get things right.

Conclusion

Communication is something we do every day, usually without thinking about it. Most of the time we get by, but we have the capacity to get things spectacularly wrong, just by being careless about language – too casual, too much jargon, or body language – too strong a handshake, avoiding eye contact. Unfortunately the first impression we make can stick with us for years, and if it happens to be unfavourable that can have a heavy cost attached.

Fortunately with just a little effort we can ensure that we almost always make the best possible impression and convey our messages clearly.

Exercise: Pat's problem

Earlier in the chapter we took a look at Pat and the tricky customer complaint she had managed to get to the bottom of. At that time, the following question was raised:

How should Pat handle the situation from this point on?

In the light of what you have learned since, use the space below to answer that question. There are some suggestions at the end of the chapter.

_____

_____

_____

_____

_____

_____

_____

_____

Clear communication checklist

- I understand what is meant by 'clear communication'.

- I make a conscious effort to listen to the other person (or people) in conversation.

- I try at all times to show respect, honesty and empathy.

- I don't either use too much force or claim 'the upper hand' when shaking hands with people.

- I return smiles I am given and offer them in greeting, and I make eye contact as appropriate.

- I subtly mirror the people I am speaking to.

- I respect the personal space of other people.

- I adhere to the nine rules of clear communication.

- I am conscious that when on the telephone I need to take great care with words, tone and inflection.

- I am not overly familiar in texts and emails.

- I use the 'introduction, situation, action' framework when writing letters.

- I use the 'contents, introduction, body of evidence and conclusion' structure when writing reports.

Case notes: Pat's problem

Poor Pat – that's quite a can of worms she's opened!

Pat has a number of issues to address here. Firstly she needs to go back to the customer and explain things. Then she must make her offer of settlement, making sure the customer shoulders responsibility for their own wrongdoings. Pat must do all this without alienating the customer; she does not want to lose custom.

Sorting out the customer is only part of the problem. When her team member returns from holiday, she will have to tackle the poor performance head on.

Finally, she must assess procedures in the department and find out how something could fester for so long under her nose.

Pat decides that since the query is complicated, she will write to the customer. This gives her a chance to set out all the facts and make sure the information flows and makes sense. She uses the letter structure to guide her.

She then rings the customer and explains she is putting information in writing and will call to discuss it fully after the letter will have been received. This gives the customer a chance to take in the information, understand the problem, and make a note of any questions that may arise.

She talks face to face with her team member when she returns from holiday, and makes sure to use open and probing questions, to listen to the replies and to show respect, honesty and empathy. Pat then takes the necessary action, including getting the team involved in a review of procedures and processes. Getting everyone involved – without pointing the finger at the culprit – may highlight some additional problem areas allowing Pat to go on to make procedural changes to suit.

Further reading

In print:

- Writing Effective Policies and Procedures: A Step-by-step Resource for Clear Communication, Nancy J. Campbell, Amacom (1997)

- Janner's Complete Letterwriter, Greville Janner, Random House Business Books (3rd edition) (1986)

- The Jelly Effect: How to Make Your Communication Stick, Andy Bounds, Capstone (2007)

- Words That Work: It's Not What You Say, it's What People Hear, Dr. Frank Luntz, Hyperion (2008)

- The Definitive Book of Body Language: How to Read Others' Attitudes by Their Gestures, Allan and Barbara Pease, Orion (2005)

- Mastering Communication, Nicky Stanton, Palgrave Macmillan (2009)

- Business Communication: Your Mentor and Guide to Doing Business Effectively, Harvard Business Essentials, Harvard Business School Press (2003)

Online:

- http://www.manageyourtime.co.uk/clear-communication-workplace.html – information on the ManageYourTime website.

- http://www.kaaj.com/psych/ – The website of Albert Mehrabian.

- http://www.inc.com/guides/growth/23032.html – article on 'Better Communication with Employees and Peers' on the website for Inc. Magazine.

- http://www.mftrou.com/communication-skills.html – information on the Management For The Rest Of Us website.

- http://lorien.ncl.ac.uk/ming/Dept/Tips/present/comms.htm – information on the Newcastle University website.

Chapter 1.3
Managing your time

Introduction

Time: most of us run our lives by the clock. We constantly try to squeeze just a few more minutes out of each day, but it all has to be paid for. Those extra few minutes in bed can mean running for the train or speeding on the motorway; the chat with a colleague on the way back from lunch may lead to working a little later at night or sneaking back to your desk and hoping the boss doesn't see you, because time is finite. Time is limited. Time cannot be slowed down or saved up.

Despite that restriction, it is possible to get more done in the time available to us, simply by being a bit smarter about it. Most of us, despite being busy, overburdened, stressed, and distracted, manage to waste huge tracts of time doing nothing useful or even especially enjoyable. (Think of the number of times a colleague has opened the morning's conversation with: 'Did you see the telly last night? Rubbish! Nothing worth watching!' You can bet that same colleague didn't turn the set off and go for a walk, read a book, or listen to some music. What a waste of time!)

Objectives

The aim of this chapter is to help you to achieve your objectives and hit your deadlines. It will help you to:

- understand what steals your time and know how to guard against it;

- set realistic goals and plan to achieve them;

- clear your workspace, get organised – and stay organised;

- be realistic about what is achievable and avoid setting yourself up to fail; and,

- get more done each day by changing how you work.

How long have you got?

No, not until the grim reaper calls – just how many hours do you have at your disposal in a week? Using a rough calculation, you start off with 24 hours x 7 days, which equals 168 hours. Sounds like a lot! Assume 8 hours getting ready for bed and sleeping per night plus a couple of extra hours for a lie in at the weekend, and that accounts for 58 hours. We're down to 110 hours already. Devote 10 hours – that's just over an hour a day – to getting up, washed and dressed and having breakfast, and we have a nice, round 100 hours to do things in.

Activity	Hours/% of time taken	Hours/% of time left
Commuting (assuming 5 days with a commute of 1 hour each way)	10	90
Work (assuming 7½ hours x 5 days, plus an hour a day for lunch)	42.5	47.5
Sustenance – cooking, eating and clearing up after meals, and grocery shopping (assuming an hour per day in the week and 2 at the weekend)	9	38.5
Housework and laundry (assuming an hour a day in the week – for tasks such as bed-making, ironing, etc. – and 3½ over the weekend)	8.5	30
Total	70	30

Looking at the table, 70 of your precious hours have gone already – 70 per cent of your available time – and you have yet to exercise, read a newspaper or a book, do the garden, walk the dog, help the kids with their homework, ring your mother or spend time with friends. No wonder you feel stressed and overburdened!

We are going to concentrate primarily here on the time you spend in the workplace, but the tips and techniques can just as easily be applied to your life outside of work. You could be pleasantly surprised at just what a difference they can make.

Good time management

Using your time effectively is a skill that can be learned, something that will, with a little effort, become habitual. Now don't get me wrong here; I'm not talking about turning you into a machine; far from it. Rather, the aim is to free you from the drudgery of always chasing deadlines and dashing about so that you can take time to enjoy the things you do.

Perhaps the most important question you can ask yourself – and you should do this several times a day, at least initially – is this: 'Is what I *am* doing now what I *should be* doing now?' During the course of writing this book, I asked myself that question many times. Many times, I was pleased to find that the answer was 'Yes'. Too many times, however, the answer involved the Guardian sudoku puzzle or online flash fiction sites. None of us are perfect (and I reckon we're all the better for it) but by asking the question, you can either skive consciously, knowing you must make up for it at some point, or get back to what you *should* be doing.

When you ask the question and you are doing something totally unrelated to the project you should be working on, then it's obvious you are doing the wrong thing. When, however, you are doing something related but not yet urgent, even though other things are, it can be easy to persuade yourself that you are actually being productive. And you may well be being productive – just on the wrong thing at the wrong time.

Case study: Vicky's dilemma

Vicky has a meeting about Christmas promotions and activities at two o'clock and she has a pile of papers to read and make notes on in preparation. Without that background information, the meeting will be far more difficult and will take much more time. Everyone attending has promised to 'do their homework' beforehand.

Vicky estimates that the reading will take an hour, but has allocated an hour and a half out of her schedule because some of the information is quite complex and she accepts she may have to read parts of it more than once. She blocked out 10.30 am to 12 noon of the day of the meeting on her daily schedule, so that the information would be fresh in her mind. She takes lunch from 12.30 pm to 1.30 pm.

It is now 11.00 am and Vicky is in the middle of a discussion with colleagues about staffing levels over the Christmas holiday period (it is September, and the difficulties faced over the summer are fresh in everyone's minds). The discussion wasn't scheduled – the meeting was pulled together on spec an hour earlier after her manager overheard people in the office moaning about the problems they'd had and asked if everyone had half an hour to spare to talk things through.

Vicky is now tapping her foot and looking at her watch. She has stopped listening to what is being said and has stopped offering ideas and suggestions because she wants the discussion to end as soon as possible.

What could Vicky have done differently an hour ago?

What is she doing wrong now?

What should she do next?

We'll return to Vicky and her dilemma shortly. Firstly, I'd like to consider why it is that we so often fail in what we set out to do.

What steals our time?

We start the day full of vim and vigour, a 'to do' list as long as our arm, and then fail and falter as the time ticks by. Some of the reasons for this are:

- We have too many distractions.
- Our work has no clear boundaries or 'finish line'.
- The goal posts keep changing!
- We suffer constant interruptions.
- Too many different projects are competing for our attention.

- We have either too much or too little information and guidance.

- We put things off.

- We do things just to make the time pass.

- We always do first those things that are quick and easy to complete.

- We are absent-minded.

- We are simply too ambitious in the first place.

Are any of those familiar to you? They certainly are to me. Let's take a look at a simple three-step action plan that we can use to combat those issues and to move steadily towards our goals. The steps are:

- Step 1 – Know where you're going.

- Step 2 – Check you are on track.

- Step 3 – Focus on success.

Let's take a closer look at those.

Three-step action plan

Step 1 – Know where you're going

Would you ever set out on a long journey without knowing your destination and arming yourself with directions, or a map, or sat-nav, and expect to get there on time and without taking several wrong turns? What you do at work and in life is no different; if you don't know where you're headed, don't be surprised if you end up somewhere you don't want to be.

Our *destinations* in work and in our private lives are *goals*. The *directions* are the *plans* we make to get us there and en route we use *milestones and monitoring techniques* to check we are still on course.

Goals may be set for the short, medium and long-term. Your work goals will normally be communicated to you as part of your organisation's strategic planning process. Such goals might include: identifying and implementing a procedure for dealing with customer complaints; reducing wastage; designing a training programme to introduce the new billing system. Your personal goals will depend on what you want to achieve in your life. Some of them will be career-orientated: earning promotion; achieving a qualification; learning a new skill. Others might not be: learning a language; owning your home outright; losing weight. All of them become more tangible when you apply a deadline and break the goal down into manageable steps.

Tips for effective goal setting

- **Challenge yourself!** There is little sense of achievement to be enjoyed by doing what you already know you can do.

- **But be realistic.** 'Challenging' is very different to 'impossible'. Don't set yourself up to fail.

- **Be specific.** If a business goal is 'to reduce waste', by how much do you want to reduce it? If a personal goal is 'to lose weight', how much do you want to lose?

- **Set a deadline by which you intend to achieve your goal.** Again, be realistic; Rome wasn't built in a day. Your business goal might now read: 'To reduce waste in the department by ten per cent within six months'. Your personal goal might be: 'To lose ten pounds by my next birthday'. Now you have a goal you can aim for rather than a vague desire to achieve something.

- **Tell someone.** Whether it's your manager at your annual appraisal or your partner over dinner, make a firm commitment to action.

- **Know why you are doing it.** Identify the benefits to the business and to yourself. There will very likely be days when the going gets tough and knowing *why* you are doing something – like putting a picture of yourself before you gained the weight you are now trying to lose on the fridge door – can help to keep you focused on the end result, especially if hitting this goal will help you move closer to achieving another. For example, if you succeed in reducing wastage, will that help you get a pay rise or put you in line for promotion? If you lose weight, will your partner treat you to a pair of designer jeans? Try always to be aware of the impact of your actions on the big picture.

Step 2 – Check you are on track

One of the ways you check you are on track when you make a journey is by looking at your map and noting your current position in relation to the route you originally planned. You may also wish to check you are going to arrive at your destination on time, by checking your watch. You need to be able to make the same checks, simply and quickly, when aiming for your goals.

The best way to do this is to have a written plan. This may be on paper or created electronically and should show the tasks that must be completed, and by when, in order that you may achieve your goal. As well as being an invaluable planning tool for you, it might also be necessary for your colleagues, staff or manager to see what is going on.

One of my goals for 2009/10 was 'Write a management book'. I had a deadline, agreed with my publisher and I had told people I was writing it, so that made it a tangible thing. My next step was to break down the goal into tasks and make a plan.

I knew how many words were required and I had already agreed what would be covered, so I had a start. What I then had to do was create a plan of action, with milestones, that indicated the order I would tackle the subjects in and by when I would have researched and written a first draft of each chapter. My plan covered many months and had time built into it for holidays and illness, plus an amount of time every so often for playing catch up should I have fallen behind for any reason. I did this because I didn't want to set myself up to fail.

Step 3 – Focus on success

One of the most important things you can do is to focus entirely on the task you are currently completing. It sounds obvious, but think of how many times you fail to do that: you are reading a report but also listening to a conversation that is going on in the office; you are speaking to a colleague on the phone, but also thinking about what you are going to say to your manager at your regular catch-up meeting. This is a behaviour almost all of us are guilty of at some point and it can cause us to have to backtrack and do again our main task.

If whatever is intruding on your consciousness is important, stop what you are doing, change your focus onto the alternative task and complete it, giving it your full attention, before turning your full attention back to what you were doing. If it is not, then do your utmost to focus your full attention on the task in hand. This is far easier said than done, but becomes easier with practice and pays off in spades once you have mastered it.

The following section includes some tips and techniques to help you clear your mind and focus on your most important task.

21 Top Tips for getting results

The following list is in no particular order of importance; what is important will depend upon your nature, your circumstances and the culture within which you operate. However, they are all potentially very useful in the battle to get more done in less time with fewer resources!

1. Combat distraction

One of my biggest time-thieves is distraction. Ever since I was small (and it made its first appearance on a school report) distraction has been a problem for me; there's just so much of interest in the world and I have a healthy curiosity! I need to keep it in check, however, and there are a number of ways I – and you, if you are also plagued by distraction – can do that.

My main technique is the 'most important question' mentioned earlier: 'Is what I *am* doing now what I *should be* doing now?' That pulls me up short if I'm drifting and I can get back on track. Another is to schedule in times when I can flick around the websites that interest me. If you, for example, regularly check the news, the weather or the sports results on the Internet, then by having set times, or using a couple of minutes to look at something as a reward for completing a task, you can avoid wasting a couple of hours effectively doing nothing. (You may not want to tell your manager about this, but if it keeps your need for news sated and the urge to check your personal email every ten minutes in check, then it's worthwhile.)

Interruptions warrant a mention here, too. As a manager, you may pride yourself on having an 'open door policy', but you may also be hampered by it. There is nothing wrong with having a set time each day or each week when your door is either actually or metaphorically shut to all but the most urgent issues.

2. Block out time for important tasks

If you were conducting a staff appraisal, you would block out the time in your diary, divert the phone and shut the door. There are times when your work warrants the same consideration. It doesn't mean you don't value your people, just that you also have a healthy respect for yourself, the organisation you work for and the results you need to achieve.

3. Learn to say 'no'

Or at the very least, 'not now'. You will not always be able to drop every-thing just because someone wants you to – and nor should you (although it must be acknowledged that if the 'someone' is someone senior, you may have little choice in the matter). All the planning and time management techniques in the world will fail if you constantly stop what you are doing because someone else is demanding attention. Be assertive: 'I have an hour this afternoon when we can talk about that'. Don't justify why you can't drop everything and do it now; there's no need. Most things will wait until you have the time to deal with them and to give them the attention they deserve.

4. Be aware of your 'prime time'

We each have a time when we are most alert, most productive and get the most done. My maternal grandmother had a saying: 'An hour in the morning is worth two in the afternoon', and so it is for me. If I get a good start to the day, it gives me the impetus I need to continue to get things done in the afternoon. If I fritter away my morning, my afternoon may well go the same way. Being aware of when you are at your best will allow you to focus on more complex tasks during those hours.

5. Get your priorities right

Attending to the trivia on your 'to do' list may allow you to cross lots of things off earlier in the day, but the chances are the bigger tasks will sit there waiting to be transferred onto tomorrow's list, and the day after, then the one for the day after that. When you look at the items on your agenda, you should make two decisions about them: how *important* is each one, and how *urgent*. Your first priority should be any task that is both important and urgent. Your last tasks should be any that might be neither important nor urgent. Such tasks may be carried forward to be completed the next day if necessary, but you should first question whether you need to complete them at all. Only do what you must; completing unnecessary work is a waste of your time.

6. Chip away at big tasks

When we discussed goal setting, we stressed the importance of breaking down big objectives into smaller, more manageable steps. For example, if you want to reorganise your workspace but cannot afford to take a day out of doing other activities in order to do it, do it a bit at a time. Got ten minutes before a meeting? Go through that pile of paperwork that's sat untouched on the corner of your desk for months. Waiting for your manager to get off the phone so you can have your weekly catch-up meeting? Go through your desk drawers while you wait. Little by little, the job gets done.

7. Organise and standardise your filing systems

Simply hunting for information swallows up much time, so it is very much in your interests to make things easy to find. Have a standardised and simple system that everyone understands for numbering and/or naming your saved information. Apply it to electronic as well as paper files and have a master copy in both formats that everyone can access.

8. Use time pressure

Schedule meetings for late morning (people will want to get away for lunch) and late afternoon (people will want to get home).

9. Take and receive useful telephone messages

How many times have you got back to your desk after a meeting or holiday and found your desk, telephone and computer screen covered in yellow notes with meaningless messages scrawled on them? This is such a waste of time! Ensure everyone records the necessary information – date, time, who called, a brief reason for the call, what they want you to do, and contact details – and does so legibly. If necessary, design a form that everyone has copies of and uses.

If you can, sharing telephone-answering duties around the team to ensure that everyone gets some call-free time is a good idea. Nothing slices through your concentration quite so effectively as a ringing phone. If you can get out of the main office when you are having a phone-free period, then so much the better.

10. Make the most of appointments

Always have objectives for your appointments and do your utmost to make sure you meet them. As well as fixing the date and time, indicate how long the meeting should take and try not to go over that. And always call ahead to confirm, to avoid making wasted journeys.

11. Overcome absent-mindedness

We all suffer from it to some degree, but even occasional absent-mind-edness can impact heavily on our time. Useful ways to guard against it include:

- **Make lists.** List making is part of my planning process. I have master lists and a daily 'to do' list for both business and personal tasks. Some people advocate having just one rolling 'to do' list, where new tasks are added to the bottom and completed ones ticked off from the top. Others start the day with a list that they rewrite at lunchtime and the end of the day, to remove completed items and make it easier to follow. Try various methods and use whatever works for you.

- **Place things logically.** That way when you need something, it should be more obvious where you will find it. For example: keep the filing index at the front of the top drawer of the filing cabinet; keep the 'bags for life' with the shopping list.

Most important of all – *concentrate* **on what you are doing.**

12. Deal effectively with paper

The amount of paper that crosses our desks can be quite daunting! I have previously advocated the 'three dots' method of dealing with paper: every time you pick up a piece of paper and don't deal with it, put a dot on it; When it gets to three dots and has still not been actioned – throw it out!

It is arguably more important, however, to deal with paperwork *appropriately*. There are a limited number of things you can do with a piece of paper: act on it now, put it to one side to act on it later, delegate it, file it, or throw it out. If you do keep it, keep it for a reason.

Rather than putting a dot on it try putting a date on it, starting with the date it first hits your desk. That way you can see at a glance when you received it and when you last had reason to retrieve it and look at it; that will help you decide whether it is worth hanging on to or needs to be dealt with in some way. (If you have done nothing with it for, say, six months, and no-one has chased you up, you are probably safe to throw it away. If someone does come back after that time, just ask if they have a copy. If it is important to them, then they will have.)

13. Know the cost of time wasting

Having a chat with a colleague in the corridor or by the coffee machine is not automatically a waste of time. It is important to nurture such relationships and you might learn something useful. What would make such an encounter a waste of time would be if your desk was piled high with important and urgent tasks and you spent half an hour talking about trivia. Ask yourself this: would you spare that half an hour out of your own time? Because if you have to take work home to make up for time lost in the office, that is exactly what you have done.

A word here about smoking breaks. I know that some organisations still allow them and that in such circumstances smokers expect and will take them. If a smoker nips out a couple of times in the morning and again in the afternoon, that's easily half an hour away from the workplace. Bear in mind, however, that it's an addiction and ask yourself would you allow an alcoholic half an hour to go to the pub? There is also a cost attached in terms of the non-smokers feeling very much discriminated against. If your smokers deserve a break, then so do your non-smokers. Everyone or no one is the best policy, otherwise you will breed discontent, and discontent steals time. (It may be that help to stop smoking for those who wish to can be built into your personnel policy.)

14. Organise your workspace

Perhaps you are tidy by nature, but depending on how long it is that you have worked for your organisation and occupied the workspace you currently have, things could be getting out of hand. If you have piles of papers, magazines and books lying around, then these need to be sorted out. If the idea of this is daunting, then break the job down into smaller tasks.

Firstly tackle the backlog. File what needs to be filed, enter on your 'to do' list that which needs to be actioned, and pass on that which is not your responsibility. Finally, and most importantly (and you should probably do this with at least half of what is on your desk) throw what is not useful to you in the bin. Be ruthless!

Next, set up a simple system to deal with what lands on your desk. Have a stack of trays, a drawer of project files, whatever is appropriate for you. Use it always, change it if it doesn't quite suit your needs, keep on tweaking until it works for you. Similarly, arrange your desk so that the things you use most often, such as your telephone, keyboard and mouse, come readily to hand.

Get into the habit of having regular tidy-up and clear out sessions – keep on top of things. Ideally, the only thing that should be on your desk and vying for your attention is the task on which you are currently working.

15. Delegate

Just because something lands on your desk it doesn't automatically follow that you are the right person to deal with it. Delegate appropriately, whether down, sideways or up.

16. Use your diary effectively

Try to use just one method of recording appointments, deadlines, scheduled work and everything else you have to deal with. Whether this is a diary or some sort of planner matters far less than that you use it consistently and effectively. The danger of multiple diaries is that you mark something up in one and not the other(s) and so miss a meeting or a deadline.

17. Set 'rules' with your manager

Double check goals and deadlines and set times for review. It is a good idea to record this, either between the two of you in an email or for your own information in a note. You might also want to set some ground rules for assistance: a manager who from your perspective is interfering and not showing trust might from his or her perspective simply be being supportive.

18. Combat 'busyness'

We probably all know someone who races around day after day and yet gets nothing done – they are far too 'busy' to actually tackle anything as mundane as work! Avoid this activity trap by using your 'to do' list, regularly asking yourself 'the most important question', and focusing all your attention on the task in hand.

19. Use the 80/20 rule to your advantage

Most people are aware of this simple but very true rule: 20 per cent of your sales force achieve 80 per cent of your sales; 20 per cent of your customers account for 80 per cent of your profits; 20 per cent of your effort produces 80 per cent of your results. This isn't a green light for spending 80 per cent of your time deliberately unproductively, however; rather, it is a warning that if we are not careful, we can lose hours every week trying to get things perfect. Your first draft of a letter to a customer is very likely good enough; maybe you can improve it by re-reading and re-working the wording once, but constantly going over and over it will not improve it sufficiently to warrant spending your time in this way. Know when to stop and move on.

Use this knowledge to your advantage and you will get more done.

20. Be realistic

Don't create for yourself a daily 'to do' list that you simply cannot achieve. By all means make it challenging, but if it is impossible, and you know it is impossible, it may very well cause you not to even try to get anything done. There is only so much you can do, even when working at peak efficiency. Acknowledge this, and set out to do a fair day's work.

This might be a good time to mention that there are some things we simply have to accept: the goal posts may well change, depending on external events that impact the business, for example. It is far easier, however, to adapt an existing and successful plan. Continuing with our journey analogy, supposing you hear on the radio that an accident has closed a road you had intended to travel on – if you know where you are right now, you can more easily change direction to avoid the pile-up.

21. Be disciplined if/when you work from home

Shirking from home – ah, the joys! I used to envy colleagues who worked from home, even if only because they avoided the daily commute and could run the washing machine while they worked. I also never really believed they put all the hours in that they should. Besides, even if I did spend time gossiping with colleagues during the working day, I still had to be in the office between nine and five.

Being able to work from home is both a privilege and a real benefit for most people; you can be more flexible about your hours and arrange your working day to suit you. Working from home offers different distractions, but you still need to take the same approach to keep on track. Ask yourself the question: is what I *am* doing now what I *should be* doing now?

Whether you work from home permanently or occasionally, you need to build trust with your manager and your colleagues: people will otherwise assume that you are watching daytime television and surfing the Internet!

Conclusion

Remember that all the time management tools in the world won't get the job done if you either don't use them or don't buckle down and get to work. You have to take control – methods and systems don't get things done: YOU get things done.

Exercise: Vicky's dilemma

Earlier in the chapter we took a look at Vicky and how she was managing her time on one particular day. At that time, the following questions were raised:

What could Vicky have done differently an hour ago?

What is she doing wrong now?

What should she do next?

In the light of what you have learned since, use the space below to answer those questions. There are some suggestions at the end of the chapter.

_____

_____

_____

_____

_____

_____

Managing your time checklist

- I regularly ask myself the 'most important question'.

- I set myself effective goals in line with organisational strategy and the needs of the organisation.

- I know where I am going and regularly check that I am on course.

- I do not waste my time by completing unnecessary tasks.

- I know when my prime time is and plan my day accordingly.

- I know what my danger areas are with regard to time management and work hard to avoid them.

- My workspace is organised and uncluttered and has the things I use most often within easy reach.

- I understand the power of the 80/20 rule and use it to my advantage.

- I challenge myself, but am realistic about what is achievable. I do not set myself up to fail.

Case notes: Vicky's dilemma

Poor Vicky! Despite her best efforts, someone else has hijacked her time!

Vicky fell into the trap she is in for two reasons: firstly, the person making the request was her manager, and secondly, she believed that she only needed to spend half an hour on the impromptu discussion, which she could afford.

The first point here is that no matter who it is that makes a request that impacts on your time, you are within your rights to either be firm about how much time you can spare or to ask if it will wait. Of course, you may still be obliged to change your plans, but at least try to stick to your schedule. Had Vicky explained the situation, is it likely that her manager would have understood and respected her need to be fully prepared for her afternoon meeting? I think the answer here is 'yes'; Vicky's meeting prep was as important, but more urgent than the ground covered in the impromptu discussion.

As the discussion progresses, Vicky feels increasingly pressured as she sees her planning, and most likely her lunch break, go up in smoke. As a result she is reacting to the stress of the situation and not focusing on what it is she is currently doing. Because she has not explained how she had planned to spend her time and why, she very likely appears disinterested, hostile and downright rude.

Vicky has three choices: she can continue feeling stressed and behaving badly; she can resign herself to the lost lunch break and participate in the discussion; or she can explain her situation and bow out, promising to put her thoughts and suggestions forward as soon as she has time to consider the situation fully. What she will do depends on two things: her nature and the culture of the organisation she works in. It seems clear, however, that whatever her underlying motivation, the first option can only damage her reputation and standing in the eyes of her manager and colleagues.

Further reading

In print:

- Getting Things Done – David Allen, Piatkus (2001)

- Successful Time Management in a Week – Declan Treacy, Hodder & Stoughton (1993)

- What's Your Time Worth? – Harold L. Taylor, Kogan Page (1992)

- Working Smarter – Graham Roberts-Phelps, Thorogood Ltd (1999)

- Time Management for Dummies (2nd Edition) – Jeffrey L. Mayer, IDG Books Worldwide, Inc. (1999)

Online:

- http://www.businessballs.com/timemanagement.htm – information on the businessballs website.

- http://www.manageyourtime.co.uk/ – information on the Manage YourTime website.

- http://www.mindtools.com/pages/main/newMN_HTE.htm – time management information on the Mind Tools website.

- http://www.iod.com/intershoproot/eCS/Store/en/pdfs/hr19 man.pdf – 'Managing your time' directors' briefing on the Institute of Directors website.

- http://www.tsuccess.dircon.co.uk/timemanagementtips.htm – time management newsletter on the Total Success website.

Chapter 1.4
Managing information and developing networks

NVQ Application:

This chapter is relevant to the following NVQ in Management Units:

- A1 Manage your own resources
- A2 Manage your own resources and professional development
- A3 Develop your personal networks
- D1 Develop productive working relationships with colleagues
- D2 Develop productive working relationships with colleagues and stakeholders
- D17 Build and sustain collaborative working relationships with other organisations
- E11 Communicate information and knowledge
- E12 Manage knowledge in your area of responsibility
- E13 Promote knowledge management in your organisation

Linked chapters:

The information in this chapter is related to information in the following chapters:

- 1.1 Planning and managing your own professional development
- 1.2 Clear communication
- 1.3 Managing your time
- 2.3 Operating within the law
- 4.2 Establishing and managing relationships
- 5.3 Managing resources

Introduction

Once upon a time manual work predominated. Time and motion studies made the manual worker more productive, as measured by output. To achieve this, an analyst first looked at the task in terms of what steps had to be completed and how much effort and time each one took. Next, anything that was unnecessary was eliminated and the remaining steps were put into a logical sequence. Finally the tools used were redesigned to support the new process and to make what had to be done as easy as possible.

Nowadays 'knowledge work' predominates. It is far more difficult to break a task down into steps; there are many variables at stake when we are looking at acquiring, analysing, organising, storing and using knowledge and information.

It may be argued that knowledge is the economy's key resource in the twenty-first century. It is also eminently portable. As such, it is essential that we not only pro-actively seek knowledge and information, but also that we ensure it is stored in such a way that it becomes a tangible and accessible resource for the organisation.

Objectives

The aim of this chapter is to encourage you to think carefully about the quantity and quality of information that, with a little effort, you are able to access. It will help you to:

- plan to keep up to date with developments both inside and outside of the organisation;

- identify and access sources of information;

- manage and use information within organisational guidelines and legal requirements;

- develop and maintain a personal network of contacts; and,

- use your network to make introductions and to tap into other people's networks.

Why do we need information?

We need information for a whole raft of reasons, including to:

- make decisions;

- solve problems;

- assess risk;

- monitor;

- compare;

- improve;

- inform;

- control;

- forecast;

- plan expansion; and,

- ensure competitive advantage.

Information is power: the power lies in how the information is used. Whilst simply knowing something changes nothing outside of yourself, good, easily accessible information has immense potential.

What do we need to know?

The list of things it would be helpful to know will depend upon the nature of your organisation. However, the following are pretty much universally useful topics:

- an accurate profile of your customers;

- details about your competitors;

- information and news about the marketplace you operate in;

- the economy; and,

- the 'zeitgeist'.

It is a good idea to brainstorm your requirements. Start generally, and then narrow down your thinking so that you define quite carefully the range, level of detail and depth of knowledge you seek. Be clear as to why you want this information, how you will gather it, what you will use it for and how you will store it, being conscious of the requirements of legislation such as the Data Protection Act. (More information on the Act may be found in Chapter 2.3: Operating within the law.)

Types of information

Information may be classified as:

- **Hard:** objective, factual, easily verifiable information, such as age, national statistics, price lists; or,

- **Soft:** subjective, intuitive information, including customer opinion and perceptions as to the quality of customer service offered.

In addition, information may be:

- for sale, e.g. lists of contact details;

- freely available, such as competitors' catalogues, information on the Internet;

- given by contacts, such as snippets from your network; or,

- for internal use only, such as in-house information used to inform strategy.

Information may be sourced externally, from the Internet, trade publications, the press and other media, or from your network; or internally, from colleagues or stakeholders.

Assessing information

Information may be divided into four broad categories:

- immediately useful – in which case act on it straight away;

- not useful – in which case you should throw it away immediately;

- useful to someone else – in which case you should pass it on promptly; or,

- of general interest, in which case file it so that it can be accessed as required.

When selecting information, it should be UPPERCRUST:

- Usable: available to you and understandable;

- Prime: the best available;

- Pertinent: relevant to your needs;

- Exact: accurate;

- Reliable: trustworthy;

- Complete: not missing key data;

- Reputable: from a good source;

- Upright: ethical and honest;

- Sufficient: enough for your needs; and,

- Timely.

Case study: Tom's challenge

Tom has been asked by his manager to research and write a report on what grants and funding might be available for a particular project. He is to give details of what is available and from whom, what would be necessary to access the finance, and what the requirements would be if such an attempt were successful. For example, if a pot of money is potentially available from a particular source, it might be necessary to prepare a bid and to show certain outcomes if the bid was successful.

Tom has also been asked to make recommendations with regard to what he finds out.

This is a completely new arena for Tom and he is struggling to know quite what to do. He doesn't want to seem stupid, but he does need help.

Where might Tom find the information he seeks?

What would be a good starting point?

Who might be able to help?

We'll return to Tom later.

Managing information

One thing you can be sure of is that a great deal of information will land on your desk on a regular basis. At first glance it might not be possible to immediately see what is useful and what is not. Even when you have tagged something as being of interest, you still need to get to the kernel of useful information contained within the whole. There are some tips and techniques you can use to help you to keep on top of things, including:

- Skim and scan documents, magazines, books and papers. Speed-reading is a useful technique and one that might be worth practising.

- Read only what you must. Remember the four categories we identified earlier; as soon as you know something is not useful to you now, stop reading and move on.

- Use online services, newsletters and so on. They pre-sort and condense information before they present it to you.

- Listen to audio books when travelling.

- Take small amounts of reading with you when travelling. (Don't take too much: it can be heavy, bulky and off-putting. Better to take a small amount and get through it than take a lot and not feel able to face it.)

- Mark up texts, and tear out pages or copy articles from periodicals and magazines to make things more compact and easy to find when you want them.

- Put the date received at the top of letters and papers that you keep. Each time you retrieve something and use it, note the date. Go through your files regularly and throw away anything you have not looked at or used for, say six months.

Interpreting information

Always read with a purpose in mind so that you actively seek useful and related information. Also, always ask yourself: 'What does this mean to me?'

Suppose you work for a business that makes lingerie and you read that the average dress size has increased: *what does that mean to you?*

Perhaps you make fitness equipment and you discover that the government is having a big drive to promote exercise: *what does that mean to you?*

Always look for the angle that makes information not merely interesting but also directly useful to the business.

Forecasting trends

As well as looking at information to see what it means to you now, you can use it to have a stab at forecasting trends. To do this you should:

- always use UPPERCRUST information;
- ask: 'What if...?' questions;

- be clear about what you base your assumptions on; and,

- avoid being swayed by personal opinions and interests.

Presenting information

There are many ways to present information to make it easy to assimilate, including:

- pie and exploded pie charts;

- graphs;

- Venn diagrams;

- Ishikawa, or 'fishbone' diagrams; and,

- bulleted lists.

As well as passing on information formally like this, be sure to pass on snippets via your network.

Storing information

There are two methods of storing information: manual and electronic. Despite the increase in electronic types of communication and storage and all the hype about the paperless office that has been aired over the years, manual systems don't look likely to become obsolete any time soon.

Whatever type of system you choose – and the chances are you will be using both types in concert – there are a few simple rules that will help with filing, storage and retrieval of data:

- Design it to be easy to use. If it is easy to file and retrieve data, then the system will be used and will work for you. If it is complicated or difficult, then people will try to avoid using it and you will work for the system. Part of this ease of use relates to the physical location of a manual filing system. I am sure I am not alone in having struggled with poorly stacked dusty boxes of random files and papers when finding what I was looking for was as much a matter of luck as anything else. Stored information ought to be easily accessible, well organised, clean and tidy.

- File regularly. Little and often is much more manageable than a once or twice a year blitz. It also means that anyone else who needs to refer to that information can find it.

- Make sure all the relevant people, whether on or off site, are able to access data (even if this is through a third person who retrieves, then scans and emails or faxes data to off-site personnel).

- Operate within the law. Be aware of what legislation affects you (for example, The Data Protection Act) and make sure you take all steps necessary to adhere to requirements. (More information may be found in Chapter 2.3, Operating within the law.)

Developing a network of contacts

In business, it is very often a case of 'not what you know, but who you know' that helps you get things done. Just as you delegate jobs because you cannot do everything yourself, you also need to employ experts and cultivate a network of contacts because you cannot personally know everything.

What is a network?

A network is simply a group of people with you at the hub as a common denominator. Each of those people will very likely have their own network, with them at the hub. The more contacts you have in your own network, the more networks you will become a part of yourself.

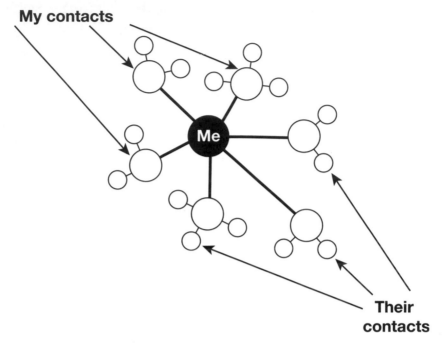

My contacts

Me

Their contacts

Network of contacts

How will I benefit?

Are you familiar with the concept of 'six degrees of separation'? If I am one step away from everyone I know, then I am two steps away from everyone they know, and so on. It's also known as the 'human web'. Interpreting mine, I am two steps away from writer Ian Rankin, three steps away from actress Susan Hampshire, and just four steps away from musician Jimmy Page.

Having a network effectively gives you access to the opinions and expertise of a range of people on an informal, free basis. As relationships develop and grow, you may benefit from snippets of information or industry gossip that could be very much to your advantage. Being consistently well-connected and well-informed will also do your own career prospects no harm whatsoever.

Where do I start?

Whenever you come into contact with other people, you have a networking opportunity. That could be within your own organisation or with people from other organisations. Prime opportunities are likely to present themselves at training events, meetings, briefing sessions, social events, and even the gym.

I used to work for an organisation that got involved in a very exciting project working with inmates at a local prison, which all grew out of a chance conversation on a train between people from both organisations who had never previously met. That project led to involvement with other local prisons – networks have a tendency to cascade.

Some networks, or networking events, are more formally arranged. The Chambers of Commerce often run such gatherings, for example, and there are likely to be other independently run local events that could prove useful to you.

How do I manage my network?

Relationships that are ignored and neglected wither away, whatever the basis for them, and business networking relationships are no exception. Whenever you get a snippet of information (provided it is not confidential) think of who in your network might appreciate the heads-up and get in touch. If you know the dates of birthdays or anniversaries, for example, either send an email or make a phone call; and if you simply haven't run into someone or had any other reason to get in touch for a while, just email or telephone them for a short chat to see how things are. People appreciate such thoughtfulness and it will keep you in the forefront of their mind should they unearth anything interesting and at the top of their 'favours due' list if you do need their help.

How do I tap into contacts' networks?

I would recommend making introductions between the people in your network whenever you get the opportunity. They will appreciate it and be very likely to return the favour. Also, if you have a 'good' contact but one who does not necessarily have the information you want, don't be afraid to contact them anyway; sound them out and see if they would be willing to put you in touch with someone in their network who can help – or even to tap into their contacts' networks to see what might be known there. Never be afraid to ask for opinions or advice from others; most of us are flattered to be asked and only too pleased to be able to help.

Conclusion

Keeping informed and up to date is a key element in management. You can't make sound decisions or judgements based on poor or flawed information any more than you can learn and develop your skills while operating in a vacuum. Be curious: you might be surprised what you find out!

Exercise: Tom's challenge

Earlier in the chapter we took a look at Tom and the project he had been set by his manager. At that time, the following questions were raised:

Where might Tom find the information he seeks?

What would be a good starting point?

Who might be able to help?

In the light of what you have learned since, use the space below to answer those questions. There are some suggestions at the end of the chapter.

_____

_____

_____

_____

Managing information and developing networks checklist

- I understand why good information is essential to good management.

- I consider what it is that I need to know and actively seek out that information.

- I know that information can be hard or soft, free or paid for, internal or external.

- When I get information, I assess it and deal with it appropriately.

- I make sure the information I use is UPPERCRUST.

- I don't just take information at face value; I consider what it means for me and for the business.

- I present information in an easy to understand format that is appropriate to the audience.

- I have easy to use and understand filing systems.

- I know why I should develop a network of contacts.

- I am alert for opportunities to expand my network.

- I nurture my contacts and actively manage my network.

- I offer information to others as well as seeking it from them.

Case notes: Tom's challenge

As Tom seems really stuck, he might be best to first go back to his manager and ask if this kind of exercise has been carried out before. If so, he needs access to the findings and it would also be a good idea to speak to the person who conducted the exercise, if s/he is available. Tom might also approach his mentor, if he has one, or select someone suitable from his network of contacts, again if he has one.

Other than that, a first sweep might be carried out online. The organisations who come to light as a result of that can then be further researched: in the company's filing system to see if they have been approached or dealt with previously, online, via the network of contacts and so on. He may also choose to approach directly those organisations that look most promising and register his interest and/or clarify facts.

Tom will need to verify what he finds out wherever possible, or else make it clear in the report that a particular comment is based on unsubstantiated data or hearsay. Once he has sufficient good quality data, he will be in a position to weigh up the pros and cons in order to arrive at his recommendations.

Further reading

In print:

- Managing Information, Peter Grainger, Manager's Toolkit Series, Kogan Page Ltd (1994)

- Beat the Bumph!, Kathryn Redway, Nicholas Brealey Publishing Ltd (1995)

- Managing Information, David A Wilson, Butterworth-Heinemann Ltd (1993)

- Management Information Systems (6th edition), T. Lucey, DT Publications Ltd (1991)

- Management Challenges of the Twenty-First Century, Peter F. Drucker, Butterworth-Heinemann (1999)

- Speed Reading, Tony Buzan, David & Charles (1992)

Online:

- http://www.ico.gov.uk – the Information Commissioner's Office website.

- http://data.gov.uk – website that aims to make government data more accessible.

- http://www.managing-information.org.uk/ – practical guide to managing information.

- http://www.doconsite.co.uk/ – the 'definitive guide to managing information and documents' (2009).

- http://en.wikipedia.org/wiki/Data_Protection_Act_1998 – summary of the Act.

- http://www.mindtools.com/speedrd.html – useful article on speed-reading on the Mind Tools website.

Part 2
Managing the business

Chapter 2.1
Leadership, culture and vision

NVQ Application:

This chapter is relevant to the following NVQ in Management Units:

- B5 Provide leadership for your team
- B6 Provide leadership for your area of responsibility
- B7 Provide leadership for your organisation
- B9 Develop the culture of your organisation

Linked chapters:

The information in this chapter is related to information in the following chapters:

- 1.1 Planning and managing your own professional development
- 1.2 Clear communication
- 1.3 Managing your time
- 1.4 Managing information and developing networks
- 3.1 Managing and implementing change
- 3.2 Innovation and opportunity
- 4.2 Establishing and managing relationships
- 4.4 Developing and motivating others

Introduction

Leadership is so often seen as a gift – something of mystical origin and very much a quality in isolation. There is the belief that you either have it or you don't. In practice, however, nothing could be further from the truth. Whilst some of us may show a natural aptitude for it, leadership, like so many things, is a skill that can be learned.

The basis of leadership is the same as the basis of good management: knowledge, skills and ability. You must have the knowledge and skills that are the basic building blocks of your business: for example, knowledge of the industry and communication and planning skills, plus the ability to put them into practice in a way that enables you and those around you to achieve the desired results in a timely and satisfactory manner.

Objectives

The aim of this chapter is to look at leadership and explain it in a business context. It will help you to:

- understand some of the many theories of leadership that abound;

- be aware of different leadership styles;

- understand culture as a concept;

- be aware of the culture and structure of the organisation in which you work; and,

- be aware of the power of communicating a clear and compelling vision.

It is fair to say that the majority of groups will, in time and without direct leadership, generate a leader from within their number. Much time can be wasted in battling for supremacy in these circumstances, however; therefore it is far better to provide a leader and to ensure that person is equipped with the necessary knowledge, skills and abilities to fulfil the role.

What is leadership?

If a group of managers are asked the question: 'What is leadership?' their answers will generally include the following:

- having a vision that everyone works towards;

- motivating staff to do what you want them to do;

- doing things for the first time or in new ways; and,

- doing or discovering something completely new.

From this we can infer that a leader must be a visionary, a catalyst and a pioneer. In addition, to be effective, a leader must have the necessary power and authority, which ought to be granted by virtue of the position held within the organisation. Finally, a leader must command respect. This is somewhat trickier, in that unlike knowledge, skills and abilities, it cannot be learned, and unlike power and authority, it cannot be granted by virtue of a person's rank or job title; respect must be earned.

The right stuff

If we think about the qualities a leader would ideally have, we might include the following:

- **Vision:** a clearly defined vision that can be communicated to others, giving a common purpose to group or team activities.

- **Tenacity:** leaders don't give up when things get tough, they dig in, take stock and forge ahead once more.

- **Adaptability:** when faced with an obstacle that can't be overcome, leaders will look for a different route to get them where they want to go.

- **Enthusiasm:** they maintain a positive attitude and help others to keep their spirits up, especially when things get tough.

- **Confidence:** in themselves, in the team, and in the vision they are working towards.

- **Integrity:** they are honest, don't have favourites and are fair in all things.

- **Warmth:** they show by their words and deeds that each member of the team is valued and appreciated.

- **Humility:** when objectives are achieved, they say to the team: 'You did this – well done', rather than: 'Look at what I did'.

Leadership vs management

There has been – and continues to be – much debate about the difference between leaders and managers. Some say that leaders do the right thing whereas managers do things right, giving a nod to Peter Drucker's assertion that doing the right thing is far more important than doing things right. Others say that leaders manage people whereas managers manage tasks. Whichever definition you prefer, it is an inescapable fact that in modern business, we have to combine both roles in order to get things done. A leader who lacks basic management skills is unlikely to get any further than a manager who cannot lead: the first can fire people up with a vision, but lacks the ability to make it into a reality; the second knows the nuts and bolts of getting things done but will have to drive or drag the team every step of the way.

Different styles of leadership

Different situations suit different styles of leadership; it is generally accepted that Winston Churchill led Britain brilliantly throughout World War II and yet had enjoyed a largely unremarkable political career before that time (he also lost the election immediately afterwards in 1945, although he led his party back to power in 1951). Steve Jobs founded Apple in his garage and turned it into one of the world's largest manufacturers of computers (having resigned after losing a power struggle with the board of directors in 1985, he is once more back at the helm following the 1997 buyout by Apple of the company he went on to found).

A number of studies have been conducted into different styles of leadership and we are going to look at two of them here: The Managerial Grid Model devised by Jane Mouton and Robert Blake, and Dr Paul Hersey's Situational Leadership® Styles Matrix.

The Managerial Grid Model

9	1:9 style								9:9 style
8									
7									
6					5:5 style				
5									
4									
3									
2									
1	1:1 style								9:1 style
	1	2	3	4	5	6	7	8	9

Concern for people (vertical axis)

Concern for production (horizontal axis)

Managerial Grid Model

In the view of Mouton and Blake, the two most important areas of concern for leaders are production and people. Looking at positioning on the grid allows us to define styles of leadership. For example:

- 9:1 style: dictatorial – an authoritarian style focusing wholly on task;

- 1:9 style: accommodating – an indulgent style focusing wholly on people;

- 1:1 style: indifferent – a minimalist style, taking little account of either people or task;

- 5:5 style: status quo – a balanced style, maintaining the status quo; or,

- 9:9 style: sound – an integrative style, taking account of both task and people.

Whilst under different circumstances different styles might be appropriate, you might find this a useful tool for identifying where you currently sit on the grid and where you would like to sit, which will help with the creation of your personal development objectives and planning.

Situational Leadership® Styles Matrix

Dr Paul Hersey combined task and people in a way that highlighted four leadership styles[1]. The styles are 'situational', depending as they do upon the team's levels of experience, ability, and willingness to accept responsibility for the task. The underlying belief is that there is no 'one best way' to lead, but that leaders need to be adaptable to the environment in which they find themselves.

	High relationship		
Low Task	**Leadership through participation**	**Leadership through selling**	High Task
	Leadership through delegation	**Leadership through telling**	
	Low relationship		

Situational Leadership® Styles Matrix

According to the model, the styles are applicable as follows:

- Leadership through telling: staff are simply directed and told what to do and how; used when staff are both unable to perform the task and unwilling to take on the responsibility.

- Leadership through selling: the manager explains things in detail and encourages staff to ask questions so that they can fully understand the process to be undertaken; used when staff are prepared to take on the responsibility but don't have the ability to complete the task.

- Leadership through participation: staff are invited and encouraged to participate in planning and decision making; this style

---

1   © Copyright 2006 Reprinted with permission of the Center for Leadership Studies. Escondido, CA 92025. www.situational.com. All Rights Reserved.

is one of engagement and encouragement and is used when staff have the ability to complete the task but are unwilling to take on the responsibility.

- Leadership through delegation: staff are allocated roles and responsibilities and allowed largely to self-manage; this style would be used with a 'mature' team that has both the ability and the willingness to take responsibility for completing the task.

The four stages can also be loosely related to the stages of team development, beginning with a team with no cohesion and poor skills and progressing to a self-managing team that can be trusted to get the job done.

The Tannenbaum and Schmidt continuum

This process is echoed in the Tannenbaum and Schmidt continuum, shown below. As we can see, as the team progresses in ability and willingness to perform, the manager relinquishes authority and the team gains freedom. Neither 'push' style nor 'pull' style is 'wrong': the style chosen depends upon the circumstances. In a crisis, for example, there may be no time for consultation and delegation.

Ideally, as this process continues, a leader would emerge from the team and the reins could be passed on.

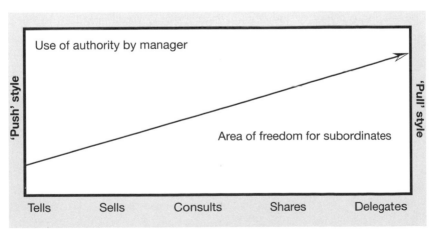

The Tannenbaum and Schmidt continuum

When I left school, my first job was as a trainee manager with a multiple grocery retailer. The company was growing and had a tried and tested method for opening new stores: the manager and deputy would be appointed early in the process and would be involved in all aspects of getting a supermarket up and running, and a team of trainee managers would go in as department heads. It was our job to set up our appointed department, perhaps to be involved in recruitment for the store, and to both be involved in initial staff training and take over continuing that training prior and subsequent to the store opening. We were there until we had identified a successor, agreed that person's promotion to department head with the manager, and trained them to the point they were confident they could run the department with only minimal management assistance.

I didn't know it at the time, but we were progressing through both Hersey's leadership styles model and the Tannenbaum and Schmidt continuum. We also had to balance the element of competition amongst ourselves at being 'first out, job done' to being confident that we had done enough to empower the new department head to do the job. If they succeeded, then the credit was theirs; if they floundered, then the blame was ours. It was a good, early grounding in the principles of management.

Action Centred Leadership

Completing our look at some of the theories of leadership is John Adair's model of Action Centred Leadership. Adair asserts that three elements are interlinked in the process of leadership, as shown in the diagram below.

Action Centred Leadership Model

The diagram illustrates centrally important needs that must be satisfied in order to have functional and productive work groups.

- **Task need:** the group comes together when things have to be done that are too much for one person to handle. *The role of the leader here may be defined as 'Achieve the task'.*

- **Team maintenance need:** the need to create and promote group cohesiveness. *The role of the leader here may be defined as 'Building and maintaining the team'.*

- **Individual needs:** physical, psychological, status, a sense of personal worth. *The role of the leader here may be defined as 'Develop the individual'.*

Adair sees these three elements as being inextricably interlinked, with performance in any one area impacting upon the others. So whilst achieving the task will impact positively in terms of building the team and offering job satisfaction for the individual, a dysfunctional team will struggle to complete the task and will cause frustration and dissatisfaction for the individual members.

The leadership roles that are indicated by the elements of the model may be broken down into functions, and Adair shows them as:

- defining the task;
- planning;
- briefing;
- controlling;
- evaluating;
- motivating;
- organising; and,
- providing an example.

Each of these is something that can be learned, which will help you to develop both as a manager and a leader.

Organisational culture

As well as making sure that you understand the structure of your organisation, you will no doubt become aware very quickly of the culture or philosophy. This has been defined as 'the way we do things around here'. Bolman and Deal assert that 'Culture is the glue that holds an organisation together'. You may perceive it as the 'personality' of an organisation and – just as with some people – it may not be something you easily get along with. If you are greatly at odds, then you may feel obliged to move on and find somewhere that is a more comfortable 'fit', as to prosper you need to be seen to 'fit in' and 'be one of us'.

I have twice faced what I would describe as a 'culture shock': the first when I moved from a corporate company to a not-for-profit organisation and the second when I took a job within a national media group. The first time I adapted, because the culture was different but not unpleasant; the second time I simply left, because it was clear to me that the values and the behaviours that were ingrained and deemed to be acceptable within that organisation would never be acceptable to me. (It should be said that how things were done was in no way related to the public face of the group. The culture was, I suspect, unique to that office and 'subversive' in nature.)

The components of culture include:

- the management structure;
- the treatment of staff;
- language and terminology;
- written style in web and paper based media;
- gender mix/dominance;
- dress code;
- surroundings;
- what is respected and rewarded;
- what people aspire to;
- what prospects exist;
- symbolism, such as logos and emblems; and,
- rituals and ceremonies.

The culture of an organisation can be a changing and evolving thing, either by design, as desired change is incorporated into the strategic plan for the business, or by influence, as 'pressure groups' create changes in attitude and behaviour. This can be for good or ill, and is something that you yourself are able to become involved with.

Suppose your organisation makes a great deal of money, which it distributes to shareholders and in bonuses to management; the culture might be perceived to be one of elitism (not everyone gets a bonus), greed (no good is done with the money), or success (look at the figures – we're doing great!). Say the elitist tag has been applied and is not welcome: changes to the bonus structure or provision of staff parties, away-days and funding for non-business related training might help share the benefits and change the culture. With greed, regular charitable donations to charities suggested and chosen by staff might help. With success, there is no related problem, although steps to share the wealth might be welcomed.

You and your image

How you look, sound, dress, and your body language all send signals to those around you about how closely you fit in at work. If you have been in your role a while, think back to the 'you' who was interviewed: in what ways have you changed since then? Has your language, speech pattern, way of dressing, working habits or leisure pursuits changed at all? If so, how much, and was it a conscious effort to 'fit in'?

Many of us know of a maverick that enjoyed success despite choosing not to toe the corporate line; we might also know of someone who started smoking when his or her age was in single figures and lived to see 100. Do you want to take the risk?

You might want to take steps to raise your profile, especially if you feel that you are being overlooked. Things you can do include:

- Be positive: even if you are dreading something. That's not to say if you have genuine concerns about the viability of a project you shouldn't voice them, but if, for example, you are required to make a presentation that you haven't really the time for and you are not confident giving presentations, don't whinge about it. Take it on the chin, make the time, prepare thoroughly, and be positive.

- Be pro-active: according to John Bird, founder of The Big Issue, 'Leading is about doing what needs to be done before you are told'.

- Act confidently: even if you don't feel it. It can be tough, but no matter how you feel inside, do your best to make sure that the image you present to the outside world is calm, capable and confident.

- Celebrate your successes: not arrogantly, but do be sure to let people know about the good things.

- Support your colleagues: we all need a little help now and then, so be there for others when they need it, whether it be advice, passing on knowledge or acting as a sounding board.

- Own up to mistakes: it is far better that news of an error comes from you, along with a suggestion as to how the situation can be remedied.

- Act with integrity: if you want to earn respect, be honest, truthful, fair and consistent. You know what is right and what is wrong and whilst cheats may seem to prosper in the short term, they are most often found out eventually and rewarded accordingly.

- Socialise with colleagues and contacts: and be sure your behaviour in a social setting stands up to scrutiny. No matter how much you act the part at work, if you behave inappropriately in a social situation it will be noted, remembered, and perhaps used against you.

Exercise: Raising your profile

Step 1: What are the main components of the culture of my organisation?

Think about the culture of the organisation you are a part of; what makes it the way it is? Who are the main influencers of 'the way we do things around here'? Is this somewhere you feel comfortable, or are there things that you are not entirely happy about?

Step 2: How am I currently perceived?

Give some thought to how people see you within the framework of the organisation. Do they see you as a rising star, a safe pair of hands, an established manager? Or have they really not noticed you at all yet? Is your name first to be mentioned when an opportunity presents itself or do the chances go to other people?

Step 3: How can I become more 'visible'?

Now think about how you would like to be perceived. What can you do to get from where you are now to where you want to be?

Use the space below to make some notes in answer to those questions. Remember, this is just for you, so be honest about how you feel and what you would like to happen.

Once you have a more definite idea of where you want to be, however, you should make a plan to help achieve that. Some of the steps will be things that you can do yourself: perhaps you want to change your style of dress or learn something new. For others, it might help to get your manager involved or perhaps to raise some of the issues at your next appraisal or one-to-one: if you make it known that you want to be considered when opportunities arise to get involved with new projects, for example, then you are at least on the list. If you want to use some of your personal development budget to gain a qualification, then you can get support with that, too.

Remember that very often all it takes to get something is to ask for it. Don't be shy!

_____

_____

_____

_____

_____

_____

_____

_____

_____

_____

Vision

Leaders are visionaries in the truest sense: they see clearly the reality they want to bring about and share that in an understandable way with those that can help them to make it happen.

This vision can be simple: to be the best sales team in the company, or it can be complex: to stimulate natural breast tissue to grow again after surgery. (A team at the Bernard O'Brien Institute of Microsurgery on Australia is currently working towards this vision. The technique will most likely be used first with cancer patients seeking reconstruction following mastectomy.) It can be quite mundane: to clear the backlog and keep it clear, or dramatic: to revolutionise home computers and how we use them.

In order to fire people up to work towards them, visions have to be both desirable and achievable. You would be unlikely to get people fired up to help you achieve your vision of 'reducing the workforce by 50 per cent in the next year'. Similarly, you would be unlikely to be able to use strategy and planning to achieve your dream of 'planting the company flag on the moon'. Your vision is your goal, and as such may involve taking a short, medium or long-term view of the future. It drives the objectives you set and feeds directly into your strategy and planning.

It is hard to remember nowadays a time when mobile phones were not ubiquitous. I recall working in the cellular telephony industry in the early days when a mobile was an expensive luxury item and to have one per household was what most people aspired to. I also recall vividly the buzz when Orange was launched and the mixture of excitement and incredulity when the vision was announced of seeing everyone in the UK, man woman and child, with his or her own mobile phone. The days of ringing an empty house were to be numbered; in future, people would ring people, from and to wherever they were at the time. We could scarcely credit the possibility – the expense, the risks of giving a child a phone that they could use unsupervised – and yet we could buy into it, because we wanted that, too.

That was a bold vision. If we had been told at the time that we would also be able to use our phones to take photographs, write documents, and access information on a world wide web that existed in cyberspace, we would very likely have flipped out! And yet here we are, living in a world that is shaped the way it is because someone had the audacity to dream it could be so.

Conclusion

Leaders achieve things with the aid of vision and within the framework of the structure and culture of the organisation within which they work. They also get results not only through their own efforts but also by encouraging others to commit to their vision and give of their best to achieve it. Similarly, an individual would not enjoy the same level of success without the motivation, guidance and encouragement of a leader. And being driven by a vision when setting and working towards our own personal goals can be a very powerful motivator indeed.

Leadership, culture and vision checklist

- I appreciate both the differences and the similarities between 'leaders' and 'managers'.

- I am aware of my own management style.

- I understand leadership styles and aim to use that which is appropriate at all times.

- I am familiar with John Adair's model of Action Centred Leadership.

- I am aware of those things that combine to create organisational culture.

- I understand the culture of my organisation and aim to impact positively upon it.

- I am conscious of the image I wish to project and take steps to achieve that.

- I have a vision: in work and in life, I know what I wish to ultimately achieve.

Further reading

In print:

- Effective Leadership (New Revised Edition): How To Be A Successful Leader, John Adair, Pan (2009)

- How to Change Your Life in 7 Steps, John Bird, Vermilion (2006)

- The Managerial Grid III: The Key to Leadership Excellence, R. Blake and J. Mouton, Gulf Publishing Company (1985)

- Management of Organizational Behaviour: Utilizing Human Resources (3rd ed.), P. Hersey and K. H. Blanchard, New Jersey/ Prentice Hall (1977)

- How to Choose a Leadership Pattern, R. Tannenbaum and W. Schmidt, McGraw-Hill Education (2009)

- Leadership for Leaders, Michael Williams, Thorogood (2005)

Online:

- http://www.situational.com/ – website of the Center for Leadership Studies, founded by Dr Paul Hersey.

- http://www.leadership-expert.co.uk/ – the Leadership Expert website.

- http://www.mindtools.com/pages/article/newLDR_84.htm – leadership styles article on the Mind Tools website.

- http://www.nwlink.com/~donclark/leader/leadstl.html information on leadership styles.

- http://psychology.about.com/library/quiz/bl-leadershipquiz.htm – leadership style quiz.

Chapter 2.2
Strategic management and business planning

NVQ Application:

This chapter is relevant to the following NVQ in Management Units:

- B1 Develop and implement operational plans for your area of responsibility
- B2 Map the environment in which your organisation operates
- B3 Develop a strategic business plan for your organisation
- B4 Put the strategic business plan into operation
- B10 Manage risk
- D4 Plan the workforce
- E8 Manage physical resources
- F3 Manage business processes

Linked chapters:

The information in this chapter is related to information in the following chapters:

- 1.2 Clear communication
- 1.3 Managing your time
- 1.4 Managing information and developing networks
- 2.1 Leadership, culture and vision
- 2.3 Operating within the law

Introduction

Management is all about planning. Whether you are planning your personal development, planning to meet your personal, team or departmental work objectives, planning to research and develop or launch a new product, or planning to take the whole organisation in a completely new direction, the basic principles are the same: it is just the scale that differs.

That is good news indeed for all of us. It means that whether our goals are lowly or lofty, we can follow a step-by-step, logical process that gives us the best chance of achieving what we set out to achieve.

Objectives

The aim of this chapter is to encourage you to make achievable plans while taking into account the impact both internal and external forces might have upon them. It will help you to:

- be aware of the planning process;

- set and plan to achieve SMART business goals and objectives;

- understand and use PESTLE and SWOT analysis techniques;

- know how to utilise scenario planning; and,

- understand risk management.

The planning process

Traditionally, the planning process is represented as a cycle.

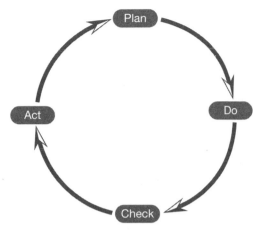

The planning cycle

However, I would suggest the following model might prove useful as an overview of the process:

Planning model

The first step is to assess the current situation and note what it is that we wish to change. We then devise a plan to bring about the desired change, implement it, and monitor progress regularly against objectives. Once completed, we review the results and this takes us back to the assessment stage: either to assess why we didn't get the results we wanted and to see where we are now with regard to that matter, or to review a different area of the business.

Case study: Colin's challenge

Following his employment as Customer Services supervisor, Colin's manager has asked him to draw up a plan showing how he will tackle the backlog of customer queries that has developed over the previous six months. Instead of meeting their target of resolving all queries within eight working days, the majority have now been outstanding for between two and ten weeks.

Colin is in charge of six teams, each comprising a team leader, a deputy, and 10 staff. The most experienced team leader is Hilary, who has been in the job for 18 months. The least experienced is Sam, who was promoted just last month.

How should Colin proceed?

We'll come back to Colin later in the chapter.

Purpose and vision

Imagine a chain of budget hotels: their purpose might be 'to provide clean, comfortable, affordable accommodation for those travelling for business and pleasure throughout the UK'. Their vision might be 'to be the biggest budget hotel chain in the country'. (This might be expressed to those outside the company as a mission statement: 'To be the UK traveller's first choice, every time'.)

Purpose tells us what the business does, whereas vision tells us where the business is going. Once the vision is defined, the next step is to set strategic objectives that will move the business from where it is now to where it wants to be.

In a stable economy, assuming a time of little or no change, then that process might be represented as a simple graph:

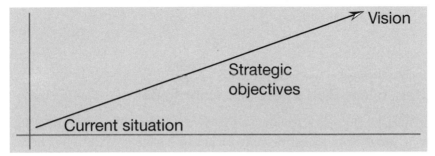

However, it is more realistic to see the process as a series of steps, each of which moves us a little closer to our vision, followed by a review of the situation:

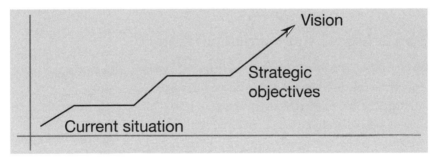

Eight steps to effective planning

As with all things, breaking the overall process down into smaller steps will help us to understand how to achieve our goal.

- Step 1: Visualise where you want the business (or your team or department) to be.

- Step 2: Assess where you currently stand in relation to that vision.

- Step 3: Set strategic objectives to help you to bridge the gap.

- Step 4: Devise a timetable to support your objectives and to provide milestones against which you can monitor progress.

- Step 5: Calculate the costs and negotiate the budget.

- Step 6: Implement the plan.

- Step 7: Monitor progress against the plan, taking corrective action where necessary.

- Step 8: Evaluate the outcome.

Step 1: Visualise where you want to be

See clearly what it is you wish to achieve. Write down and define and refine your vision; this is your primary objective. You will need to be able to communicate this clearly and concisely to others in order that you get the support you need for your plan. Practise an 'elevator pitch': imagine you enter the lift in the lobby and have just the amount of time it takes to reach the top floor to explain to a fellow traveller what your vision is.

Step 2: Assess your current position

Think of this as a journey, and, as with any journey, when you are planning your route there are two things you need to know: where you are starting out from and where you are going to. This step allows you to see how much ground you must cover to achieve your goal.

Step 3: Set strategic objectives

Break down your route into bite sized pieces by setting strategic objectives that move you nearer to your goal. In the example of our hotel chain, they might want to set quarterly sales objectives for each region and monthly targets for each hotel.

When you set strategic objectives, they should be SMART. That is: Specific, Measurable, Achievable, Realistic and Time-bound. Let's take a closer look.

Specific

It is essential that you are very clear about what you wish to achieve, it should be possible for anyone to grasp what you are doing as a result of reading your objectives and so you must make sure that they reflect that lack of ambiguity. Examples:

- To reduce overall bad debt by 10 per cent within six months.

- To increase sales by 20 per cent in the next 12 months.

- To reduce customer complaints by 10 per cent in the first quarter.

Measurable

You need some independently verifiable way of proving success. Having set specific objectives in the first place, you should easily be able to see what it is that must be measured to demonstrate progress.

Achievable

It may be that you cannot achieve your ideal in the time or with the budget available. If that is the case, then scale down your objectives accordingly and be prepared to have a 'stage 2' if necessary to finish the job. If you choose objectives that are specific and measurable, yet unachievable, they will be demotivating to staff and you may achieve less than had you lowered your sights in the first place. Anything you know to be unachievable is a dream, not an objective. Dreams have their place, but not in this context.

Realistic

Is what you aim to do feasible in the light of all else that must be taken into account? Projects do not exist in a vacuum and your activities must complement the activities of the rest of the business.

Time-bound

You need to know by when you wish to achieve your goal otherwise it can drag on forever. There should be an end to activity, by which – ideally – things will have come to a natural and satisfactory conclusion.

Step 4: Devise a timetable

Provided all your objectives are SMART, then your timetable should come together quite naturally. The master timetable will have the advantage of highlighting times when you have too much (or too little) to do, allowing you to make whatever amendments may be necessary.

Step 5: Calculate the costs

Take everything into account when you draw up your budget and be prepared to negotiate if necessary.

Step 6: Implement the plan

The best planning technique in the world won't get results if the plan isn't put into action. If you are introducing new machinery, launching a new product or expanding the business then you might want to make a big splash, although many plans get started in an atmosphere of quiet efficiency and cause no ripples whatsoever at this stage. The important thing, however, is to make sure that you start work when your timetable decrees, otherwise you will be playing catch-up from the outset.

Be flexible; it is always better to bend than to break. Remember that management guru Peter Drucker asserts that it is more important to be doing the right thing than to be doing things right.

Step 7: Monitor progress

Monitor progress against milestones and investigate variances. Where necessary take corrective action.

Step 8: Evaluate the outcome

Your final task is to evaluate how successful you were in working towards and achieving your objectives. There are always lessons to be learned and one of the most important tasks is to make sure that those lessons are recorded and not lost; that way in the future new methods can be tried to replace those that were less satisfactory and those that worked well can be repeated and developed.

PESTLE analysis

A PESTLE analysis is a structured way of considering external forces that have a bearing on the business. PESTLE is the acronym for the type of forces to be taken into account:

- Political;

- Economic;

- Socio-cultural;

- Technological;

- Legal; and,

- Environmental.

This model was known initially as a PEST analysis, then became STEEP with the addition of environmental forces, and is now PESTLE, following the addition of legal forces.

Political forces

These include such things as government legislation; EU legislation; employment law; tax policy; trade restrictions; data protection issues; trade union action; and threat of terrorist action.

Economic forces

These include such things as inflation; interest rates; exchange rates; taxes; unemployment levels and so on. It is the global economy that has to be looked at here, not just the UK; whatever is happening elsewhere now may well have an impact on the UK in time. This is perhaps especially true of what happens in America.

Socio-cultural forces

These include such things as demographics; disposable income levels; fads and trends; and patterns of leisure and shopping.

Technological forces

This is potentially the area of most dramatic change and will include such things as advances in IT and communication; availability of information; robotics; equipment and machinery; and science.

Legal forces

These include such things as government and EU legislation; employment law; consumer legislation; health and safety issues; and policies preventing discrimination.

Environmental forces

These include such things as sustainability; recycling; energy efficiency; waste management; intensive vs. organic farming; and ecologically sound housing.

SWOT analysis

To conduct a SWOT analysis simply means to consider the business in a certain context and to identify what strengths, weaknesses, opportunities and threats exist.

Outsourcing customer telephone queries

Strengths	Weaknesses
There'll be a dedicated team	Not 'our' people
It's cheaper	They're based off site
We're currently struggling	Lack of knowledge
It will give 24/7 coverage	Don't understand ethos/culture
Opportunities	**Threats**
Existing staff can be employed elsewhere	Competitors don't outsource – customers might prefer them
Money saved can be used elsewhere in the business	Staff resistance/morale

Scenario planning

Scenario planning is a strategic planning tool that helps in the production of a range of flexible, medium to long term plans for the business. You can use as a starting point the results of your PESTLE and SWOT analyses, and then:

- take each point in turn and consider what are the drivers for change;

- describe how things might look if the situation should change according to those perceived drivers;

- identify what opportunities and threats exist in the new vision of the future; and,

- consider what would be the best response for the business to that situation.

Scenario planning is all about posing 'What if...?' questions and imagining possible futures in which your business might find itself operating. You should decide on what overall assumptions the scenarios you intend to create should be based. It can be helpful to look back over a similar period to that for which you are planning ahead and see how things changed. This should give you an idea of the direction in which things are going and can be used to kick-start a brainstorming session to come up with some ideas as to what might happen in the future: will progression be linear and steady? Is it likely to speed up or slow down? Might things go off at a tangent? Are any new developments likely?

It can be helpful to distil the information generated by your brainstorming session into three or four full scenarios; provided they make sense in themselves, they can help you to make sense of the future.

Risky business

In simple terms, risk management is a three-step process involving:

- identifying potential risks;

- assessing the likelihood and implications of those risks occurring; and,

- planning to either prevent them from happening or to minimise the impact on the business if they should occur.

Business risks may be inherent in the marketplace or due to a specific series of events or course of action. There are three basic ways to manage risks:

- **Avoidance**: simply don't do whatever it is that exposes you to risk. For example, if I go out on a day when rain is forecast, there is a strong risk that I will get wet. I do not want to get wet, so I am not going to go out.

- **Mitigation**: this involves taking steps to counter the risk and includes such tactics as outsourcing activities such as perhaps call handling or manufacturing. In my example, I might buy an umbrella and take it with me – or I could send you out instead!

- **Acceptance**: if the cost of avoidance or mitigation is considered to be too high, then we may simply have to take the risk and accept the hit if the worst happens. So if umbrellas suddenly become very expensive or the price you want to charge me to go out in my place is too high, I would have to face the elements and take my chances.

Risk management strategy needs to be an integral part of organisational process and procedure. It is a good idea to have a written policy and to make risk assessment a requirement of all new projects and initiatives. No business will ever be risk free; the trick is to take risks that are calculated.

Conclusion

Making plans and working to achieve goals can be exhilarating – provided that the plans are well thought out and the objectives are SMART. If we commit ourselves to plans that are unworkable we set ourselves up to fail. Of course, nothing we ever do is free from risk, so we must consider and understand the risks we face and work out what we will do if the worst happens. Thinking things through, working within a framework and taking a calm, logical approach will give us the best chance of success.

Exercise: Colin's challenge

Earlier in the chapter we took a look at Colin, who had been tasked with drawing up a plan to tackle the outstanding customer queries. At that time, the following question was raised:

How should Colin proceed?

In the light of what you have learned since, use the space below to answer that question. There are some suggestions at the end of the chapter.

_____

_____

_____

_____

_____

_____

Strategic management and business planning checklist

- I understand the planning cycle.

- I understand the planning process.

- I can define both purpose and vision for the organisation.

- I use the eight steps when making strategic plans.

- I set SMART objectives for my team and myself.

- I know how to conduct a PESTLE analysis.

- I know how to conduct a SWOT analysis.

- I use scenario planning to consider possible future developments.

- I take risks into account when setting objectives and making plans.

Case notes: Colin's challenge

Colin has inherited a tricky situation. The first thing he needs to do is to gain a sound understanding of how the situation came about and what is achievable for the team. He also needs to make sure that he is aware of the full extent of the problem; if the team leaders have been juggling the figures or hiding anything for fear of reprisals, then his plans will be worthless.

His first act is to get the team leaders together and get the facts. Hilary in particular should be helpful here. Once he knows exactly how things stand, he can make an accurate assessment of how long it will take to achieve his vision of clearing the backlog. This will form the basis of his SMART objectives. These objectives are likely to be set for the department as a whole and then broken down by team, so that it can be seen if any one team is experiencing greater difficulties than the others.

He must also consider whether it would be useful to get the staff to work overtime or to hire some temporary staff for a period of time, and add that cost in to his budget.

He needs to make sure that the reporting mechanism for age and volume of queries is sufficient for his purposes, so that he can check whether things are on target and take corrective action if things slide.

Finally he must investigate and address the cause of the problem so that it doesn't simply flare up again.

Further reading

In print:

- Strategy Safari: The Complete Guide Through the Wilds of Strategic Management, Henry Mintzberg, Financial Times/Prentice Hall (2008)

- Essential Tools for Operations Management: Tools, Models and Approaches for Managers and Consultants, Simon Burtonshaw-Gunn, John Wiley & Sons (2010)

- Harvard Business Essentials: Strategy, Harvard Business School Press (2005)

- What is Strategy and Does it Matter? Richard Whittington, Thomson Learning (2000)

- Principles of Strategic Management, Tony Morden, Ashgate Publishing Limited (2007)

Online:

- http://www.thinkingmanagers.com/business-management/strategic-management.php – Edward de Bono & Richard Heller's 'Thinking Managers' site.

- http://www.planware.org/strategicplan.htm – information plus a free to use online strategic planner on the PlanWare website.

- http://managementhelp.org/plan_dec/str_plan/str_plan.htm – information on strategic planning on the Free Management Library website.

- http://www.cwc.org/market/mkt4.htm – useful article on strategic planning.

- http://www.netmba.com/strategy/ – information on strategic planning on the NetMBA website.

Chapter 2.3
Operating within the law

Linked chapters:

The information in this chapter is related to information in the following chapters:

- 2.2 Strategic management and business planning
- 4.1 Employing people

Introduction

Businesses nowadays have to comply with a whole raft of legislation, more so then ever before. It is also subject to change at an alarming rate. Consequently this chapter is intended to give an overview and then sign-post you to reliable sources of online information that ought to be kept up to date, thus ensuring that you have access to contemporary data.

Objectives

The aim of this chapter is to make you aware of the main areas of legislation with which you must comply. It will help you to:

- know what the main responsibilities of your organisation are;
- keep up to date with the requirements you are expected to meet;
- take action to comply with them; and,
- know how to stay informed.

Employing people

When a business employs people there are many requirements that must be met, starting with verifying that the employee has the right to work in the UK. If they haven't and you take them on, then your organisation is liable for a fine or even a criminal conviction. You cannot simply avoid the issue by choosing not to interview or employ people who sound or appear to be 'foreign', either, as you would then (quite rightly) fall foul of laws against racial discrimination.

This is a very tricky area as historically the necessary checks have not been either simple or straightforward for employers to make, despite which the responsibility for checking and accountability should an error be made both lie with the employer. However, the law in this area is evolving. New technology is making passport checking possible for employers and identity cards are being issued. Over the next year or so, more changes are expected that should combine to make things easier for employers and make their responsibilities much fairer and easier to meet than they have been so far.

Related legislation

- Asylum and Immigration Act 1996

Further information

- The UK Borders Agency: www.ukba.homeoffice.gov.uk

- The Department for Business, Innovation and Skills: www.berr.gov.uk

- Government public services information website (England and Wales): www.direct.gov.uk

- Free business support and advice: www.businesslink.gov.uk

Employment rights

People you employ have certain rights that you must ensure are upheld. These range from those of a basic nature (access to a toilet and drinking water) to more complex ones involving hours worked, remuneration and time off for various reasons. Some legislation applies only to businesses over a certain size.

The main areas are arguably the national minimum wage and the working time directive. There is no defence against not paying someone at least the national minimum wage – although many self-employed people work for far less than this – but employees can choose not to be governed by the working time directive and so work more hours per week than legislation stipulates. You must not, however, pressure people to opt out or discriminate against them if they choose not to.

Related legislation

- The Factories Act 1961
- Rehabilitation of Offenders Act 1974
- Employment Protection (Consolidation) Act 1978
- Transfer of Undertakings (Protection of Employment) Act 1978
- Transfer of Undertakings (Protection of Employment) Regulations 1981
- Employment Rights Act 1996
- Working Time Regulations 1998
- Human Rights Act 2000
- Employment Relations Act 2004
- Work and Families Act 2006
- Working Time (Amendment) Regulations 2007
- Employment Act 2008
- Information and Consultation of Employees Regulations

Further information

- The Department for Business, Innovation and Skills: www.berr.gov.uk

- Government public services information website (England and Wales): www.direct.gov.uk

- Free business support and advice: www.businesslink.gov.uk

- The Advisory, Conciliation and Arbitration Service: www.acas.org.uk

- HM Revenue and Customs: www.hmrc.gov.uk

Contracts of employment

The contract between employer and employee is effectively established when a job offer is made and accepted. It does not have to be in writing, but it is good practice to record terms. Whilst it is not necessary to provide a contract, employees are with very few exceptions entitled to a written statement within two months of starting work.

The statement must include the following:

- organisation name;

- employee name;

- date employment begins;

- the duration of the contract, if it is not a permanent position;

- hours of work;

- job title and/or a brief description of duties;

- place of work;

- the pay and how often it will be awarded;

- holiday entitlement;

- sick leave/sick pay entitlement;

- details of pension scheme/contracting out options;

- details of any collective agreements that are in place;

- details of disciplinary and grievance procedures; and,

- notice of termination required on both sides.

It is a good idea to cover terms and conditions of employment in the induction for new staff so that people are clear from the off what to expect from you and what you expect from them.

Related legislation

- Employment Rights Act 1996

- Employment Act 2008

Further information

- The Department for Business, Innovation and Skills: www.berr.gov.uk

- Government public services information website (England and Wales): www.direct.gov.uk

- Free business support and advice: www.businesslink.gov.uk

- The Advisory, Conciliation and Arbitration Service: www.acas.org.uk

Equality and diversity

You must take positive action to promote a diverse workforce and also ensure that everyone enjoys the same respect and consideration and has the same chances of advancement.

By law, you cannot discriminate against anyone on the grounds of:

- gender, or gender reassignment;

- pregnancy or maternity;

- sexual orientation;

- marital or civil partnership status;

- age;

- disability;
- race, nationality, ethnicity or national origin;
- religion or belief, or lack of it;
- trade union membership, or non-membership; or,
- status as a fixed term or part-time worker.

There are four main types of discrimination, which are:

- direct: e.g. 'men only';
- indirect: e.g. with a height restriction or requirement;
- victimisation: unequal treatment for whatever reason; and,
- harassment: bullying or picking on someone for whatever reason.

At the time of writing (January 2010) a high street clothing retailer is under fire for advertising for 'cool, good-looking' staff. In 2009 the same firm was obliged to pay compensation to a previous employee who claimed she was bullied into quitting because she had a prosthetic arm. Whilst the firm denies discrimination, the publicity surely cannot be doing their business any good whatsoever.

Related legislation

- Sex Discrimination Acts 1975/86
- Race Relations Act 1976
- Disability Discrimination Act 1995
- Race Relations (Amendment) Act 2000
- Fixed Term Employee Regulations 2002
- Employment Equality (Religion or Belief) Regulations 2003
- Employment Equality (Sexual Orientation) Regulations 2003
- Age Discrimination Regulations (2006)
- Employment Equality (Age) Regulations 2006
- Employment Equality (Age) (Amendment) Regulations 2008

Further information

- The Department for Business, Innovation and Skills: www.berr.gov.uk

- Government public services information website (England and Wales): www.direct.gov.uk

- Free business support and advice: www.businesslink.gov.uk

- The Advisory, Conciliation and Arbitration Service: www.acas.org.uk

- The Equality and Human Rights Commission: www.equalityhumanrights.com

Bullying and harassment

Instances of bullying and harassment in the workplace must be taken very seriously indeed. People being bullied often don't realise they have protection against such treatment, or might be wary of seeking help as bullies are so often in a senior position to their victims. Bullies might not realise that their behaviour constitutes bullying – or, more likely, will hide behind a defence of 'she's too sensitive', 'he needs to toughen up', or 'that's just how it is here'.

Please don't be naïve when it comes to issues of bullying; it can happen in the best of organisations. What makes the difference is how it is handled when it does occur. And it is far more prevalent in the workplace than you might think; I have certainly witnessed it on more than one occasion and, despite the fact that I am neither timid nor easily intimidated I too have been the victim of workplace bullying.

Bullying behaviour includes:

- undermining someone;

- nit-picking;

- belittling a person;

- assigning tasks that cannot be completed for some reason, e.g. the deadline given is unrealistic;

- changing deadlines at short notice, or changing them and not telling people;

- overloading someone with work;

- withholding necessary information;

- offensive or insulting behaviour;

- verbal abuse; and,

- acts of physical violence.

Harassment includes:

- the expression of bigoted views (e.g. homophobic, racist);

- lewd comments and jokes, and innuendo;

- sending offensive emails; and,

- name-calling.

It is a good idea to draw up a policy, and on a personal note, I would advocate zero tolerance. Have clear guidelines for people who are being bullied and make sure there is more than one route of complaint; if in the first instance the matter must be taken up with the line manager, for example, and the line manager is the bully, then a lack of complaints will certainly not indicate a lack of bad behaviour. It is also a good idea to monitor staff turnover rates and to hold exit interviews.

Vicarious liability

Under certain circumstances, employers are not only responsible for the behaviour of their staff in the main place of work, but in all work situations. This includes office parties; official functions, business trips and so on. Employers may be liable for a claim of (for example) age discrimination if it can be shown that they knew, or should have known, about it and failed to take action to stop it or prevent it from happening again.

Related legislation

Covered at least partially by anti-discrimination laws.

Further information

- The Department for Business, Innovation and Skills: www.berr.gov.uk

- Government public services information website (England and Wales): www.direct.gov.uk

- Business Link: www.businesslink.gov.uk

- The Advisory, Conciliation and Arbitration Service: www.acas.org.uk

- The Equality and Human Rights Commission: www.equalityhumanrights.com

- Workplace Bullying – non-profit site working to provide a legal resource to those working against bullying or harassment of any kind in the workplace: www.workplacebullying.co.uk

- Bully Online – perhaps the first and claiming to be the world's largest resource on workplace bullying and related issues: www.bullyonline.org

Trade Union recognition

Whilst it is no longer legal for any Trade Union to operate a 'closed shop' (i.e. every employee must become a member of the union), the unions still have a valid role to play within British business.

Employees have the right to become members of Trade Unions if they wish: employers, however, are not automatically required to recognise the unions.

Recognised unions represent workers in discussions with the employer. This can be done collectively, for example, in pay negotiations; or individually, for example in bullying or disciplinary cases. Most unions that are recognised are done so under a voluntary agreement with the employer. If the employer will not voluntarily recognise a Trade Union, then the union can follow a statutory procedure for recognition.

People cannot be discriminated against on the grounds of Trade Union membership, or lack of it.

Related legislation

- Trade Union and Labour Relations (Consolidation) Act 1992

- Trade Union Reform and Employment Rights (TURER) Act 1993

Further information

- The Department for Business, Innovation and Skills: www.berr.gov.uk

- Government public services information website (England and Wales): www.direct.gov.uk

- Free business support and advice: www.businesslink.gov.uk

- The Advisory, Conciliation and Arbitration Service: www.acas.org.uk

Redundancy

Redundancies are carefully regulated. They may only be instigated for the following reasons:

- the business ceases trading at a particular site;

- the business ceases trading altogether; or,

- a particular type of work is scaled down or phased out completely.

There are strict guidelines to follow with penalties for an employer if errors are made. It is a good idea to take legal advice if your organisation is considering making redundancies. The following are advisable:

- know the law and follow it;

- have a written procedure that is communicated to all staff;

- remember that communication is key – people will be under enough pressure if jobs are under threat: don't add to it by handling things badly;

- be sensitive; and,

- keep records.

Related legislation

- Transfer of Undertakings (Protection of Employment) Act 1978

- Transfer of Undertakings (Protection of Employment) Regulations 1981

- Trade Union and Labour Relations (Consolidation) Act 1992

- The Collective Redundancies and Transfer of Undertakings (Protection of Employment) Regulations 1995

- The Collective Redundancies and Transfer of Undertakings (Protection of Employment) (Amendment) Regulations 2006

- The Collective Redundancies (Amendment) Regulations 2006

Further information

- The Department for Business, Innovation and Skills: www.berr.gov.uk

- Government public services information website (England and Wales): www.direct.gov.uk

- Free business support and advice: www.businesslink.gov.uk

- The Advisory, Conciliation and Arbitration Service: www.acas.org.uk

Health and safety at work

The essence of health and safety is simply to provide a clean, comfortable and safe working environment for staff and anyone else that comes into contact with your business. Having sound health and safety policies and procedures makes good business sense: the cost of implementation is likely to be considerably lower than the costs attached to accidents, ill health, and possible closure due to a lack of compliance with the law.

The principle statute in this area is the Health and Safety at Work etc., Act 1974. The Act sets out general principles for the management of health and safety in the workplace. As a result of this framework further, more specific regulations were created, so tailoring the legislation to a specific industry sector. These regulations, known as 'Statutory Instruments' include the Personal Protection Equipment (PPE) at Work Regulations 1992 and the Control of Substances Hazardous to Health Regulations 2002 (commonly known as COSHH). The Statutory Instruments also provide for compliance with the law of the European Union, and the Act is the principal means for ensuring the requirements of the Council Directive 89/391/EEC on health and safety at work are met.

The objectives of the Act are stated to be:

- securing the health, safety and welfare of persons at work;

- protecting persons other than persons at work, against risks to health and safety or arising out of or in connection with the activities of persons at work; and,

- controlling the keeping and use of explosive or highly flammable or otherwise dangerous substances, and generally preventing the unlawful acquisition, possession and use of such substances.

The original enactment of the bill also covered noxious emissions, but this has since been repealed and is now covered by the Environmental Protection Act 1990.

The general duties of the Act call for employers to ensure (so far as is reasonably practicable) the health and safety of all employees with regard to plant, systems of work, buildings and facilities. Similar provision must also be made for the safety of contractors, clients, visitors and the general public. Safety representatives may be appointed and consulted, and since 1996 employees must also be consulted on safety matters.

Employees in turn have a duty of care to themselves and others with regard to health and safety and to co-operate with those carrying out duties or fulfilling requirements under the Act.

Related legislation

- The Health and Safety at Work etc., Act 1974

- The Personal Protection Equipment (PPE) at Work Regulations 1992

- The Control of Substances Hazardous to Health Regulations (COSHH) 2002

Further information

- The Health and Safety Executive: www.hse.gov.uk/

- Free business support and advice: www.businesslink.gov.uk

- The Department for Environment, Food and Rural Affairs: www.defra.gov.uk

- The World Health Organisation: www.who.int/en/

- Government website offering free environmental advice: www.netregs.gov.uk

- The Department for Business, Innovation and Skills: www.berr.gov.uk

- Government public services information website (England and Wales): www.direct.gov.uk

Risk assessment and management

Risk assessment is the process of determining the likelihood of a risk happening and the magnitude of the damage if it did. Likelihood and severity can be given ratings, which would then be multiplied to give a probability rating of the risk occurring. This process involves objective evaluation of each risk or hazard in turn. The Health and Safety Executive identifies five steps that must be followed when undertaking a risk assessment. These are:

- identify the hazards;

- decide who might be harmed and how;

- evaluate the risks and decide on precautions;

- record your findings and implement them; and,

- review your assessment and update if necessary.

Risks are categorised as:

- physical: including the dangers of noise, heat, light and radiation;

- chemical: exposure to chemicals at work carrying the risk of burns, poison and disease;

- biological: created by exposure to bacteria, viruses, spores and dusts which may be human, animal and bird, or vegetation in origin; and,

- ergonomic: usually muscular-skeletal and due to poor posture, badly laid out work area or repetitive movement.

Risk management looks at the potential risks, perhaps identified as a result of conducting a risk assessment, and then puts health and safety measures in place to control them.

Related legislation

- The Health and Safety at Work etc., Act 1974

- The Personal Protection Equipment (PPE) at Work Regulations 1992

- The Control of Substances Hazardous to Health Regulations (COSHH) 2002

Further information

- The Health and Safety Executive: www.hse.gov.uk/

- Free business support and advice: www.businesslink.gov.uk

- The Department for Environment, Food and Rural Affairs: www.defra.gov.uk

- The World Health Organisation: www.who.int/en/

- Government website offering free environmental advice: www.netregs.gov.uk

- The Department for Business, Innovation and Skills: www.berr.gov.uk

- Government public services information website (England and Wales): www.direct.gov.uk

Business insurance

All businesses require insurance. Some insurance is required by law, other types are simply prudent. The most common types are:

- Employers' Liability Insurance;

- Public Liability Insurance;

- Product Liability Insurance (which may be included with Public Liability Insurance as a package);

- Professional Indemnity (for certain professions only, e.g. accountants and lawyers);

- Key Person Cover;

- Directors and Officers Insurance (to protect directors of limited companies, who can, in certain circumstances, be personally liable);

- Goods in Transit;

- All Risks Buildings and Contents;

- Business Assets and Equipment;

- Legal Expenses Insurance;

- Money Policies; and,

- Credit Insurance (protects against debtors becoming insolvent).

Related legislation

- Employers' Liability (Compulsory Insurance) Act 1969

Further information

- The Health and Safety Executive website has a comprehensive guide for employers covering the requirements of the Act: www.hse.gov.uk/

- The Department for Business, Innovation and Skills: www.berr.gov.uk

- Government public services information website (England and Wales): www.direct.gov.uk

- Free business support and advice: www.businesslink.gov.uk

Handling sensitive data

A survey undertaken in 2009 for National Identity Fraud Prevention Week found that around one third of UK employees fail to shred sensitive documents, choosing instead to simply throw them in the bin; more than one third did not know or were unsure as to whether a comprehensive policy was in place for handling potentially sensitive documents; and almost three-quarters feel that more could be done by the organisations they work for to protect clients' sensitive information. This is worrying news indeed and indicating that a great number of UK businesses could fall foul of the requirements of The Data Protection Act 1998.

The Act requires businesses to comply with eight principles designed to ensure that personal information is:

- fairly and lawfully processed;

- processed for limited purposes;

- adequate, relevant and not excessive;

- accurate and up to date;

- not kept for longer than necessary;

- processed in line with peoples' rights;

- secure; and,

- not transferred to other countries without adequate protection.

The Act also awards rights to individuals, including the right to find out what personal information is held on computer and in many paper records. This means that all employees must be mindful that whatever they write on a file or in an email, not necessarily to but simply about a customer, might at some point be read by that customer.

Legal admissibility

Organisations must be able to show that any documents or data held electronically have not been changed since time of storage in order for them to be legally admissible. So, if you routinely scan customer correspondence and shred the originals, should a customer take you to court (or vice versa), you will be required to prove that the documents you are holding are exactly as received and have not been altered or amended in any way.

Best practice is shown in the 'Code of Practice for Legal Admissibility and Evidential Weight for Information Stored Electronically' (BIP0008) published by the British Standards Institute (BSI).

According to COLA (as the code is commonly known), you should have in place five key information management components:

1. representation of information (i.e. an information management policy);

2. a duty of care;

3. business procedures and processes;

4. enabling technologies; and,

5. audit trails.

Full information is available on the BSI website.

Related legislation

- The Data Protection Act 1998

- The Civil Evidence Act 1995

Further information

- The Information Commissioner's Office: www.ico.gov.uk/

- The British Standards Institute: www.bsigroup.com

- The Department for Business, Innovation and Skills: www.berr.gov.uk

- Government public services information website (England and Wales): www.direct.gov.uk

- Free business support and advice: www.businesslink.gov.uk

Business and the environment

Businesses have a legal and – arguably – a moral responsibility to monitor, limit and control the impact their activities have in the environment. Over and above this, however, many customers actively seek out businesses that act in an environmentally responsible manner, meaning that this actually makes good business sense and, far from being merely a 'cost' exercise, can, over time, positively impact the bottom line.

Three main regulators enforce environmental legislation in the UK:

- The Environment Agency (England and Wales);

- The Northern Ireland Environment Agency; and,

- The Scottish Environment Protection Agency.

A range of environmental rules exist with which businesses must comply, including those on:

- emissions;

- waste storage and disposal;

- statutory nuisance (noise, odour, fumes etc.); and,

- storage and use of hazardous substances, and disposal of hazardous waste.

Under certain circumstances permits or licences are required. For example, if your business is responsible for handling or disposing of waste, discharges effluent or tainted water into the sewage system, or uses hazardous substances.

Related legislation

There is a huge amount of legislation in this area, with different requirements for England, Scotland, Wales and Ireland. The best source of information is the NetRegs website, where you can read up on current and future legislation that could affect your organisation.

Further information

- Government website offering free environmental advice: www.netregs.gov.uk

- The Department for Business, Innovation and Skills: www.berr.gov.uk

- Government public services information website (England and Wales): www.direct.gov.uk

- Free business support and advice: www.businesslink.gov.uk

- Department for the Environment, Food and Rural Affairs: www.dcfra.gov.uk

Exercise: Legal requirements

Drawing on the information you have read, make a list of the main areas of legislation that your organisation is affected by. Do some research of your own and make a note of any industry-specific requirements.

How are these dealt with? Who is responsible for ensuring adherence? How often is the performance reviewed to confirm suitability?

_____

_____

_____

_____

Part 3
Managing change

Chapter 3.1
Managing and implementing change

NVQ Application:

This chapter is relevant to the following NVQ in Management Units:

- C4 Lead change
- C5 Plan change
- C6 Implement change

Linked chapters:

The information in this chapter is related to information in the following chapters:

- 1.2 Clear communication
- 2.1 Leadership, culture and vision
- 2.2 Strategic management and business planning
- 4.2 Establishing and managing relationships
- 4.3 Building and leading the team
- 4.4 Developing and motivating others
- 5.3 Managing resources
- 6.4 Project planning and management
- 6.5 Problem solving and decision-making

Introduction

We live in a rapidly changing world and change of one sort or another is something we all face regularly in both our work and our private lives. It can be welcome or it can be very hard to bear, it can start out looking like one thing and turn out to be another, or it can seem like a whole load of trouble just for things to stay basically the same. Whatever it is and whatever the outcome, it generally involves an amount of stress and worry because change, by its very nature, involves uncertainty. Change is uncomfortable and people tend to react to it in different ways. The ability to plan and facilitate change, and to manage the process well is an essential management skill, one of the most useful in your toolkit.

Objectives

The aim of this chapter is to consider the reasons for and effects of change. It will help you to:

- understand why change is necessary;

- know why people resist change;

- plan to implement changes effectively; and,

- monitor and evaluate the benefits of change.

Triggers for change

Triggers for change may be due to external forces, such as advancements in technology, changes in legislation or action taken by competitors; or internal forces, such as failure of systems, the launch of new products or services, or restructuring.

The change can be something that affects the whole organisation, just your department, just your team or perhaps just you. Whilst it is of some comfort if you are not the only one going through change, research has shown that faced with change, even in a group, people generally feel alone in coping. It is certainly true that we are each responsible for our own reactions and behaviour, and if one is finding change difficult, to see colleagues apparently handling things with ease can be both isolating and dispiriting.

Levels of change

Change can be categorised as either:

- **extreme**: dramatic change, either as the result of a crisis or a planned but major change, such as relocation or a restructure involving job losses;

- **moderate**: planned and affecting a significant number of people, perhaps on an operational level, such as introducing new machinery or increasing responsibilities; or,

- **mild**: perhaps minor changes to systems or procedures.

Barriers to change

These might also be thought of as reasons for resisting change. The main ones are:

- fear (I won't be able to cope, they won't need me, they don't know what they're doing, I won't have a say);

- lack of knowledge (they haven't told us the full story, what about so-and-so, have you heard the rumours);

- disaffection (oh great – another hare-brained management scheme, have you heard which idiot's in charge of it, I don't see why I have to change); and,

- a preference for the status quo (there's nothing wrong with how things are).

The section below headed 'Managing the process' will tackle these and provide a framework that will help everyone involved to cope with planned change.

Case study: Out with the old…

Chris works as a customer services supervisor for a telecoms company that has recently merged with another business. Due to consolidation, all customer service queries are now dealt with at the site where she works. Many of the 'new' customers have long-unresolved queries that they are determined to get resolved under the new regime, so the call rate is much, much higher than had been expected and planned for. Their accounts are on an earlier version of the same system the staff are used to, so whilst they can more or less find their way round the screens, they have to swap databases depending on whose customer the caller was originally and this all takes extra time. The situation will be resolved when the new billing system comes in, but they will have to live with regularly changing between systems for the next several months.

Staff are used to seeing queries through from initial call to resolution, investigating problems, making calls, writing emails and letters as necessary. They enjoy this as it both gives them a break from the phones and also provides a sense of ownership and job satisfaction. With the new situation, however, that system simply isn't working.

After discussion, it has been decided to introduce a new query handling system: front line and back line. Front line staff are to stay on the phones and take calls constantly. They will answer whatever they can there and then, but record details of any more involved queries and pass them on to the backline staff. Backline staff will investigate and resolve the more complicated customer queries and will only get on the phones to investigate queries or to call customers back.

How can Chris bring in the changes with the least possible upset and disruption?

We'll return to Chris in a little while.

Looking for things to change

You should make a point of being alert to areas of potential improvement, ideally as part of a culture of 'continuous improvement'. You can do this informally by being observant and listening to what people have to say, or formally by having in place a system of review or perhaps a staff suggestion scheme. The kinds of things to look at include:

- **staff:** knowledge and skills, staffing levels, team and department structures;

- **processes and procedures:** duplication of work, bottlenecks;

- **equipment and machinery:** faults with, new developments;

- **sales and marketing:** quality and availability of supporting materials, response from buyers to price etc.

- **location:** complaints about accessibility, distance from similar businesses and so on.

Managing the process

Change is a process and as such is something that we can plan for and manage. Even if we find ourselves 'fire fighting', there are certain steps we can take to reduce stress, encourage participation and increase our chances of success. Those steps are:

1 communicate clearly;

2 show congruence;

3 involve and engage; and,

4 provide help and support.

Let's take a closer look at those.

1. Communicate clearly

At times of change, you need to communicate more, and more effectively, than ever before. Change can be represented as a force field diagram, with drivers and barriers shown as opposing forces. This can be a powerful way of both acknowledging people's concerns and highlighting the reasons why change is necessary.

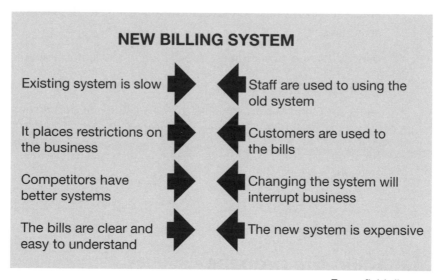

Force field diagram

One of the biggest causes of fear, itself a massive barrier to your success, is lack of understanding of what is happening, how and why. Tell people. Sell the benefits – make sure they know what is in it for them. People are much more likely to accept a period of learning and disruption if they can see that at the end of it, they will be better off. Keep them informed at every step of the way and be mindful of the fact that what they do not hear from you, they will hear from someone else, who may well embellish or invent facts. This is potentially dangerous, as rumour and innuendo can be hard to stamp out. The more you deny something, no matter that you are telling the truth, the less people will believe it. Stick to the facts and don't give 'rumour control' the chance to get their oar in.

Do tell people as much as you can as soon as you can. The recent crisis in the financial sector caused a great deal of upheaval and a great many job losses. One of the Trade Unions involved complained bitterly of the way information was drip-fed from management, who – presumably – were in possession of an overall strategy and plan, saying that the constant flow of announcements of changes and batches of redundancies was like 'death of a thousand cuts'.

The ways in which you can disseminate information include:

- one-to-one meetings;
- team briefings;
- department briefings; and,
- newsletter or intranet.

It is good practice to tell everyone what is going on, even if they are not directly affected (although it makes sense to inform those who are directly affected first of all).

2. Show congruence

Congruence may be thought of as consistency. Being consistent in what you say and do will generate trust, establish your sincerity and boost your credibility. People will have confidence in what you are doing and your ability to achieve results.

3. Involve and engage

This follows on quite naturally from the previous two points. If people are informed and are receiving a consistent message, they will have to actively resist becoming involved and engaged. If you are working through planned change, then as part of the planning process seek feedback and input from people. You might be surprised by what you find out! The one situation in which this might not be possible is if you are fire fighting and simply do not have time to get input from more than a handful of others; if that is the case, people will understand – provided you communicate clearly and show congruence.

4. Provide help and support

There are times when this is crucial: during a period of redundancy, for example, when both those who are leaving and those who are staying all require support. Those making the decisions and conducting the redundancy interviews will also need support, but be sure to choose those people carefully and brief them fully. They may well be handling the process for the first time, but it is not acceptable for them – as has happened in my experience – to say at the end of the interview: 'Phew! That's the hardest thing I've ever done. I'll need a drink tonight.' A little respect and consideration is the least people who are losing their jobs – and their livelihoods – should be able to expect.

Methods of support include:

- allowing time for people to work on their CVs, fill in application forms and go to job interviews;

- help and advice with regard to the above;

- information about training, further education, or self-employment; and,

- financial advice and counselling.

When you are the change…

This can be such a tricky situation! There you are, full of vim and vigour as a result of landing a new job or a promotion, and when you bounce into the department all you see are frosty faces. You are energised and enthusiastic and your team are sullen and uncommunicative.

The instinctive thing to do might be to write them all off and see who you can get rid of, or try to squeeze one or more friendly faces into the team to try to redress the balance. This isn't necessarily the best way to deal with the situation, however.

Firstly, think why it is that people may feel as they do. Perhaps they have had change thrust upon them without clear communication, congruence, being involved and engaged, and being provided with help and support. Perhaps on top of that, one or more of their number felt they were in with a chance of getting the job themselves and they don't understand why someone from outside was chosen in preference to someone who already knew the team, the department and the company. They may also feel threatened or intimidated by you. See things from their perspective and you may well understand just why they feel as they do.

If this is the case, start by communicating and involving people. Don't be afraid to ask their advice and to acknowledge their skills and experience. I don't mean let them do your job for you; that would just breed more resentment. But don't make mistakes for the sake of asking how things are done and do give credit where it's due. Remember that the successes are shared while the mistakes are yours alone.

N.B. If any adverse reaction you experience is due to racism or sexism, for example, then it should not and must not be tolerated.

Monitor and evaluate benefits

Monitor key indicators to check that things are going according to plan. This gives you two opportunities:

- the chance to take corrective action if things aren't quite right, but before they get completely off course; and,

- the chance to trumpet successes to whomever might be interested. Depending upon what it is that is being done, that might be to colleagues within the team, the company, stakeholders or even the world at large in the form of a press release.

Conclusion

Change can be daunting, frightening, or just plain depressing if handled badly. Handled well, it can be one of the most motivating experiences you and your team can go through. One thing is for sure: it cannot be avoided.

Managing and implementing change checklist

- Triggers for change can be both internal and external.

- Change may be something we actively seek to do as part of a process of continuous improvement.

- I consider change and identify whether – for me, my team or my department – the change is extreme, moderate or mild.

- I understand barriers to change and try not to let my own fears affect how I try to deal with it.

- I support others to help them overcome their barriers.

- I use the four-step framework to manage change.

- I can illustrate drivers using a force field diagram.

- After a process of change, I undertake an evaluation to see what might be learned.

- I let people know when change has gone well.

Case notes: Out with the old...

Chris has her work cut out! She can see that there will be resistance to this change and that it will be very unpopular, and she understands why. The initial perception will be that the front line jobs are less prestigious, that there is more of a 'factory' feel to the work. It will also be relentless: there are more calls than ever before, as soon as one call is finished, another one comes through, and as there is currently no lull – only a dip in the number of calls that go unanswered – the only breaks will be scheduled ones. Front line staff will also be deprived of the satisfaction of seeing a query through to the end.

Back line staff have it easier in many ways, but will have to try to understand the notes taken by front line staff to get to the bottom of the query. One person's shorthand might make no sense whatsoever to another person. If back line staff have to ring customers up to seek clarification, then any time advantage of the new system will be lost.

Chris prepares a force field diagram. She will talk things through with her team leaders in the first instance and knows that a visual representation can be very powerful. She will also take care to use the four steps, and to sell the benefits.

Chris has the option of allowing team leaders and/or staff to have some say in how things are handled. Perhaps they would prefer to have one or two weeks on the front line, then swap to back line, and vice versa. Giving people some power in the decision making process will help the new system to be accepted. Also, whilst the intention is only to use this system for as long as is necessary, she knows that if it proves successful, senior management may well choose to keep it. Consequently she wants it to be as popular as possible.

Further reading

In print:

- Making Management Simple, Frances Kay, Helen Guinness and Nicola Stevens, How To Books Ltd (2005)

- Managing Change, Roger Plant, Gower Publishing Company Ltd (1987)

- Coping with Change at Work, Susan Jones, Thorsons (1995)

- Winning at Change, George Blair and Sandy Meadows, Pitman Publishing (1996)

- Managing Innovation: Integrating Technological, Market and Organizational Change, Joe Tidd & John Bessant, John Wiley & Sons (2009)

Online:

- http://www.businessballs.com/changemanagement.htm   – information on change management on the businessballs website.

- http://www.mindtools.com/pages/article/newPPM_82.htm – Kotter's 8-Step Change Model.

- http://www.leadership-and-motivation-training.com/managing-change-in-the-workplace.html – useful article on managing change on the workplace.

- http://www.businessknowhow.com/manage/leadwithin.htm – useful article on change on the Business Know-How website.

- http://www.strategies-for-managing-change.com/managing-change-in-the-workplace.html – useful information on managing change.

Chapter 3.2
Innovation and opportunity

NVQ Application:

This chapter is relevant to the following NVQ in Management Units:

- C1 Encourage innovation in your team

- C2 Encourage innovation in your area of responsibility

- C3 Encourage innovation in your organisation

Linked chapters:

The information in this chapter is related to information in the following chapters:

- 1.2 Clear communication

- 2.1 Leadership, culture and vision

- 4.3 Building and leading the team

- 4.4 Developing and motivating others

Introduction

Nothing creates an opportunity quite so much as a problem: just think of Post-it notes or Blu-tack. Each of those came about following a failure in the development of the product the research and development teams were working on, in the case of Blu-Tack, a sealant that didn't seal and in the case of Post-it notes, a glue that was only 'low-tack'. Both were also the result of a reaction, however. The fact is that the opportunity for developing these new products always existed, there simply wasn't the impetus for people to see it. The ability to change a problem into an opportunity is a powerful gift: the ability to see the opportunity without that stimulus is arguably a greater one.

Objectives

The aim of this chapter is to encourage you be on the alert for new ideas. It will help you to:

- generate new ideas;

- encourage creativity in the team;

- assess ideas that are generated or put forward fairly and accurately; and,

- look for areas where individuals and teams can work together to cross-fertilise ideas.

Defining 'innovation' and 'opportunity'

When I checked the definitions of these words, I found that the dictionary definition of 'innovate' is 'to bring in new methods, ideas etc.; make changes'. The thesaurus liked 'innovation', for which it suggested the synonyms 'alteration', 'change', 'modernisation', 'newness', and 'variation', among others.

'Opportunity' is 'a good chance; a favourable occasion; good fortune'; and also 'break', 'chance', 'look-in' and 'opening'.

So, what we seem to be looking at here is the ability to be creative, both in devising new ways of doing things and in knowing how to best take advantage of any good fortune that comes our way.

Giving creativity a bad name

I don't know about you, but I hate cliché and jargon. When someone starts talking about 'blue-sky thinking', 'thinking outside the box' or 'pushing the envelope' my heart sinks. It's a shame, because the fact that these phrases are straight out of 'The Office' shouldn't obscure the fact that the thing they represent – innovation – is both desirable and beneficial to both individuals and businesses.

How innovation comes about

Let's just think about the different ways in which innovation may come about and some of the things that those types of innovation have brought us.

Innovation by chance

When Alexander Fleming stacked the cultures of staphylococci he had been working on and locked up his laboratory to spend August 1928 on holiday with his family, little did he know that it would lead to the discovery of penicillin. On his return he found that one of his cultures was contaminated with mould and that the cultures of staphylococci immediately surrounding it had been destroyed. 'When I woke up just after dawn on September 28, 1928, I certainly didn't plan to revolutionise all medicine by discovering the world's first antibiotic, or bacteria killer,' Fleming later said, 'But I guess that was exactly what I did.'

Innovation by mistake

In 1879 a Procter and Gamble worker went for lunch and forgot to turn off the mixing machine he was using to make soap. When he returned, he saw that the batch of soap he was working on had been whipped into a froth. Afraid of being scolded and knowing that the basic constituents of the soap and its cleansing action would be unaffected, he poured the whipped batch of White Soap into moulds and it was shipped out with the usual mix.

Over the next several weeks, P&G received many letters asking for more of the 'soap that floated'. The additional air mixed into the batch left in the mixing machine for too long by mistake caused the soap to float. Seizing on the opportunity this presented, P&G added extra mixing time into the preparation stage and launched 'Ivory Soap', one of their most successful products ever.

Innovation by accident

In 1839 Charles Goodyear dropped a lump of the India rubber infused with sulphur that he was experimenting with onto the top of the stove and created vulcanised rubber.

Around 1946, Dr Percy Spencer of the Raytheon Corporation was testing a vacuum tube known as a 'magnetron' when he discovered that the bar of chocolate in his pocket had melted. Intrigued, he placed some popcorn kernels near the tube and watched in delight as they popped. The microwave oven had been invented.

Innovation by design

We take it for granted nowadays that we can listen to music whenever and wherever we choose, but it was not always so. In the late 1970s Sony set out to create a brand new market by developing and offering to people something that they didn't even know they wanted. The product was the Sony Walkman and it is the forerunner to any and all portable music players that are available today.

Whilst no one would turn down the sort of good fortune that innovation by chance, innovation by accident, and innovation by mistake represent, we are going to focus our attention here on innovation by design.

Creativity

Creativity is a process, not just a series of flashes of insight. When you are actively seeking to be creative, you have an objective in mind. For example:

- to produce something for a certain price;
- to improve or enhance an existing product or service;
- to solve a problem; or,
- to meet a need.

With your objective in mind, you can plan to come up with something to help you to achieve your goal. The following should provide you with a framework you can use:

- **Step 1 – Break it down**: before you can get creative, you need as full an understanding of what it is you wish to achieve as possible. Without that, you might create something that in itself is innovative and impressive – but that does not help you to achieve your current objective.

- **Step 2 – Try alternatives**: you are starting to generate possible solutions here, and whilst it is possible that your first idea will be 'the one best way', it is not likely. Ideas are being thrown into the mix, assessed, picked apart, discarded outright or put on the back burner for more thought.

- **Step 3 – Pace and mutter**: like a dog with a bone, you work away at your problem trying to shake something useful loose from the jumble of thoughts and ideas.

- **Step 4 – Let it be**: give up. Go for a coffee. Finish that report you've been putting off. Think about other things.

- **Step 5 – Eureka!** That moment of insight you've been waiting for finally happens! You have it!

- **Step 6 – Detail the solution**: back to analysing and breaking down, as you turn your flash of insight and inspiration into a proposal and/or workable plan.

Generating new ideas

Let's move on to consider some of the tools and techniques that you have at your disposal when you are actively seeking to generate new ideas.

Lateral thinking

The dictionary suggests that lateral thinking is a means of solving problems by apparently illogical methods. Dr Edward de Bono, the father of lateral thinking, describes it thus: 'You cannot dig a hole in a different place by digging the same hole deeper.' Lateral thinking involves 'fuzzy logic', it is the kind of thinking that computers can't do (yet!).

Lateral thinking gets us to look at things from different perspectives, to explore different options and challenge our preconceptions.

For example, imagine you are a supermarket manager and you are wondering how you can get the checkout queues down. Lunchtime is a particular problem as your staff are taking their lunch breaks at the same time as everyone else. What can you do?

Logical thinking might come up with such suggestions as: change the staff's working hours so they take lunch before or after the rush; hire part-time staff to cover the lunch period; train the staff to be quicker, and so on. Lateral thinking might well suggest that if you don't want people to jam up the aisles while they wait to be served by an operator, let them serve themselves! And as we have seen, that is exactly what is happening in many supermarkets now. Other kinds of stores are also adopting the self-service checkout; in fact, I can now pay for my petrol at the pump if I so choose, I don't have to go into the kiosk at all.

Brainstorming

Brainstorming is a long-established method for helping groups to generate new ideas. The rules are simple: anything goes, the wilder and more crazy the ideas, the better! During the ideas generation stage, no assessment is allowed; ideas are simply sparked off by the general atmosphere of creativity.

Brainstorming is a useful activity, but there is always the danger that what people are striving to do is simply to come up with the most extreme idea.

If you run a brainstorming session, it can be a good idea to use a warm-up exercise. Try something simple, such as 101 uses for a CD or quickest way to make £1 million.

Asking questions that help

Provocation is essential to creativity. Using structured questions can help provoke people into seeing or thinking about things in a different way. For example:

- How can we...?

- What if...? Or What if I...?

- Is there a better way to...?

The power of provocation – Crandall's olive

In the 1980s Robert L. Crandall, then head of American Airlines, asked himself the question: 'What if... we removed just one olive from every salad served to passengers?' He wondered if anyone would even notice. The airline tried it, and no one did notice – but the airline saved $40,000 a year!

Looking for opportunities

Read the newspapers and news sites, trade journals, magazines, watch TV, listen to the radio, and talk to people. Keep an eye out for trends and always look for the angle that will give you an advantage.

- What are people talking about? *What does that mean for me?*

- What is the zeitgeist? *What does that mean for me?*

- What's happening in America? *What does that mean for me?*

- What qualities are likely to be valued in the future? *What does that mean for me?*

Have regular 'What if…?' sessions with staff. It can also be helpful to run staff suggestion schemes.

Looking for opportunities is rarely a regular part of anyone's job role or job description; consequently you need to motivate your people to do it. Lead by example, but also think about how they can be rewarded. What's in it for them? This needn't be in terms of money: people also value recognition and praise, for example, and extra holiday is always appreciated. It might be worth considering whether, if the budget doesn't run to a payment, you can afford to award a day off for especially good ideas.

I have an idea… what now?

So once you have an idea, what do you do with it? Well you now need to decide if your idea is good enough to be put forward to management for serious consideration. There are four stages to the process:

- **Describe:** write down all the details of your idea. Walk around it and look at it from all angles. Make your description as detailed as you can.

- **Evaluate:** take a long, hard look at your idea. Does it stand up to close scrutiny? Is it as good as it first seemed?

- **Accept or reject:** if it doesn't pass muster, either reject it outright or go back to the thinking stage. Perhaps it is essentially sound but something in the process of thinking it through and describing it is wrong, or it may need a wee tweak here and there. If it holds water, move on to the next stage.

- **Present:** write a report or prepare a presentation – whatever is necessary to take your idea to the next stage.

The process can be represented as a flow chart:

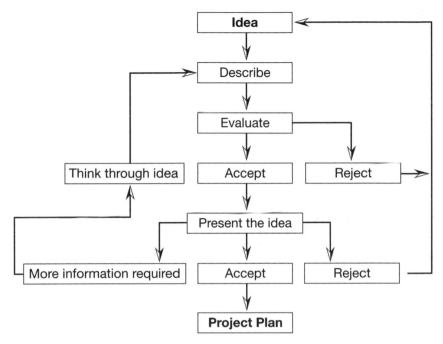

Developing and presenting an idea

Reasons for rejection

- Too expensive: sometimes even the best ideas are simply too costly to implement.

- Flawed thinking: there is a problem with the basic assumption, skewing the logic of subsequent thinking.

- Been done before: whilst this shouldn't automatically lead to rejection, it often does because bias against an idea remains. However, many things might have changed in the interim – the economic climate, changes in technology, even just the team involved in implementation – that would tip the scales and make the difference.

- Emperor's new clothes: where something promises benefits or results that are illusory, but because of the rank or status of the originator of the idea, no one has dared to speak up.

- Not practical: some ideas are simply unworkable, even if the outcomes might be desirable.

Quiz: Lateral thinking

1. A baby falls out of the window of a 22-storey building and lives. How can this be?

2. A man and his son are in a car crash. The father is killed and the boy is seriously injured. An ambulance arrives and takes him to hospital for treatment. When he gets there, the surgeon says, 'I can't operate on this boy – he is my son!!!' How can this be?

3. In the middle of the ocean is a luxury yacht. Floating in the water nearby there are a number of bodies. What happened?

4. A man lives on the twelfth floor of an apartment building. Every morning he takes the elevator down to the lobby and leaves the building to go to work. When he returns in the evening, he takes the elevator to the tenth floor and walks the last two flights of stairs to his apartment unless there is someone else in the elevator or it rained that day, in which case he travels all the way to the twelfth floor. Why does he do this?

5. Look at the grid of dots below. Without taking your pencil off the paper, draw four straight lines that between them pass through each dot.

Conclusion

Innovation can happen by chance, but it is not wise to rely solely on fortune for new ideas and approaches. It's the same with new opportunities. Being in at the start of something, or being the catalyst for something new, can be hugely rewarding, however, and it only takes one or two successes to start to get everyone fired up and enthusiastic about looking for new openings and new ways of doing things. It is everyone's responsibility to be alert to opportunity and taking steps to develop a culture of creative awareness should go a long way to encouraging that and should also impact positively on the bottom line.

Innovation and opportunity checklist

- Innovation involves introducing new methods and ideas.
- Opportunity involves spotting openings and capitalising on luck.
- Creativity is the cornerstone of both.
- Innovation can come about by chance, by mistake, by accident or by design.
- Creativity is a process, which means we can use a framework to help us to be creative.
- Lateral thinking is the kind of thinking that computers can't do.
- Brainstorming can be a useful group exercise for ideas generation.
- We can ask questions that provoke new ways of looking at things.
- Opportunities abound; we need to actively seek them out.

Answers: Lateral thinking quiz

1. A baby falls out of the window of a 22-storey building and lives. How can this be?

   A. The baby fell out of a ground floor window.

2. A man and his son are in a car crash. The father is killed and the boy is seriously injured. An ambulance arrives and takes him to hospital for treatment. When he gets there, the surgeon says, 'I can't operate on this boy – he is my son.' How can this be?

   A. The surgeon is the boy's mother.

3. In the middle of the ocean is a luxury yacht. Floating in the water nearby there are a number of bodies. What happened?

   A. The occupants of the yacht decided to all go for a swim, but forgot to drop a ladder so they could climb back aboard the yacht. They all drowned.

4. A man lives on the twelfth floor of an apartment building. Every morning he takes the lift down to the lobby and leaves the building to go to work. When he returns in the evening, he takes the lift to the tenth floor and walks the last two flights of stairs to his apartment, unless there is someone else in the lift or it rained that day, in which case he travels all the way to the twelfth floor. Why does he do that?

   A. The man isn't tall enough to reach the buttons for any floors higher than the tenth. If someone else is in the lift, or if he has his brolly, with which he can reach the buttons, he can travel higher.

5. Look at the grid of dots below. Without taking your pencil off the paper, draw four straight lines that between them pass through each dot.

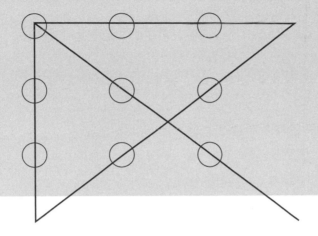

Further reading

In print:

- Serious Creativity, Edward de Bono, HarperCollins Publishers (1992)

- Innovation X: Why a Company's Toughest Problems are its Greatest Advantage, Adam Richardson, Jossey Bass (2010)

- Change by Design: How Design Thinking Creates New Alternatives for Business and Society, Tim Brown, Collins Business (2009)

- The Art of Innovation: Success Through Innovation the IDEO Way, Tom Kelley, Profile Business (2002)

- The Leader's Guide to Lateral Thinking Skills: Unlocking the Creativity and Innovation in You and Your Team, Paul Sloane, Kogan Page (2006)

Online:

- http://www.edwdebono.com/ – Dr. de Bono's website – get the low-down on creativity direct from source.

- http://www.creativitymeansbusiness.com/articles/innovation.html – useful article on the business benefits of creativity on the Creativity Means Business website.

- http://www.management-issues.com/creativity.asp – useful article on creativity and innovation on the Management-Issues website.

- http://www.1000ventures.com/business_guide/innovation_mgmt_main.html – Innovation Management website.

- http://www.fastzone.com/Innovation-Opportunities – 'Seven sources for innovation opportunities' article on the FastZone website.

Part 4
Managing people

Chapter 4.1
Employing people

NVQ Application:

This chapter is relevant to the following NVQ in Management Units:

- D3 Recruit, select and keep colleagues

- D4 Plan the workforce

- D15 Initiate and follow grievance procedure

Linked chapters:

The information in this chapter is related to information in the following chapters:

- 1.2 Clear communication

- 2.2 Strategic management and business planning

- 2.3 Operating within the law

Introduction

The whole area of recruitment and selection can be a minefield. Some people interview well and perform poorly, others interview less well but are world class employees, some CVs and applications are works of pure fiction, others may be scrupulously accurate but look less impressive if assumptions are made that 'everyone exaggerates when applying for a job'. Then there are references: will an employer who wants to help a mediocre employee move on really give an accurate reference, or will they 'big them up' to make them seem like a more attractive prospect?

You cannot defend yourself against everything and you will most likely make mistakes of your own from time to time, but having sound policies and procedures to follow will minimise the impact on the business.

Objectives

The aim of this chapter is to enable you to take into account all elements involved in ensuring the business attracts and retains the best possible people. It will help you to:

- assess workforce requirements;

- prepare accurate and useful job descriptions and person specifications;

- recruit effectively and select appropriately;

- review and evaluate procedures;

- monitor staff turnover; and,

- deal with staff grievances.

People are generally a business's greatest expense and biggest asset: they can make or break a business. Getting the right people – not just into the company, but also into the right roles and at the right level – is crucial to business performance. Recruitment and selection impacts significantly, for good or ill, the bottom line.

Case study: There can be only one!

Charlie is recruiting for a new salesperson and he and Mary from HR have just finished the first round of interviews. For Charlie, there are only two candidates worth seeing again, even though in his original plan he had aimed to shortlist five people from the dozen interviewed in the first round.

Charlie is so impressed with his two favourites that he is considering trying to find the money to take them both on. This would be a squeeze and would also mean restructuring territories, but for two good sales-people and the additional business they would bring in, he feels it would be worth it.

What should Charlie do next?

Should he stick with his original plan or go with his gut instinct?

We'll come back to Charlie in a little while.

Reasons for taking on staff

There are three main reasons for taking on new personnel:

- to replace staff who have moved on;
- to expand an existing function; or,
- to introduce a new function, either to the business or to the site.

You will always have staff turnover to a greater or lesser degree. A buoyant jobs market could tempt people to look for more money elsewhere, some will leave to care for children or other relatives, others may start a business of their own, or dissatisfaction with the company may drive people out.

Similarly, if the business is growing then functions within it will grow. Consolidation of the business across sites may also cause a department to increase in size. The introduction of a new function will involve creating a department from scratch.

When you are faced with a request for more personnel, the first place to look is inside the company; is there existing capacity to take on the additional workload? Perhaps another department is over-staffed and redeployment of personnel would solve the problem at little extra cost. It can also be worth advertising posts internally first; that way, whilst you will still need to train staff in the new procedures they will have to follow, they will at least be familiar with the company and the culture. Also, don't underestimate or write off the knowledge and experience of others in your organisation; getting them involved at any or all stages of the process can save you a great deal of heartache.

Some years ago I was working for an organisation that was launching a new product from another site, with its own customer services and other related functions. The part of the organisation at the geographical location I was working for had well established policies and procedures and a wealth of experience; we waited in vain for the call inviting us to get involved and help set up the new business. The reason, we found out later, was that those involved didn't want their shiny new business 'tainted' by ours. Which was fine, until it all imploded within a week of launch because their poorly prepared and inadequately trained staff couldn't cope. At that point, we had to arrange for half of our staff to go to the other site, have a quick briefing on the new system and so on, and get on the phone to save the day. This meant arranging for an army of temporary staff to come onto our site and be trained up double quick to fill the breach. All of this could have been avoided if the existing knowledge and experience had been used. The message here is clear: beware superiority and intellectual snobbery!

Assessing requirements

If you are boosting an existing function, then data relating to, for example, how many more customers need to be catered for will help. Say you have ten people caring for the existing customer base and due to consolidation this will grow by 50 per cent. You may simply need five more people or, depending on whether people currently are struggling or have spare capacity, either six or four. Estimating how many staff you need is often a 'best guess', at least to start with, but gathering whatever data might be available – or generating some, if none exists – will help. You might do a check as to how many calls, on average, an operator takes per day, or how many complaints are resolved, how many accounts chased up – whatever is relevant.

Say you are buying an additional piece of machinery; how many staff are used to man existing machines? What will be the impact on maintenance staff, or on staff further down the production line, or in packing? Think through all the implications of an event like this, talk to the relevant people and do your best to assess impact accurately.

Whatever the situation, be sure to keep full and accurate records of what you do and evaluate the process after the event. That way, lessons learned may be put into practise to help with future requirements.

Profiling the post and the person to fill it

When you have a vacancy or vacancies to fill, you need to get an idea of who you want, in terms of knowledge, skills, abilities, experience and so on, to fill the post. The first step is to gain an understanding of the job itself. To do that, we need to gather information from people who already have an understanding or an insight into what would be required. This is likely to include the manager or team leader, anyone already doing the job, whether on site or elsewhere, and members of the team in which the post to be filled will be based. If possible, gather everyone together and conduct a group analysis; with everyone around the same table, the job can be seen more clearly, from the overarching purpose to the detail of the tasks to be performed. If that isn't possible, then at least talk to as many people as you can, either face to face or on the phone, and share your draft job profile for comments before finalising it.

When drafting the profile, look at categories of information such as:

- What level of education is required?

- What experience should people have?

- What level is the post at, and what is the reporting line?

- What are the essential knowledge, skills and abilities?

- Are any specialist skills, such as languages, required?

- Is the job customer facing?

- Is the job office based or will travel be a requirement?

Take time over the job profile as it is key to getting the right person into the job; if your understanding of what is required is flawed, then the whole process of recruitment and selection will be flawed because you will not be looking for the right person.

Job description

The job description will largely fall out of the job profiling exercise, as will the person specification, which we will look at next. A job description defines broadly the responsibilities and duties of the post-holder, along with the department or function it sits within, the grade it is at, and the accountability it carries.

Below is a simple example of a job description.

Job title:	Admin support officer
Function/dept:	Customer Services
Grade:	4
Reporting to:	Customer Services admin team leader
Staff responsibilities:	None
Main purpose:	To work as part of the admin team to provide support to the Customer Services function.
Main duties:	1. To collect and distribute post on a daily basis. 2. To deal with routine email correspondence. 3. To ensure adequate stocks of supporting materials are available. 4. To provide data input support. 5. To file information, as required. 6.... 10. Any other duties that are deemed appropriate.

Person specification

Preparation of a job description leads quite naturally into the preparation of a person specification. Once you have both profiled the job and created the job description, you have a pretty good idea of what is required, albeit still in broad terms. If the job description is the skeleton, then the person specification helps to puts flesh onto the bones.

The main thrust of a person specification is to define the required knowledge, skills, abilities and attitude. Break it down into those that are essential and those that are desirable, and do be specific.

Below is a simple example of a person specification.

Job title: Admin support officer			
	Essential	**Desirable**	**Measured**
Education:	GCSE Maths and English	5 GCSEs	5
Experience:	Minimum 6 months working in an office environment	2 years office experience in a customer focused environment	1 2 3
Knowledge:		Filing systems	1 2
Skills:	Numeracy Literacy	Problem solving	1 2 4
Abilities:	Use of email and word processing packages	Use of databases	1 2 3 4 5
Attitude:	Shows initiative		1 2 5
Measured: 1 = application form 2 = interview/assessment centre 3 = references 4 = testing 5 = other evidence (e.g. certificates)			

Remember that the information contained within the job description and person specification isn't just for you: it should also be provided to applicants, some of whom, on the strength of that information, may decide not to apply as they don't fit the bill. Make it as accurate as possible, or else you risk the right person not applying.

Review regularly those job descriptions and person specifications you have on file, perhaps using a rolling programme that ensures they each get assessed at least once a year as a matter of course. Do keep on top of it; jobs change, industries change, and out of date specs help no one.

Attracting applicants

The process of attracting as many suitable applicants as possible, whilst deterring the unsuitable ones, is called 'recruitment'. 'Selection' comes next, and is the process of whittling down a pool of candidates, using a system of selection criteria, until you are left with the most suitable person(s) for the available job(s).

A variety of recruitment methods are available to you, including:

- advertising inside the organisation;
- external advertising, either on the web, in a local or national newspaper, or on the radio or even television;
- employment agencies;
- employment fairs;
- careers service/local schools;
- the Job Centre; or,
- training schemes, such as Modern Apprenticeships.

You may also receive speculative applications from time to time. If you do, acknowledge them and have a system for storage and monitoring, so that they come to your attention when and if something appropriate comes up.

When you are recruiting, you need to give certain information to people in the first instance to help them to decide whether to enquire further. This should include:

- who you are;
- what you do;
- where you are based;
- what the grade/salary of the job is;
- a brief description of the job, with title;
- specific candidate requirements; and,
- how to register interest or get more information.

There are a number of ways you can take applications forward, including:

- providing downloads from the company website;

- inviting requests for information via telephone, email or post;

- inviting people to contact you for an initial telephone interview or aptitude test;

- requesting CVs.

CV vs. application form

If I am applying for a job, I much prefer those that will accept my CV. I tailor it to suit, of course, but even after doing that and writing the covering letter, I can still be finished my application in relatively little time.

If I am involved in the recruitment process, however, I favour application forms. The reason for this is that comparing CVs can be like comparing apples and pears, as people set them out differently, use different grades of paper, different fonts, emphasise different information and so on, whereas comparing application forms at least involves looking at the same information in the same order, making scanning, reading and comparing much easier. You can also design your form so that it gives you the information you want, and only that information, in the order you want it in. (This won't stop some folk from writing exactly what they choose to, of course, but that also tells you something about them!)

Designing an application form

When designing an application form, remember that the purpose is to gain sufficient information to know whether to invite someone for interview, not to cover all the ground that your interview questions will anyway. Consequently, you should keep it as brief as possible. That makes it more likely that people will go on to complete it and also makes it easier for you to read through the ones you receive. The kinds of information you should ask for include:

- personal details;

- educational achievements;

- work experience, especially the most recent;

- knowledge, skills and abilities; and,

- specialisms.

It is a good idea to use questions that ask for examples, such as: 'Think of a time when you had to rely on your initiative. Describe briefly what happened.' You might also ask: 'Describe how you believe you match the requirements of the post, giving examples of work and life experience to back up your assertions.' This kind of approach both helps candidates to know what you want and allows you to see that they have demonstrated the attributes you are seeking. When you send out application forms, include copies of the job description and person specification; that will help candidates to supply information that best shows how they meet the requirements of the post.

Finally, do not play games with people. I recall submitting an application by email into which I put a lot of work and which vanished into a black hole. Perhaps it was a test to see who would follow up their application if they were ignored first time around; perhaps the company in question simply was incompetent or rude. I am also aware that when a lot of applications are received, there are those who will halve the pile indiscriminately in order to make the job of dealing with them more manageable. I am loathe to write off things into which I have put time and effort, but I prefer to have nothing to do with companies that play games, are incompetent or are rude, particularly when it happens right at the outset.

The selection process

There are likely to be at least three and possibly more steps to your selection process depending upon the level of the vacancy and the way your organisation likes to handle the process. We are going to look at the most likely steps here in order to give a framework to the selection process. The steps we are going to look at are:

- Stage 1 – the application;

- Stage 2 – face to face;

- Stage 3 – shortlist; and,

- Stage 4 – the job offer.

Stage 1 – the application

Whether CV or application form, your first stage selection will be paper-based (although if you conducted a telephone interview and sent out forms only to those who passed, it is effectively your second stage). Before you start to go through the pile of applications on your desk, it is a good idea to:

- decide how the selection process will be handled: for example, will it fall to one person or a team, will everyone involved look at every application, or will they be shared out between them for a first sift, and so on;

- establish a scoring system weighted in favour of the more important aspects of the job so that you can compare applicants more easily; and,

- know in advance how many applicants you wish to long-list.

Once you have assessed the applications and long-listed the most suitable, write to the unsuccessful people as quickly as possible with a short, polite rejection.

Stage 2 – face to face

Having created your long-list, you will want to meet people face to face. The main choice you face here is between an interview or an assessment centre.

An assessment centre involves getting all of the applicants together for a day or a half day and putting them through a series of tasks, tests, exercises and interviews, then comparing how they fare. You will also be able to see how they cope with pressure, how they interact with others and so on. Assessment centres take a bit of organising but can be extremely useful and rewarding, both for organisers and applicants.

The most common form of face to face selection, however, remains the formal interview. With interviews, preparation is key. The things you need to consider include:

- who should interview: will it be just one person or a team, and what role will they each play;

- when and where should the interviews be held;

- how long should the interviews last;

- what questions will you ask; and,

- will you require people to complete any other tasks or tests while they are with you: for example, tests of literacy or numeracy, psychometric assessments or presentations.

Your first task is to ensure the necessary staff and appropriate room(s) are available on your chosen date(s) and to get those booked and diarised. When you schedule your interviews, allow sufficient time between each so that you can reflect and make notes while the information and your impressions are still fresh in your mind. Cramming too many into a day will leave everyone feeling short-changed and frazzled – especially the interviewers!

Once you have this information, you can allocate time slots to people and write to your candidates inviting them to attend. Your letter should include:

- details of the job you are interviewing for;

- when and where the interview is to be held;

- how long they should expect to spend with you;

- what, if anything, they need to bring with them;

- who to ask for on arrival;

- what to do if the time and date are unsuitable;

- a map and/or directions; and,

- whether expenses will be paid.

Finally, make sure the room is prepared, that you have sufficient materials and stationery, and that water is available. Read over all the documentation in advance and make notes to remind yourself of anything you particularly want to discuss in detail with a candidate.

A structure for interview

Having a simple structure for interview will help you to ensure all candidates get the same treatment and information. I would suggest the following as being suitable:

1. **Greet.** Welcome the candidate and introduce everyone present. Spend a minute or two on small talk to break the ice and help put the candidate at ease.

2. **Give information.** Before you start asking questions, give some information to the candidate about the organisation, the reason for the post being vacant, and the main objectives of the role.

3. **Question.** Run through the planned questions with the candidate. Use open and probing questions to find out more where necessary. Allow the candidate time to consider answers, don't automatically jump in if there's a silence.

4. **Invite candidate questions.** Give the candidate the opportunity to clarify anything she is unsure of and to offer any further information.

5. **Part.** End the interview by telling the candidate what will happen next and thanking her for attending.

Immediately after the interview, have a brief discussion with any fellow interviewers, make notes and write a brief paragraph detailing your thoughts and impressions.

Avoiding bias

When interviewing, you should leave your personal prejudices at the door. We all have some; perhaps we have a down on Morris dancers or we favour people who like jigsaw puzzles. (Legislation exists to cover the legal aspects of bias and prejudice and this is covered in chapter 2.3, Operating within the law, which should be read in conjunction with this one.) The person offered the job should fit most closely the person specification irrespective of star sign, hobbies or hair colour.

Stage 3 – shortlist

It may be that you feel able to make a job offer following an assessment centre or single interview, but many firms like to hold a second round of interviews with short-listed candidates. This gives the opportunity to confirm first impressions and to get others involved in the selection process. It also gives the chance to ask more specific questions and to get to know the candidate better. Draw up your short list as soon as possible after the interviews and write to all the candidates. Be sensitive when rejecting people and remember to give full information to those you are inviting back.

When you are making your final selection after interview, stick to your selection criteria. Although it's human nature for instinct to play a part in the selection process, stick as far as possible to the facts and be aware of any personal bias you may have.

Stage 4 – the job offer

Previously when writing to candidates, you have rejected before you accepted, because those letters were the most straightforward and you didn't want to keep people hanging on. With the job offer, it can be a good idea to do it the other way around, or at least to delay rejecting your second and perhaps third choice candidates. Send out your offer letter first, then if your chosen candidate rejects you, you can move on to your second choice without having lost face.

The offer letter should be specific about the package being offered, detailing salary, holidays, car, pension – whatever is applicable. Ask the candidate to reply within a period of time, remember you have other people waiting to hear. Once you have your acceptance, you can move on to send letters of rejection, bearing in mind that having come this far, people may be very disappointed to receive them. Make them personal and offer feedback if possible.

Keep everything on file for at least three months.

Induction and probation

Most jobs have a probation period, usually three months, perhaps longer, depending upon the seniority of the post. Probation works both ways: not only does it give the company a chance to fully get to know the new employee, it also gives the employee a chance to weigh up the company. Having adhered to a sound recruitment and selection process will reduce the risk of that period ending in separation.

Most jobs also have an induction, which might be anything from a 'welcome' meeting with the manager to a month of structured training. Do whatever is appropriate, and where necessary test competence before an employee goes fully into a role for which they have just been trained. Make sure enough on-job support is in place.

Evaluation

Immediately after recruitment and selection, it is a good idea to evaluate the process and to identify any area that might be handled better next time. Seek feedback from as many of those who were involved as possible, including your new recruit(s). You might want to use a form or checklist so that you can collect easily comparable data, hold informal interviews or perhaps have some mix of the two.

After a period of time that allows them to settle in, check the suitability of the person or people you employed. How do they measure up? Do they confirm the efficacy of the processes and selection criteria followed? Keep records and learn from what has happened.

Monitor staff turnover

Whenever someone leaves your organisation, hold a leaving interview to find out why they are moving on. Look for trends and problem areas and be prepared to fully investigate and take corrective action if necessary.

It can also be useful to conduct a climate survey, to find out what your staff really think. This is an anonymous survey asking about how people feel about their job, the company, the department they are in and so on, and is effectively an opportunity for staff to 'appraise' the organisation. Don't be defensive if you do this and you receive bad news; it takes courage for people to speak out. Welcome the opportunity to put things right. (If no corrective action will be taken based on findings, then it would be unwise to undertake the procedure.)

Grievance procedures

Even the best run and most well organised businesses can suffer problems from time to time. It makes good sense to have robust grievance procedures in place for such occasions.

A major bonus of grievance procedures is that they can alert you to problems that you can take steps to resolve. For example:

- communication issues;

- office environment problems – noise, temperature, equipment, etc.;

- difficulties with tasks people are required to complete and procedures they are expected to follow; and,

- cultural and behavioural issues, such as racism, bullying, homophobia, sexual harassment, etc.

Make sure your grievance procedures are workable. One organisation I worked in had a first appeal to the line manager, with a further appeal, should things not be satisfactorily resolved, to the board of directors. In practice, staff felt they had no representation and no viable course of redress when things went wrong. The interpretation at board level might have been that there were no major grievance issues, but this was far from the case.

It can also be dangerous to invite people to air grievances in a group situation if the message that will be given afterwards – no matter what the issues raised – will simply be to like it or lump it.

The grievance process should be both straightforward and easy to understand, and not be intimidating. People can feel nervous enough speaking out; perhaps they are shy by nature or fear it may threaten their job security. It is indefensible to then face them with a system that is unwieldy and needlessly stressful. It should also be quick: The Advisory, Conciliation and Arbitration Service (ACAS) recommends that no longer than seven working days should be taken to come back with an answer.

Aim not to have too many stages to the process: the first stage will most likely be to raise the issue with the immediate line manager, with a second stage appeal to a senior manager. This ought to be sufficient. You may choose to allow staff to approach an alternative manager if the issue relates to their own line manager (particularly pertinent if the issue is to do with bullying) and people should have the right to be accompanied by a colleague or a Trade Union representative if they so wish. Make sure records are kept and shared with the employee in question.

Whilst you must always take grievance issues seriously and treat them sensitively, I also want to add a word of warning: be alert to both someone who is 'trying it on' and to the deeper issue underlying the one raised. In the case of the former, it is a sad fact that there are some people who will complain about everything and anything, and who also use procedures such as this to make waves. Properly handled they will soon be exposed and if they persist in their behaviour you can take appropriate action. In the latter case, remember that people do not always express themselves directly. They may not feel able to raise the main issue and so look for something else in order to open a dialogue, in the hope that either someone else will speak up as a result or that the investigation process will bring the underlying issues to light. Think of it this way: if someone is persistently late, it might be that they need to get to bed earlier, buy a better alarm clock – or are subconsciously trying to avoid a tricky situation in the office. It is part of the process to get to the bottom of things.

Where it is difficult or impossible to achieve a consensus, consider concil-iation. ACAS can help, although you must consider who will have the final say.

Conclusion

Good policies and procedures give you a framework to operate within and so can help greatly with recruitment and selection. Within this framework, however, you should still be alert for anyone who, although they might not 'fit' exactly, shows initiative and potential, whether that person is inside or outside the organisation.

Exercise: There can be only one!

Earlier in the chapter we took a look at Charlie, who was part way through the recruitment process and felt that he had two candidates that he really should employ. At that time, we asked:

What should Charlie do next?

Should he stick with his original plan or go with his gut instinct?

In the light of what you have learned since, use the space below to answer those questions. There are some suggestions at the end of the chapter.

_____

_____

_____

_____

_____

Employing people checklist

- I understand the reasons for taking on new personnel.

- I have a structure for assessing staffing requirements.

- I know how to profile a job.

- I know how to write and use both job descriptions and person specifications.

- I consider the available methods of attracting applicants and use the most appropriate.

- I give necessary information when advertising for staff.

- I know what to include on an application form.

- I consider and use appropriate selection methods.

- I know how to plan and conduct an assessment centre.

- I know how to plan and conduct an interview, and I use the five step process: Greet; Give information; Question; Invite candidate questions; and, Part.

- I am aware of my own personal bias and do my best not to let it influence my decisions.

- Induction and probation periods are built into the process for new starters.

- I always evaluate the recruitment process and am alert for lessons that may be learned.

- I have systems in place to monitor staff turnover.

- There is a robust grievance procedure in place.

Case notes: There can be only one!

Whilst it is good that he is both enthusiastic and optimistic, Charlie is getting carried away with his initial impressions. Mary from HR should act as a brake on his recklessness.

Charlie would be better advised to stick to his original plan and to ask five people back for a second interview. To determine who they should be, he and Mary should go through their interview notes and assess all 12 first round candidates against their pre-determined criteria.

It would be a good idea for Charlie to have a second interviewer in with him for the next round of interviews too, to confirm his impressions of candidates. It may be that he still wishes to employ one or both of his current favourite candidates, but by operating within the framework, his decision to do so will be based on logic and will be justifiable.

Further reading

In print:

- Finding and Keeping the Right People – How to Recruit Motivated Employees, Jon Billsberry, Pearson Education (2000)

- People Resourcing: Contemporary HRM in Practice, Stephen Pilbeam & Marjorie Corbridge, Financial Times/Prentice Hall (2006)

- Hiring and Keeping the Best People, Harvard Business Essentials, Harvard Business School Press (2003)

- A Manager's Guide to Hiring the Best Person for Every Job, DeAnne Rosenberg, John Wiley & Sons (2000)

- HR Strategy: Creating Business Strategy from Human Capital (2nd edition), Paul Kearns, Butterworth-Heinemann (2009)

Online:

- http://www.acas.org.uk/index.aspx?articleid=924 – Advisory, Conciliation and Arbitration Service (ACAS) publication 'Employing people: a handbook for small firms'.

- http://www.businesslink.gov.uk/bdotg/action/layer?topicId= 1073858787 – information about employing people on the Business Link website.

- http://www.prospects.ac.uk/cms/ShowPage/Home_page/Self_ employment/How_to_set_up_your_own_business/Employing_pe ople/p!elkbefa – information on employing people on Prospects, the UK's official graduate careers website.

- http://www.financehub.org.uk/managing_money_and_resources /employing_people/default.aspa – information on employing people on the Finance Hub website.

- http://humanresources.about.com/od/recruitingandstaffing/u/ employ_people.htm – 'Everything you need to know about employing people' on About.com.

Chapter 4.2
Establishing and managing relationships

NVQ Application:

This chapter is relevant to the following NVQ in Management Units:

- D1 Develop productive working relationships with colleagues
- D2 Develop productive working relationships with colleagues and stakeholders
- D10 Reduce and manage conflict in your team
- D17 Build and sustain collaborative relationships with other organisations

Linked chapters:

The information in this chapter is related to information in the following chapters:

- 1.2 Clear communication
- 1.4 Managing information and developing networks
- 4.3 Building and leading the team
- 4.4 Developing and motivating others
- 4.6 Effective negotiation

Introduction

We all juggle many different types of relationships in our lives, some of them with people we spend a great deal of time with, others with people we never actually meet; some with people we care deeply about, others with people with whom we have the vaguest of ties. Whatever their basis, relationships need to be nurtured or they will wither and die. This is something not all of us find easy to do or to find the time to do – how often have our closest friends drifted away when we no longer go to school or college, or work together every day? We spend more waking hours with colleagues than we do with family and friends. Bearing that in mind, it is worth putting a little effort into the state of those relationships.

Objectives

The aim of this chapter is to help you establish and develop productive working relationships with people you work with both inside and outside of your organisation. It will help you to:

- have a framework within which to operate;
- consider how you can be a good contact for others;
- be aware of power in relationships;
- understand how conflict can arise and know how to deal with it; and,
- have a working knowledge of Service Level Agreements.

Working relationships

You don't get paid for being popular, so why bother putting a load of effort into getting along with people you work with, especially those you only see once every month or two? Well, for a start, because so many organisations run on goodwill and co-operation. Call it what you like – going the extra mile, putting yourself out, being a star – organisations have their own terminology for such things, both formal and informal. What it boils down to is people doing that little bit more for the benefit of other people. We need the help of others to achieve our objectives. We get satisfaction from being able to help in return. We cannot exist in a vacuum, not even those of us who work alone, from home, there are always people to interact with.

That being the case, we might amend our earlier 'why bother?' to a heartfelt, 'How come people *don't* get along, then?' Well, for a whole host of reasons, including:

- **They have a different approach.** I had a very dear friend of whom it was said she would not stand when she could sit, she would not walk when she could drive, and she would not run, ever. I have worked with people like that, too, people who do things at their own pace no matter what, and whilst it was a pleasure to have a friend with that outlook, it has at times driven me crazy to have colleagues with it. Not that I tear about like a headless chicken; I like to think I am organised and methodical, but I do everything as fast as for me it can be done. Whether I'm putting the groceries away, doing the ironing or working on a project, I don't dally. When I compile training packs for a course, I lay everything out in order to make it easy to select what I need and I work as fast as I can. If there is a group of us involved, then while some take things at a steady pace and use the task as an excuse for a chat, my competitive streak comes to the fore and I try to either finish first or do more than anyone else. There is no wrong or right way, necessarily, just differences in approach and it is these differences that under certain circumstances can breed resentment.

- **Objectives are unclear.** If people are not sure of what it is they are required to do, then they will decide that for themselves. This will almost always result in conflicting priorities, no one will know what others are working towards and tempers will fray.

- **Poor communication.** The root cause of so many problems! If it's not that something has been expressed in an ambiguous manner, it's that someone didn't hear what was said. Or didn't listen. Or made assumptions. All of these will result in frustration and conflict.

- **Personal bias.** When someone doesn't like tall people, sci-fi fans, people from the next town, people who wear pink… the 'horns' part of the 'horns or halo' effect.

Good relationships need:

- clear communication;
- trust;
- give and take; and,
- honesty.

Conversely, poor relationships cause:

- stress;
- unhappiness;
- self-doubt; and,
- loss of self-esteem.

So, how can we overcome these issues and actually work at establishing good working relationships?

Establishing and managing relationships is something that we all do, and have done since we were small. Whatever works with family and friends will, with perhaps a few minor amendments to take into account the different context, work with colleagues, stakeholders and customers. Remember that everyone needs and appreciates attention being paid to them.

Any kind of attention you can get from or give to another person may be termed a 'stroke', and strokes are essential to our sense of wellbeing.

Strokes, which are physical, verbal or non-verbal, are also positive or negative, conditional or unconditional.

Positive strokes enhance your feeling of wellbeing: praise, admiration, thanks, interest.

Negative strokes erode your feeling of wellbeing: criticisms, ridicule, ingratitude, and disinterest.

Worst of all is zero strokes. Solitary confinement, if prolonged, will lead to a degree of mental damage.

Strokes are generally balanced, and an imbalance can cause feelings of neglect or discomfort. For example, when you get to work there are a number of people you say good morning to. With some of those people, that is pretty much all you say to them. Following a period of absence, however, you talk for longer. 'Good morning' leads to 'how was your holiday?' and so on. Next day, you are back to the old routine, because your longer chat restored the stroke balance. If someone tries to have a longer conversation two days in a row, or chooses not to have a longer one after a break, then it feels odd as the stroke balance is out of kilter.

Establishing good relationships with colleagues and work contacts is vital to confidence, peace of mind and success. Practise offering strokes and people will respond positively. If you get a negative reaction to a positive stroke, then that person needs more strokes; people need as many or more positive strokes as negative strokes.

Ego states

Eric Berne conducted studies into what he termed 'Transactional Analysis' and identified three separate 'personalities' or 'ego states' in people's behaviour, which he classified as 'parent', 'adult' and 'child'.

If you have ever found yourself saying things that your parents used to say to you, or reacting to a situation in the same way they would or did, then that is your parent ego state coming to the fore. Parents can either be 'controlling' or 'indulgent'.

If, on the other hand, you have made an independent appraisal of a situation and subsequently expressed your feelings and opinions, conclusions and recommendations in a fair, calm and non-prejudicial manner, then that is your adult speaking. Adults are rational and unbiased.

If you react to something, as you would have done when you were small, that is your child. Children are playful and fun loving.

All of the ego states are necessary and are useful in different circumstances; problems arise, however, when the 'wrong' ego state is prevalent at any one time. I used to work with a man who used his 'child' ego state most of the time. Because he was so much fun, none of the team minded this so much and we accepted that he was less productive than the rest of us. Problems occurred, however, when the team was under pressure. Whilst everyone else would buckle down and work harder and longer until things got back to normal, he would simply carry on as before – and in the process, drive his team-mates crazy. He had no sense of urgency, no 'internal barometer' that prompted him to switch behaviours to suit the circumstances.

Body language

Body language can reinforce your verbal message or discount it. It is often the basis upon which people decide whether or not you are worth listening to. You may be able to bring to mind occasions when important messages have been undermined by the speaker's body language. Use the following tips to avoid this type of pitfall:

- Face the other person, but at an angle; do not stand in direct opposition.

- Maintain a natural, receptive posture.

- Lean slightly towards the other person.

- Place yourself close enough so that you are both comfortable.

- Match the body language of the speaker without obviously imitating or mimicking.

- Avoid extremes of dress or behaviour unless you are in the business of drawing attention to yourself.

Remember that much of our behaviour has a basis in our biology. Much of body language is about communicating non-threatening behaviour to others of the same species who once would have seen our very presence as a challenge (there is more information on body language in chapter 1.2, Clear communication).

Case study: Cut in the corridor

Becky is a team leader in her organisation and is hoping to advance further. As part of this aim she routinely offers to take on extra tasks, to gain additional experience, raise her profile and build good relationships with people. She recently helped Anne, a team leader in a different department, to solve a problem she was facing. Shortly afterwards Anne was interviewed for a supervisory position, which she got, due in no small part to her successful problem solving. Becky hasn't spoken to Anne since, but Anne sent her an email thanking her for her help and promising to catch up soon.

Becky is walking back to her department from the canteen when she sees Anne heading her way. She smiles and stops for a chat, but Anne holds her hand up, says: 'Busy!' and keeps on going without so much as a smile or making eye contact.

Becky feels hurt and angry to be cut dead so rudely.

How should Becky deal with the situation?

We'll come back to Becky later.

Power

We tend not to think about it – or even to *like* to think about it – but all relationships are power-based. Good relationships arguably have power in balance, and we operate most of the time from a standpoint of equality. When something happens to upset the status quo, however, power is likely to surface and be used.

Types of power

In the 1950s, the research of sociologists French and Raven identified five bases of power:

- **Reward power:** the ability to reward or offer benefit to someone in exchange for the desired behaviour;

- **Coercive power:** the ability to punish unacceptable behaviour;

- **Legitimate power:** the right to demand that certain behaviours be either demonstrated or avoided based on legitimate authority (a variation is information power, based on a person's ability to control availability and accuracy of information);

- **Referent power:** power awarded by admirers; and,

- **Expert power:** power awarded on the basis of recognised expertise or specialist knowledge.

Most relationships have more than one type of power. Your boss has legitimate power by virtue of his position. He has reward power and coercive power, which he can use in a 'carrot and stick' way to influence behaviour. He may also be awarded expert and/or referent power, but so might a member of your staff, as these aren't dependent upon hierarchical position.

Think about some of your other relationships: what types of power do others hold over you? What types of power do you hold?

Conflict

Conflict might not always be a bad thing, but it almost always makes people feel awkward and uncomfortable. It upsets the status quo and causes change. If the change is ultimately for the better, perhaps because it results in unwieldy systems and procedures or poor communication channels being sorted out, for example, then that is a good outcome and we can say that the conflict has been constructive. Too often, however, the conflict remains unresolved or becomes a battle of personalities, and the change consists of people withdrawing from what has become an unpleasant situation.

Constructive conflicts tend to centre on interests rather than needs and to be dealt with openly. The outcome is 'win-win', with both parties meeting their objectives.

Destructive conflicts tend to centre on people's needs and on personalities; the strategy will be attack and counter-attack, rather than an attempt to find common ground. The outcome may not always have a winner, (it can be 'lose-lose') but will always have a loser ('win-lose' is the alternative).

Stages of conflict

Conflict might seem as if it comes out of nowhere, but even though we aren't usually aware of it – especially if we are personally involved – there is actually a pattern to events. Consider the following:

- **Stage 1:** Everyone is happy – or pretending to be. The situation is one of either genuine harmony or active conflict avoidance.

- **Stage 2:** One or more parties feels very strongly that something is wrong, but feels unable to express it or unwilling to admit to it.

- **Stage 3:** Finally someone speaks out and identifies and articulates the problem. Once conflict is out in the open like this, it can be handled well or handled badly. Handled well, a 'win-win' outcome can be achieved and everyone will be happy. Handled badly, things will escalate further.

- **Stage 4:** The focus is taken away from the root cause as the parties involved start to bring in other issues and perhaps to involve other people.

- **Stage 5:** Those involved begin appealing to third parties for help and support. This can be tricky for anyone getting involved, as either or both of the conflicting parties may turn on them. Despite this, at stages 4 and 5, a 'win-win' outcome is still achievable – with care.

- **Stage 6:** A very destructive stage that invokes the 'fight or flight' response. Aggression may be verbal or physical and withdrawal may involve simply walking away, or resignation or transfer. Emotions will be running high.

- **Stage 7:** The start of a vicious cycle of events as conflict repeats itself. The parties involved will try to externalise the conflict and talk about 'rights' and 'principles', as if they were not to blame for what happened. They will be trapped in the last two stages and unable to bring things to an amicable end.

When you are in conflict

Despite our best efforts and our best intentions, most of us at some point will become involved in conflict, even if we do nothing to knowingly or intentionally provoke it. What we must not do is allow it to escalate, as described in 'Stages of conflict' above. Acknowledge it, address the issues, and move on.

Managing conflict between others

This is both easier as there is arguably less emotion in it for you and harder as people may try to draw you in. Also you may genuinely have more sympathy or liking for one of the parties involved. You must remain impartial, however, otherwise rather than helping to resolve the situation you may add fuel to the flames.

Dealing with conflict

There are things you can do to manage conflict no matter what your role in the proceedings. Let's look first at those things you should avoid doing.

Bad ways to manage conflict:
- deny that a problem exists;
- bully people;
- take sides;
- use your power to force compliance;
- abuse the other person, either verbally or physically;

- avoid taking responsibility by blaming the other person;

- make inflammatory statements (It's your fault! You are wrong!);

- give in to avoid a fight; and,

- demand your own way at all costs.

Good ways to manage conflict:

- confront it;

- make an effort to understand the other person's point of view;

- seek to find a compromise;

- be fair and impartial;

- show that you value the relationship;

- accept you are at least partly to blame;

- qualify your concerns (I don't think that will work *because*...);

- be assertive; and,

- use RDA statements.

RDA statements

RDA stands for 'resent, demand, appreciate'. RDA statements give a framework for addressing bad behaviour whilst showing respect for the other person combined with an appreciation of good behaviour.

You might say to someone:

- I resent that you were out of the office all yesterday afternoon with no explanation.

- I demand that you tell me when you are going to be out, where you are going and how long you expect to be.

- I appreciate the business that you brought in last month. You worked very hard – well done.

When speaking to people familiar with RDA, by all means use exactly this terminology. If, however, you are speaking to someone unfamiliar with it, you might want to choose language that conveys the spirit of these messages without using such emotive language. 'Resent' and 'demand' are strong words and may provoke a 'fight or flight' response. Under those circumstances it would be far better to say, for example: 'It's not acceptable for you to be absent without explanation' or: 'In future you must let me know your plans'. This gets the message across in unambiguous terms but without provoking an unwanted response.

Service Level Agreements

Service Level Agreements (SLAs) are formal agreements that cover the various aspects of a relationship between a customer and supplier. They can be with external suppliers, or internal, if, for example, another department provides some sort of service to your department. The sorts of things they cover include:

- responsibilities on both sides;
- the service to be provided;
- timescales;
- payment terms;
- dispute resolution; and,
- termination of agreement.

SLAs put a relationship on a more formal footing and can help avoid problems and misunderstandings by providing a framework within which all parties will operate.

Contracts

In essence, a legally binding SLA. Make sure you read the small print and take legal advice if necessary.

Conclusion

A lot of what we do in establishing and managing relationships is second nature. We have to remember to work at them and we must also bear in mind that we are paid our salary partly on the basis that we will behave in an acceptable manner – and getting along with colleagues is part of that behaviour.

Exercise: Cut in the corridor

Earlier in the chapter we took a look at Becky and Anne. At that time Becky was feeling hurt and angry and we asked:

How should Becky deal with the situation?

In the light of your own experience and what you have learned since, use the space below to make some notes. There are some suggestions at the end of the chapter.

_____

_____

_____

_____

_____

_____

Establishing and managing relationships checklist

- I appreciate the actions that need to be taken to establish good working relationships.

- I am not responsible for the behaviour of others, but I am responsible for how I react to it.

- I consider the types of power that might be at play in my relationships with others.

- I do not abuse power in relationships.

- I stand up for myself when I am treated unfairly.

- I have a strategy for dealing with conflict should I get caught up in it.

- I use a range of behaviours and tools to deal with conflict.

Case notes: Cut in the corridor

It is understandable that Becky feels hurt and angry. Anne has been exceptionally rude and no matter how busy she might be, there is simply no excuse for her behaviour.

How she reacts, however, is Becky's choice.

She can choose to ignore Anne from then on, which might be understandable, but will potentially damage her career prospects within that organisation and will also prolong the upset for her.

She can give Anne a piece of her mind, either face to face, over the phone or by email, but that will have the effect of escalating the situation. As with the first option, it will also very likely damage the relationship beyond repair.

She can choose to forget it and pretend it never happened, although we tend not to be able to completely forget such things and it may well fester for a long while and resurface at a later date.

She can talk to Anne about it, being honest about how Anne's behaviour made her feel, but making it clear that she values the relationship. She might say: 'When you cut me dead in the corridor it was very hurtful and it made me angry. I don't deserve to be treated like that. I appreciate that you are busy and are getting to grips with new responsibilities, and if there's anything I can do to help, let me know.'

Of course, if Anne stops to think, she will realise that she has behaved badly and apologise to Becky as soon as possible.

Further reading

In print:

- The Games People Play, Eric Berne, Penguin Books (1970)

- The Bases of Social Power, J.R.P. French and B.H. Raven, in Studies in Social Power, D. Cartwright (ed.), Institute for Social Power (1959)

- Managing Business Relationships, David Ford, Lars-Erik Gadde, Hakan Hakansson & Ivan Snehota, John Wiley & Sons (2003)

- The Essential Guide to Workplace Mediation and Conflict Resolution: Rebuilding Working Relationships, Nora Doherty & Marcelas Guyler, Kogan Page (2008)

- Managing Relationships at Work (ILM Super Series), Institute of Leadership & Management (ed.), Pergamon Flexible Learning (2003)

- Difficult Conversations: How to Discuss What Matters Most, Bruce Patton, Douglas Stone & Sheila Heen, Penguin (2000)

Online:

- www.workrelationships.co.uk – information on work and relationships that covers a wide range of issues.

- www.nickheap.co.uk – lots of free resources to help with development.

- http://www.ogc.gov.uk/delivery_lifecycle_managing_relationships. asp – information on managing relationships from the Office of Government Commerce website.

- http://www.microsoft.com/education/competencies/comp_mana gingrelationships.mspx – information on managing relationships from Microsoft Education.

- http://www.managementhelp.org/intrpsnl/basics.htm – information on conflict management from the Free Management Library.

- http://www.businessballs.com/transactionalanalysis.htm – information on the theory on the businessballs website.

What makes a team?

So at what point does a group of people stop being a group of people and become a team? Is it as simple as calling them such?

Well, yes and no. Naming is certainly a part of it, the start of defining a team identity, but there is more to it than that, as we shall see.

Teams can be said to have certain characteristics, which include (but are not limited to) the following:

- **A common purpose:** Every member of a team shares in the common purpose of that team. With a sports team, that purpose may simply be 'to win'. With a sales team, the purpose may be 'to get as many sales as possible'. This may also turn into rivalry with other sales teams and become 'to get more sales than team B'. Within the team, rivalry may also exist: 'I want to get more sales than Freddie' (this may help or hinder).

- **A shared vision:** Teams generally work towards a clearly defined medium to long-term goal. In sports, this may be 'to be top of the league' or 'to win the cup'. In business, it may be 'to beat last year's annual sales figure' or 'to reduce customer complaints by 20 per cent'. The shared vision will be supported by the common purpose.

- **Core values:** Team members will overlook all other differences such as age, colour, religion or whatever, and develop core values. Think back to when you were a child: did you have a special group of friends who shared a catchphrase, sense of humour, style of dress, or who had some other common feature? In the same way that you had your core values – the things you shared that set you apart as a 'gang' – so do teams. Everything else becomes secondary to the badge of membership, whatever that may be.

Team strengths and weaknesses

People are naturally disposed to feel comfortable in small groups. It is, after all, how we experience the world as we grow up, with immediate family, extended family, groups of friends, classmates, and interest groups, such as Brownies or a chess club. Arguably this means that we are also pre-disposed to working in small organisations, or work teams within larger ones.

Of course, the flip side of this is that as well as benefiting from the social 'glue' that bonds us together in such groups, we can also experience the bickering, resentment, in-fighting and power plays that also go on. Generally, if a family or social group has a strong, charismatic leader, then this kind of behaviour is sublimated, and so it is with work teams. With work teams, however, team members also have a duty of care to the team, the task and the employer and there is a not unreasonable expectation that people will behave in a fair and honest manner.

Team strengths	Team weaknesses
Productivity may be boosted	Can waste time bickering
Can increase job satisfaction	People may have hidden agendas
Can engender a sense of pride	Can get caught up in politicking
Can promote a sense of identity	Factions and cliques can develop
Can boost commitment	Can become dysfunctional

Teams are useful when:

- There are clear objectives.

- Achieving those objectives requires diversity.

- Tasks cannot be completed by just one person.

Group dynamics

An enormous amount of research has been conducted into how people and groups interact, throughout which Bruce Tuckman's four stage model still holds good. The four stages he identified are:

- **Forming:** the group comes together and people begin to assess the rules or core values of the group and to work out what their role within it might be.

- **Storming:** the difficult but necessary phase where people test boundaries, ground rules and loyalties, and compete for the most favoured position.

- **Norming:** the rules and boundaries begin to be accepted and people settle into their roles within the team.

- **Performing:** people start to work in earnest to achieve the team's objectives.

Some people add a fifth stage, mourning, to the model, which is appropriate to project teams, for example, that will disband once their work is completed.

Case study: The bubble burst

Ed has just been employed as a team leader in an organisation he really wanted to work for. He is elated! The organisation is well respected and Ed feels he got the job because he took a strategic approach to his personal development: just one year ago he got his first office job, having worked in retail before that (he enjoyed retail, but wanted the weekends off to spend with his fiancée and had to accept that wasn't an option unless he switched jobs).

Now that he has taken up his position, however, the bubble has been well and truly burst. His team are surly and uncommunicative, they haven't met an objective or hit a target in months and they spend more time bitching about their colleagues or gossiping about what was on television than they do actually working.

Ed is conscious that he is on three months probation and he fears that if he doesn't sort things out and start getting results, he will lose his job. He can't afford for that to happen. He and his fiancée have just bought their first house and they need both salaries to pay the mortgage and other bills.

What can Ed do to sort out his team and secure his job?

We'll come back to Ed later.

Team types and theories

We have already observed that people feel comfortable in small 'family' groups. Within these groups, people have definite roles (mother, brother), responsibilities (run the household, walk the dog) and expectations, both of others (I expect my parents to take care of me) and from others of themselves (my parents expect me to behave well). Work teams have similar roles, responsibilities and expectations. Teams are generally made up of people with complementary skills and abilities in order that they may work together to perform perhaps complicated tasks.

Many theories have been put forward as to how a team should look and operate. Some of the more well known are:

- Belbin team roles: Dr Meredith Belbin's work has identified nine clusters of behaviour, each having its own strengths, weaknesses and contribution to make to the team, which he terms 'team roles' (information on Belbin's theory is signposted in the 'Further reading' section at the end of the chapter).

- Beddoes-Jones Cognitive Team Roles: focuses on understanding how individuals' thinking preferences drive their behaviour and the impact these preferences have on their motivation, values and relationships at work.

- Margerison-McCann Team Management System: identifies the strategic work roles people like to fulfil and can be used effectively in both team and leadership development capacities.

- Management Team Role Indicator (MTR-i): a team-roles questionnaire and model that aims to show what kind of contribution each member makes to the team. Like the Myers Briggs Type Indicators (MBTI), the MTR-i team roles are based on Jungian theory.

The working team

You may be able to handpick your team, but it is more likely you will inherit. You may be lucky and get a happy, functional group of people with a full and complementary range of skills and abilities with which to tackle the job you all have to do, or you may get a bunch of disaffected folk with skills gaps, personal issues and axes to grind. Most likely, your team will sit somewhere between these two extremes and it will be a big part of your job to create an effective, successful team.

Three steps to building the team

There are three basic steps to take when you want to build a team:

- review and assess the current situation;

- devise and implement a plan of action; and,

- monitor and evaluate progress

Like many management tasks, on the surface of it team development is simple: know where you are now, know where you want to be, take steps to bridge the gap. And like many management tasks, it really is that simple! What makes it complicated are the external pressures and events over which you have no control and over which you may have to try to exert some influence. Let's take a closer look at the three steps.

Review and assess the current situation

When you take charge of a team, what you need to achieve will be communicated to you in the form of objectives. These in turn should form a part of the overall strategic plan of the organisation and should support the achievement of that. Once you know what tasks your team must undertake, you are in a position to determine what mix of skills and abilities your team must have in order to be successful.

Your first step, therefore, is to see what the existing situation is: what skills and abilities your people currently have. Armed with that information, you are in a position to move to the next step.

Your assessment should involve the whole team; the chances are, they are painfully aware of their own – and the team's – weaknesses and development needs. Don't forget to celebrate strengths the team has, rather than focusing solely on shortcomings, and be sure to see those shortcomings as 'development needs', not 'problems'.

Devise and implement a plan of action

Your plan of action may have many elements: perhaps you need to boost the numbers of your team, you may need to engage a specialist or consultant, almost definitely you will have a range of training needs that must be addressed.

The nature and volume of the work you plan to do will be dictated by organisational objectives. The way in which you organise your team to meet those objectives is down to you and, to a lesser extent, your team.

Within the structure of a team, people take on one or more of the various roles that have to be fulfilled. These are likely to include:

- Leader: the leader has overall charge of the team and gives direction, allocates work and monitors progress.

- Expert: people in this role will have particular knowledge and skills and will bring to the team something that no one else involved can supply. Experts may come from inside or outside of the organisation.

- Functional: this is based on role – what a person does day to day to contribute to the achievement of team goals and objectives; for example, buyer, trainer, salesperson.

- Administrative: this refers to those who carry out supporting activities such as filing, taking minutes of meetings, distributing information and so on.

Depending on the type of team and the nature of the organisation, people may fulfil different roles in different teams. For example, whilst a salesperson in a work team will always fulfil the same role, they may change from telephone to field sales, and objectives and targets may change as campaigns change. An expert may take the role of expert in a number of teams, just as admin people may support the work of several teams. You may find yourself leading one team and fulfilling an expert or functional role in another. Consequently, you should clearly define areas of responsibility and limits of authority. Set objectives and define the required standards, and make sure those things are fully understood.

A word to the wise with regard to team-building courses: be careful! I don't know if the cost of the damage done to businesses by ill-advised team-building training has ever been assessed, but I'm confident that figure would be pretty high. Some of the training is excellent, without a doubt, but some is pointless, damaging and even downright dangerous. Be sensible when choosing your teambuilding; there is a world of difference between someone feeling challenged and someone feeling threatened.

Many years ago I worked for an organisation that was growing rapidly. Several positions for team leader existed and there were a number of us ready for that promotional step. It was announced that we would all be taken to Kielder Forest for a day's 'assessment and team-building'. This was the first such exercise any of us had ever encountered and we naturally wanted to know what it was all about. The training manager fobbed everyone off, which aroused suspicion that there was more to it than met the eye, but off we all went anyway – we wanted those promotions!

The day itself consisted of the now familiar routine of standing on upturned milk crates, playing with scaffolding poles and running around like idiots. No one felt they got much from it – apart from a deep distrust of the training manager, a sense of futility and far too many midge bites. Nevertheless, I did get my promotion – despite (or perhaps because of) the fact I stood up to the bullying, ex-military 'instructor' and refused to let my team attempt an exercise that we all considered to be too dangerous. Much to his intense irritation, we completed it as a theoretical rather than a practical task.

Monitor and evaluate progress

Your plan should include milestones and markers that you can use as quick checks to see you are on the right path. Make sure that you gather enough of the right information both to be confident that you and your team are performing satisfactorily and to be able to demonstrate that you are. This is for the benefit of both the team, as a motivator, and management, as part of your regular reporting process.

If you find that you are drifting off course or not performing to the required standard then this approach will quickly alert you to the fact, allowing you to take steps to get back on track. If it turns out that you were overly optimistic when you made your plans, then this will also be highlighted. If that does turn out to be the case, then re-forecast and go back to senior management with the new figures and outcomes. Your discussions might not be comfortable, but they will undoubtedly appreciate being told early on that objectives are not achievable rather than getting several months down the line and finding out how bad things have got. Whatever you do, do not lie, distort the figures or cover things up; that may keep things on an even keel for a short time but will only make things worse in the long run.

Delegation

Management may be defined as 'the art of achieving results by directing the efforts of others': 'to employ', after all, does mean 'to use'. People are the most valuable assets a manager has: not in terms of platitudes and flattery (be nice to them and they won't rebel) or some sort of politically correct 'corporate speak' (it's what the stakeholders expect to see in the mission statement) but in actual point of fact: you simply cannot do everything that needs to be done on your own. If we accept this definition as true, then delegation is arguably the most essential management skill. It is not something that everyone finds easy or does well, however, and poor delegation can cost time, money and staff.

Why delegate?

We delegate for the simple reason that it is not possible to do everything that needs to be done ourselves; as managers, we need to be able to take a strategic view – to see the big picture – and that can be hard to do when you're bogged down by routine tasks. In fact, as managers we generally aren't paid to carry out routine tasks: it is our responsibility to see that they get done, but not our responsibility to do them. Delegation is also a great way to develop and motivate staff, and to allow people to try out new tasks, roles and responsibilities in a safe environment.

Golden rules of delegation

- Do it in good time. Don't delegate tasks that are close to deadline just to get them off your desk or 'to do' list: that simply isn't fair, especially when people are doing things for the first time. Allow extra time so that if snags do occur, there is still time to meet deadlines. If things are completed in advance, that's a bonus.

- Delegate what has to be done, not how it must be done. People have their own methods of working and your way may turn out not to be the best after all. Delegation should be carried out on the grounds of accountability: you are looking for the end result. How people achieve that result is – within limits – up to them.

- Delegate choice assignments, too – not just the bad stuff that you want rid of. Beware also of hanging onto tasks you enjoy when your job or level of responsibility means you should be passing them on to someone else.

- Consider the employee to whom you delegate specific tasks. Match skills, abilities and areas of interest as much as possible. If you discussed at appraisal one staff member's interest in the company web site and a project to redevelop it comes up, don't assign a place on the project team to anyone else without very good reason.

- Demonstrate trust: you need to communicate with the team whilst they work on their various tasks, but without spying on them. Give them room to manoeuvre and allow them to make and correct their own mistakes (again, within limits). I used to work in an office where the manager searched everyone's desks after they had gone home for the night – something I found out when I noticed things on my and colleagues' desks were regularly disturbed and then asked enough questions to get to the bottom of it. We had nothing to hide, but if you treat people as if you don't trust them, they may well become untrustworthy.

- Use a framework for delegation. A simple three step process should help both you and your staff know what to expect:

  - **Step 1:** Explain the background and the task, so that the team member knows how it fits into the overall strategy for the business and/or department. Encourage discussion.

  - **Step 2:** Set objectives and agree deadlines, so that the team member knows exactly what is expected. Remember it is the outcome you are delegating, not the process by which that is achieved, although it can be a good idea to ask how the delegate thinks they might proceed with the task. (Remember that they may need time to think about things, especially if it is a new or complicated project.)

  - **Step 3:** Agree monitoring and reporting procedures. Build in regular feedback sessions, time checks on milestones and so on. That way you can be confident that things are running according to plan or be alert to issues that need action without breathing down someone's neck.

Pitfalls and perils

The biggest threats to effective delegation are poor relationships and communication. If you have a relationship with a lack of trust, then that will impact adversely on everything you try to do. Remember that your staff will mask their feelings in much the same way you do and be honest – at least with yourself – when considering the state of the relationships you have. (There is more on this in chapter 4.2, Establishing and managing relationships.) If you communicate poorly, then do not be surprised if people do not achieve the results you were hoping for.

You might also experience guilt, if you are delegating work to someone who is already working to capacity. At times we must all dig deeper, however, and if you are also stretched then it can help to build team spirit.

You may feel fear at losing control over tasks and processes. This is natural, especially the first few times you delegate work, but stick to the three steps and you retain control.

Staff appraisal

Performance appraisal is a part of working life, with regular interviews built into the calendar. It can be a useful exercise or a dispiriting one, depending largely upon the relationship between the appraiser and the appraisee. Most commonly appraisals are held once a year, but may be held twice yearly, quarterly, or even monthly. Some organisations hold a formal annual appraisal tied in to pay awards, with regular less formal meetings throughout the year.

What is appraisal?

Appraisal may be seen as many things, including:

- a check up;

- a chance to take in the big picture;

- a time to reflect;

- an opportunity to reinforce praise; and,

- a chance to celebrate successes.

Why do it?

If appraisal can be such a headache, why do we bother? Surely we can jump on bad behaviour and dole out praise as we go along? Well, yes, and indeed we should. Appraisal, however, gives us a formal opportunity to reward and acknowledge good performance and business success and to record it, too. As we move on from challenge to challenge, it can be easy to forget that we have enjoyed some great successes over the months.

Appraisal can also be motivating; staff get their opportunity to have a one to one with a manager who can at other times be largely unavailable. I remember a colleague being understandably upset when her appraisal was interrupted: 'That's *my* time,' she complained, and she was right. People expect their appraisal time to be awarded and not interrupted or cut short.

Appraisal is an opportunity to look to the future, to share visions and goals and to plan work for the coming period. This allows people to get on with their bit of the process whilst understanding where it is all leading.

The structured appraisal

As with so many management tasks, having a structured approach can pay dividends and appraisal is no exception. The following three-step process should help:

- **Review:** look back at what has happened since the last appraisal;
- **Set goals:** look forward and plan the next period's work; and,
- **Check understanding** and gain commitment.

Before the appraisal interview, explain the process to all staff so that they know what to expect. Repeat it at the start of the appraisal, too. If you want people to self-appraise, get the forms out to them in good time. (Some organisations have both the appraisee and appraiser fill in identical forms, then seek to achieve congruence in the appraisal.)

Review

If there is one golden rule about appraisal it is this: no surprises! You should address problems and offer praise as and when the need arises. When you review what has happened since the last formal appraisal, you should be remembering highlights and, perhaps, difficult times, too. Don't gloss over difficult issues or brush them under the carpet. There is no need to dwell on them, but you must acknowledge them otherwise the appraisal will lack honesty.

The bulk of the time in many an appraisal is spent in looking back; I would advocate that you avoid doing that. If you have addressed things as they arose, there really is no need. It is far more motivational to look forward.

Set goals

You can neither praise nor reprimand anyone fairly or credibly when they don't know exactly what it is that they should be doing. Some organisations seem to have a 'sink or swim', 'survival of the fittest' culture; this does not generally work in the best interests of either the organisation or the individuals within it.

At this stage in the appraisal, it is your opportunity to explain what the organisation and departmental plans and goals are for the coming period. These can then be reduced to team and individual objectives, which can be seen to contribute directly to the overarching goals of the business.

Look at any development needs that those objectives create: what additional knowledge, skills and abilities will be required? How will these needs best be met?

Check understanding and gain commitment

Make sure that the appraisee understands exactly what is required of them and what help they will be given to help them to meet their objectives.

Giving feedback

The main rule when it comes to giving feedback is to go for the ball, not the player. 'Your performance' or 'Your behaviour', not 'You' – especially if the feedback is critical of performance or behaviour.

To be credible and useful, feedback must be specific: give examples, praise areas of improvement, and suggest areas for development.

Danger areas

Things to beware include:

- The recency effect: remembering only that which has happened in the last few weeks, which can change perception of performance for good or ill;

- Horns or halo: liking or disliking someone because of how they look, speak or dress;

- Fear: lacking the courage to address difficult issues in particular;

- Talking too much: the appraisee should do more than half of the talking in an appraisal;

- Interrupting: as a general rule (chatterboxes excepted) you should never interrupt a junior member of staff. Do it once too often and they might stop trying to contribute altogether!

Disciplinary action

Sadly, the need for disciplinary action is inevitable. It can also be a time that provokes strong feelings, anger, outrage and fear among them. Consequently having a set of guidelines and procedures will help us to deal with the issues whilst putting to one side the emotion.

Establishing rules and standards

When drawing up standards for conduct, look to cover the following areas:

- behaviour;

- safety of self and others;

- presentation in and out of work; and,

- preservation of assets.

Formal procedures

Formal procedures, like rules and standards, should be unambiguous, easy to understand and fair. They should cover:

- Number and type of warnings that will be given: most systems start with a verbal warning, after which, should behaviour or performance not improve, there will be a first written and then a final warning issued. Certain offences, such as theft or fraud, will be designated as 'gross misconduct' and warrant immediate dismissal.

- Who can attend to support: this may be a union representative, colleague or family member.

- The hearing process: what an offender can expect to happen if misconduct is uncovered.

- Duration: how long the process will ideally take to complete and how long a warning remains on record.

- A list of offences that constitute gross misconduct.

Taking disciplinary action

When something is brought to your attention, you must first investigate the circumstances. Sadly there are some who will distort the facts – or even lie outright – to get another person into trouble so your first responsibility is to verify that there is a charge to face. You must also be sensitive to the person raising the issue, especially if a staff member has raised concerns about a manager, as that will likely have taken a lot of soul searching and an amount of courage.

As part of your investigation process, you must also talk with the person who has been accused of wrongdoing, explain what has been alleged and get their side of the story. Only after you have as much information as possible and have had a chance to weigh things up should you decide whether to make things formal and take action.

Having decided to take disciplinary action, you then need to assess the seriousness of the offence and decide what is to be done. Your options include (but are not necessarily limited to):

- verbal warning;
- first written warning;
- final warning;
- fine;
- suspension from duty;
- demotion; and,
- dismissal.

Give notice of the official interview and prepare thoroughly. Remember that this is not a bullying session and neither are you a head teacher or judge: aim to be fair and impartial – but firm. You are tackling the ball, not the player, so don't make a personal attack. Remember to recognise the rights of the individual and, even if you are dismissing someone, treat them with respect.

You will also need to think about the appeals process: whether appeals will be allowed and if so, what form will they take. If you have to go to arbitration, there is always ACAS, and indeed, their web site contains a lot of very useful information.

Conclusion

In the words of Steve Jobs, when asked about his business model on '60 Minutes': 'My model for business is The Beatles: They were four guys that kept each other's negative tendencies in check; they balanced each other. And the total was greater than the sum of the parts. Great things in business are not done by one person, they are done by a team of people.'

Exercise: The bubble burst

Earlier in the chapter we took a look at Ed and his dysfunctional team. At that time, we asked:

What can Ed do to sort out his team and secure his job?

In the light of what you have learned since, use the space below to make some notes. There are some suggestions at the end of the chapter.

_____

_____

_____

_____

_____

_____

_____

Building and leading the team checklist

- Team characteristics include having a common purpose, shared vision, and core values.

- I appreciate team strengths and weaknesses.

- Teams generally go through four stages: forming, storming, norming and performing.

- There are many team types and theories, including Belbin's team roles and the Management Team Role Indicator.

- I use the three-step framework for building a team: review and assess the current situation, devise and implement a plan of action, and monitor and evaluate progress.

- I follow the golden rules of delegation and don't keep all the 'best' jobs for myself.

- I adhere to the three-step framework for delegation: explain background and task, set objectives and agree deadlines, and agree monitoring and reporting process.

- I understand the value of staff appraisal and know that appraisal time is important to staff.

- I use the three-step framework: review, set goals, and check understanding.

- I know what the disciplinary code and procedure is for my organisation.

- I do not hesitate to use it if circumstances warrant it.

Case notes: The bubble burst

Poor Ed – he's certainly got his work cut out!

His best bet is to work within the framework suggested earlier: review and assess the current situation; devise and implement a plan of action; and, monitor and evaluate progress.

Ed needs to start talking to people and gathering information. Once he has a good grasp of what the problems are, he can get to work and address them. He will need to use his relationship-building skills, too – this team seems to have some deep-rooted issues!

Taking a step-by-step, methodical approach and working on the relationship with the team should start to pay off. Monitoring progress should give him some good news to report to his boss when his probationary assessment comes around, even if he hasn't turned things around completely.

Further reading

In print:

- Team Roles at Work, R. Meredith Belbin, Elsevier Butterworth-Heinemann (1993)

- Reframing Organisations, Lee Bolman and Terence Deal, Jossey Bass (1990)

- Soul of a New Machine, Tracy Kidder, Little-Brown (1981)

- How to be a Better Teambuilder, Rupert Eales-White, Kogan Page (1996)

- Building Effective Teams (Leading from the Centre), Duke Corporate Education (ed.), Kaplan Business (2005)

Online:

- http://www.belbin.com/ – Belbin Team Role Theory website.

- http://www.cognitivefitness.co.uk/ – website of the Cognitive Fitness Consultancy.

- www.acas.org.uk – the website of the Advisory, Conciliation and Arbitration Service.

- http://www.businessballs.com/teambuildinggames.htm – free team building resources from the businessballs website.

- http://humanresources.about.com/od/involvementteams/a/twelve _tip_team.htm – team building tips from About.com.

Chapter 4.4
Developing and motivating others

NVQ Application:

This chapter is relevant to the following NVQ in Management Units:

- B5 Provide leadership for your team

- B9 Develop the culture of your organisation

- D5 Allocate and check work in your team

- D6 Allocate and monitor the progress and quality of work in your area of responsibility

- D7 Provide learning opportunities for colleagues

- D8 Help team members address problems affecting their performance

- D13 Support individuals to develop and maintain their performance

Linked chapters:

The information in this chapter is related to information in the following chapters:

- 1.1 Planning and managing your own professional development

- 1.2 Clear communication

- 2.1 Leadership, culture and vision

- 4.3 Building and leading the team

- 5.3 Managing resources

Introduction

There are those who simply don't see the point of staff development: after all, if you take on people who can do the job in the first place, there ought to be no need. Others see it as a money pit, a cost that does nothing for the bottom line. However, that outlook doesn't take into account either the motivational benefits of planned development or the need to react to rapid change. Just as we need exercise to keep our bodies fit and healthy, staff development is essential if we are to keep the business fit and healthy. Staff costs are most likely your highest costs, therefore doesn't it make sense to invest a little more to help them to be the best they can be?

Objectives

The aim of this chapter is to facilitate the processes of development and motivation. It will help you to:

- consider the benefits of developing staff;

- identify development needs;

- consider the pros and cons of different types of training and learning;

- be aware of some of the theories that exist with regard to motivation; and,

- understand what motivates people, and also what might demotivate them.

Barriers to development

Before we move on to look at how and why we can develop staff, it is worth taking a moment to consider why it is that people are resistant to the process. Resistance is often due to fear. Managers are afraid of:

- incurring a cost with no discernible benefit;

- wasting time on the 'wrong' training; and,

- staff becoming more skilled, knowledgeable and competent than them.

Staff are afraid of:

- failure;

- success; and,

- change.

What do people need to know?

Training is about increasing capacity, making someone better, quicker, more efficient, more accurate. The best way to find out what someone needs to learn is to look at what the optimum job requirements are, assess the current performance level of the individual, then work out what is required to help bridge the gap.

The areas to look at are knowledge, skills and attitude (KSA). Training should impart knowledge, instil and/or develop skills, and encourage or change attitudes. Let's take a closer look at those areas.

Knowledge

People need to know about:

- the organisation;

- the job(s) and task(s) they are required to carry out;

- the standards they are to meet; and,

- clients and customers.

Skills

Skills may be either occupational or 'soft'. Occupational skills are to do with the processes undertaken and the tools used. Soft skills include:

- communication;

- negotiation;

- problem solving;

- decision-making; and,

- time management.

These skills are increasingly considered to be key to success when it comes to people management.

Attitude

Attitude, or how we think and project our feelings, is one of the pillars of performance in business. There has been much debate about attitude, and having a positive mental attitude (or PMA) is seen to be both desirable and essential. What does it boil down to? 'Attitude' revolves around:

- openness;

- empathy;

- respect;

- self-confidence;

- self-awareness; and,

- patience.

When deciding what KSA profile staff are required to have, your best starting point will be the job description and person specification that were developed for the role in question.

Methods of development

A range of options is available to you when considering how best to develop your staff. Which you choose depends upon a number of things, including:

- budget;

- cost;

- the nature of the training need;

- what has been done in the past; and,

- the urgency of the situation.

The methods you can choose from include:

- formal group training courses, whether internal or external;

- coaching, which may be one to one or group; and,

- learning by osmosis.

Let's take a closer look at those options.

Formal group training

Formal group training courses, whether run internally or externally, can be very successful. People get the chance to share their experiences and can also remind each other of learning points when they return to the workplace.

It is a good idea to keep a database of available training courses along with evaluation by those who have attended. This will save you starting from scratch every time you look to meet a training need. With internal training, there should be a menu of available courses to view on (for example) the intranet. With external courses, you may find that you have to find out for yourself – although the training function may take care of that, too. Your network of contacts may prove very useful here and be able to recommend (or otherwise) useful courses, too.

Coaching

Coaching may be conducted on a one-to-one basis or in small groups. A manager, supervisor, team leader or staff member may carry it out: any of these might be senior to, junior to, or the peer of the trainee(s).

There is rather more to coaching than 'sit them with Johnny'. A coaching session should be conducted with a specific objective in mind and, as a result of it, the trainee(s) should experience a change with regard to KSA.

Learning by osmosis

What I mean by this is the way that new people will pick up the business terminology, team language, company culture and the general 'vibe' just as a result of being in a particular department or organisation. Daily routines are observed and absorbed, and the strengths and weaknesses of different members of staff are learned. This isn't a case of dumping people at a desk and letting them get on with it, it is a natural part of becoming integrated in new surroundings.

Designing your own training workshop

There may be times when you choose to develop your own workshop. If so, then this loose framework should keep you focused on your objectives. In fact, that is exactly where you begin: your starting point for any training initiative is what you hope to get out of it. It is only when you know what you want to achieve that you can make choices as to the best way to get the right message across.

The framework consists of three steps:

- set objectives;
- select appropriate methods and activities; and,
- prepare a detailed schedule, with timings.

It is said that you should 'tell them what you're going to tell them; tell them it; then tell them what you told them' and this holds true. Open your session with introductions and an icebreaker, then state the objectives. Explain how the session is structured and say what will be covered.

The 'tell them it' phase is the session itself, where you go through all of your training material. Finally, you should recap the session. This is an especially useful step: when people get to the end of a workshop they very often heave a sigh of relief, not because they're glad it's over, but because a lot of ground has been covered and they have spent more time actively engaged and thinking than they might during a routine day. Taking them back along the path of the journey shows just how much they have experienced and learned.

Set objectives

We've already mentioned objectives. They should be specific and tell people exactly what they should get out of participating in the workshop. For example:

Aim

The aim of this session is to improve participants' skills as givers of service, to raise awareness of the importance of customers to the success of any business, and of the role of quality customer service in gaining and keeping customers.

Objectives

The session will enable participants to:

- *present a confident and positive image to customers at all times;*
- *identify and satisfy core customer needs;*
- *encourage customer complaints;*
- *handle difficult customers effectively; and,*
- *develop a customer service strategy.*

Anyone attending this workshop would know exactly why they were there and also what they could hope to get out of it in terms of KSA.

Select methods and activities

The basic methods available to you are:

- lecture;
- demonstration;
- debate;
- theoretical exercise;
- practical exercise; and,
- hands-on, practical experience.

You should choose whatever is most appropriate. For example, if you are training people in the use of a computer system or software, then whilst the workshop will undoubtedly have some elements of lecture, demonstration and debate, the bulk of the training should be hands on practical experience.

Prepare a detailed schedule

You need to be able to tell people how long the workshop will last and you also need to be sure that you can fit everything in. The best way to do this is to decide in what order you will do things and assign a realistic amount of time for each element of the workshop. That way, you can keep an eye on the clock and make sure you don't overrun. Having said that, if a particular discussion, for example, is going well and people are sharing experiences and learning from them, by all means let it run on a little longer. Flag up when time will run out (we can give this another five minutes) or agree to return to the topic over lunch (we can take 15 minutes less for lunch and pick this up again then): whatever suits you and your trainees the best.

Ten tips for trainers

1   use people's names;

2   make eye contact;

3   avoid jargon;

4   use visual images;

5   use analogy and metaphor to illustrate learning points;

6   use case studies;

7   allow people to share their experiences, both good and bad;

8   be prepared to share your own experiences, both good and bad;

9   if people are starting to nod or to drift off, shake things up; if you can't think of anything else, get them to run around the room, stretch, touch their toes, move one place to the right – anything to get them moving and liven up a bit; and,

10 make your training fun! People learn more and have better recall when they enjoy the experience.

Training evaluation

Whatever type of training has been conducted, it ought to be reviewed and evaluated. Without these steps you don't know what's working and what isn't. If you are seeking to evaluate training that you have conducted, it is worth preparing an evaluation sheet that you can leave with the trainee(s) to complete afterwards. You can ask people to grade individual exercises out of (say) five, ask them what they enjoyed most and least, what they will do first as a result of attending – whatever suits your needs. Do look over the forms afterwards and see if there are any trends emerging: if people consistently give a low grade to or enjoy least a particular exercise, you may want to take a look at it and see how you can improve it. If they consistently grade highly or enjoy most an exercise, you can identify what is good about it and aim to use that in other workshops.

Other methods of evaluation include:

- one-to-one discussion;

- quizzes and questionnaires; or,

- monitoring statistics (if call rates increase and/or query levels drop after relevant training, it is safe to say there has been an improvement).

Motivation

There are a lot of synonyms for the word 'motivation', including:

- ambition;

- drive;

- hunger;

- incentives;

- inducement;

- inspiration;

- spirit; and,

- stimulation.

Motivation starts with oneself – if we aren't personally motivated, then we cannot motivate anyone else. Enthusiasm breeds enthusiasm. Apathy breeds apathy. It is all about attitude, having a positive outlook, being open-minded, not always assuming the worst will happen.

Maslow's hierarchy of human needs

Working in the USA in the 1950s and 1960s, Abraham Maslow developed a theory that people are driven by inner needs. He identified five categories, which he arranged in a hierarchical pyramid. Starting at the bottom, they are: physiological, safety, social, esteem and self-actualisation.

The most basic needs – prepotent needs, as he termed them – generally had to be satisfied before any higher needs could even be considered.

Frederick Hertzberg

Frederick Hertzberg looked at aspects of work and identified two categories of influences, which he termed 'motivators' and 'hygiene factors'. Motivators cause job satisfaction and include:

- achievement;
- recognition;
- responsibility; and,
- advancement.

Hygiene factors cause job dissatisfaction and include:

- working conditions;
- relationships with colleagues;
- management style; and,
- company policy.

In essence, hygiene factors relate to Maslow's lowest two categories of need and motivators to the top two: the middle one is a bit of each.

Douglas McGregor

Douglas McGregor formulated two models: Theory X, which assumes that people are lazy, dislike work and must be coerced, directed and controlled; and Theory Y, which assumes that people will strive to meet their goals if organisational rewards exist, and therefore must be supported by organisational conditions. Theory X may be thought of as 'the stick' and Theory Y 'the carrot'. All organisations have an element of Theory X about them, with standards for behaviour and reprisals for those who fail to meet them; the best organisations have given as much thought to Theory Y elements.

There are two basic types of motivation:

- intrinsic, where one does something for its own sake; and,

- extrinsic, where one does something for some other reason.

McGregor's models are basically to do with extrinsic motivation: people do what they do to gain reward or to avoid punishment.

Drivers

There are a number of drivers that can motivate us. With drivers, it's all about how much you want or value something. If you want or value it a lot, then your motivation is high. The types of things that typically motivate us include:

- Money – which ought not simply to be given, but earned on the basis of performance or results, for example. People should not be paid just for 'presenteeism'; they should understand how and why their salary is earned and awarded.

- Targets – but the caveat is that these must be realistic. If there is no chance of achieving something, there is no motivation to try.

- Participation – allowing people to contribute to process design, or to generate and contribute ideas is a powerful motivator.

- Recognition – giving feedback, praise, promotion and/or further financial reward.

Exercise: What makes you tick?

Think about your own experiences with your current and with any previous employers you have had. Take a little time to make some notes under the questions below.

What motivates you?

_____

_____

_____

What demotivates you?

_____

_____

_____

Now consider the people you currently manage. Be realistic when you answer the next question. For example, many people are motivated by money, but if your budget is squeezed, it won't currently help you to list bonuses or pay rises as factors that could prove useful to you now.

How can I use this knowledge to motivate others?

_____

_____

_____

Conclusion

Some teams stumble along from day to day complaining about their workload and each other, and seem to operate in an endless spirit of resentment. Others award each other nicknames, have in-jokes and even a team language. They get the job done and they have fun while they do it; they have team spirit.

Individuals can be much the same – focused, happy and busy or very much not. It can help to safeguard your motivation to take a strategic view and to have a medium to long-term plan so that you know why you are doing the day-to-day stuff. To put it simply, are you breaking rocks out of a quarry, or are you building a cathedral?

Developing and motivating others checklist

- Thinking in terms of knowledge, skills and attitudes (KSA) gives us a framework for training needs analysis.

- A range of development options is available for use, including formal training and coaching.

- If we design our own training interventions, then we start by looking at what we want to achieve. This tells us what should be in the workshop.

- Whatever training our staff or we undertake, we will get more out of it if we review and evaluate it afterwards.

- Motivation is a personal thing and starts with the self.

- Maslow identified a hierarchy of human needs; lower needs must be met before higher needs become important.

- Hertzberg identified motivators and hygiene factors: motivators should be put in place and hygiene factors met to the satisfaction of the workforce in order to best ensure that goals will be met.

- Douglas McGregor's theories give us a way to organise the workplace: Theory X will mean the organisation is driven by fear of reprisals; Theory Y, by the desire to attain reward.

- Motivational drivers include money, targets, participation and recognition.

Further reading

In print:

- The Tao of Motivation, Max Landsberg, HarperCollins Business (2000)

- Work and the Nature of Man, Frederick Hertzberg, Granada (1974)

- Motivation and Personality, Abraham Maslow, Harper and Row (1954)

- The Human Side of Enterprise, Douglas McGregor, McGraw-Hill Higher Education (1960)

- Leadership and Motivation: The Fifty-fifty Rule and the Eight Key Principles of Motivating Others, John Adair, Kogan Page Ltd. (2006)

Online:

- http://www.businessballs.com/motivation.htm – information on motivational theory and activities from the businessballs website.

- http://www.accel-team.com/motivation/index.html – information on the theory and practice of employee motivation from the Accel team development website.

- http://www.money-zine.com/Career-Development/Leadership-Skill/Motivation-Theory-and-Leadership/ – useful article on the money-zine.com website.

- http://www.leadershipexpert.co.uk/leadership-motivating-others.html – useful information from the leadership expert website.

- http://humanresources.about.com/od/motivationsucces3/a/motiv atestaff.htm – 'Motivating your staff in a time of change' on the About.com website.

- http://netmba.com/mgmt/ob/motivation/maslow/ – information on Maslow's Hierarchy of Needs from the Internet Center for Management and Business Administration.

Chapter 4.5
Ensuring productive meetings

NVQ Application:

This chapter is relevant to the following NVQ in Management Units:

- D11 Lead meetings

- D12 Participate in meetings

- E11 Communicate information and knowledge

Linked chapters:

The information in this chapter is related to information in the following chapters:

- 1.2 Clear communication

- 1.3 Managing your time

- 1.4 Managing information and developing networks

- 4.6 Effective negotiation

- 6.4 Project planning and management

- 6.5 Problem solving and decision-making

Introduction

Everyone hates meetings. Well, pretty much everyone. If you have lots of time to fill and not much to do, they can be a boon, but for the majority of us, the invitation to yet another meeting can be a heart sinker. Why is this, do you think? In the majority of cases, it seems that the reason is that the meetings we most often attend are little more than talking shops, with nothing achieved as a result. No wonder then, when you are already struggling to get done everything you want to in the course of your day, that the thought of a meeting doesn't fill you with glee.

It has been estimated that managers spend about half of their time in meetings, with the figure rising to about three-quarters for senior management. Think of the cost attached to that! When companies run cost cutting exercises, why is it they downgrade hotels and travel, and cut back on stationery budgets rather than taking a long, hard look at what happens in meetings?

In tough economic times, many companies balk at spending a few thousand pounds consulting an expert; instead, to save money, they have a series of management meetings to find a way forward. Let's assume three meetings each lasting half a day are deemed necessary, with eight managers at varying levels attending each one. Let's also assume that they each spend about an hour preparing for each meeting and two to three hours on tasks arising, and that the average salary is £60,000. That's getting on for five weeks worth of time, at a cost of around £6,000, and there's no guarantee anything will happen as a result, never mind the right thing.

You may be relieved to learn, however, that there are positive steps you can take to ensure that the time you spend in meetings is worth your while.

Objectives

The aim of this chapter is to cut down the amount of wasted time you spend in meetings. It will help you to:

- judge whether calling a meeting is the right thing to do;

- know how to act before, during and after a meeting in order to get the best results;

- create an agenda and a structure for meetings;

- successfully chair a meeting; and,

- produce useful records of meetings.

So when *is* a meeting appropriate?

To help decide that, it might first help to consider what a meeting actually is and, equally importantly, what it is not. A meeting isn't simply getting a group of people together to tell them something and perhaps take some questions afterwards: that's a briefing session. Nor is it a group of people getting together for a general chat: that's a catch-up session. And nor is it getting together with a person or people to tell them where you are in relation to where you thought you'd be at this point in time with a particular project: that's an update session.

What differentiates a meeting from all the other reasons people might assemble around a table is that a meeting has an objective: meeting groups *do* things. Meetings are dynamic events to which there should be a definite purpose and a tangible outcome. A meeting might well incorporate briefing, catch-up and review sessions, but will also involve discussion, suggestion, challenge and much other behaviour in order that the objective is achieved.

Why meetings fail

There are a number of reasons why meetings don't achieve what they set out to do – or indeed, anything at all! These include:

- the objective is unclear or non-existent;

- there is no agenda;

- no one is in control of the meeting;

- the wrong people are in attendance;

- the meeting is held in an unsuitable environment;

- a meeting wasn't necessary;

- the meeting was held too late to make a difference;

- no minutes or action points were circulated afterwards;

- no one did what they were supposed to do following the meeting – and no one chased them up about it;

- lack of preparation prevented a full discussion;

- underlying factors caused resentment amongst attendees;

- the meeting tried to achieve too much in the time allowed;

- there were either too many or too few people in attendance; and,

- people didn't speak up for fear of reprisal.

Case study: Nicola's to-do list

It's Monday morning and accounts department supervisor Nicola has three items on her to-do list that require prompt attention.

Item 1: the organisation has chosen a new credit checking system. It will be fully operational in about six months time as the old system is phased out and staff are trained in using the new one. Nicola must let her team leaders know about the decision before the scheduled weekly meeting on Wednesday as she doesn't want them hearing about it from elsewhere.

Item 2: Nicola must let her boss have the monthly report showing last month's performance figures. Her boss needs the information for the monthly management meeting on Tuesday; Nicola has a catch-up session with her boss pencilled in for Friday afternoon.

Item 3: Nicola has been invited to join a project team that is being put together to look at the company website and update the content. The first meeting is on Thursday. She has received a lot of information relating to the project and she knows both that it is important and that her boss is keen for the department to have a say; however, Nicola is struggling with her workload and, especially with the new system coming in, she hasn't really got time for the website project. One of her team leaders mentioned recently that the website was looking dated and expressed an interest in sorting it out.

How might Nicola handle each of the three items?

We'll come back to Nicola shortly.

A structure for success

In order to give yourself the best possible chance of running and participating in productive meetings, there are a number of tasks and behaviours to complete and consider both before, during and after the meeting itself. There is far more to ensuring productive meetings than simply turning up more or less on time clutching a dog-eared agenda. The work involved will pay off in spades, however, if it ensures that rather than presiding over or participating in another 'talking shop', you actually achieve what you set out to achieve. Tangible results make useful bargaining tools at appraisal time!

As with so many management tasks, having a framework within which to operate can help immensely. We are going to take a three-step approach to meetings here, the three steps being:

- Step 1: Tasks to complete before the meeting;

- Step 2: What to do during the meeting; and,

- Step 3: Tasks to complete after the meeting.

Step 1: Tasks to complete before the meeting

The process of ensuring productive meetings begins long before the meeting itself. Putting in the groundwork beforehand should make the meeting itself shorter and more effective, and therefore more satisfactory for all attendees, which will make them more inclined to participate should you call a further or future meeting. There is a series of tasks you can work through to ensure your meetings achieve the best results:

- question whether calling a meeting is the right course of action;
- define quite clearly the purpose of the meeting;
- decide who should attend;
- identify any pre-meeting reading or preparation that would help things along;
- create an agenda, with timings;
- send out all relevant information in a pack to invitees; and,
- book a room and order refreshments, if necessary.

Let's look at those in a little more detail.

Question whether calling a meeting is the right course of action

What is it you want to achieve as a result of the meeting? If you wish simply to inform, but not consult, could you send an email instead? The answer to that may depend largely on the culture of the organisation you work in, but if you do gather people together to inform them of something, stress it is a briefing session; that way they will not turn up expecting to be able to contribute to a decision that has already been made.

If you can avoid calling a meeting, then I would suggest you always do so; that way when you do call one, people will know there is a definite purpose to it and that it is worth their while to attend.

Define quite clearly the purpose of the meeting

It goes without saying that if you do not know why you are doing something, then you will have difficulty explaining the purpose to those you hope to persuade to do it too. Meetings are held to:

- decide on a plan of action;

- find a solution to a problem;

- resolve conflict;

- negotiate a deal;

- bring about change;

- improve a situation; or,

- achieve movement.

Whatever your objective, a meeting should always have a purpose.

Decide who should attend

Once you know why you are calling a meeting, it should be easier to decide who should participate in it. Invite only those people who can make contributions that will drive things forward. Company culture might again rear its head here, in that attending certain meetings may be seen as a status symbol and those left out – irrespective of whether their presence would be beneficial either to them or to the outcome – might feel slighted. Use your judgement, but try to avoid inviting people just so they can say they were there.

Similarly, you should question the invitations you receive to attend meetings; can you say, hand on heart, that you can make a valid and valuable contribution and that the meeting would be less effective if you weren't there? Never be afraid to ask why you were invited or to turn down an invitation if you don't feel it would be best use of your time. When we looked at time management, I proposed that you should regularly ask yourself the question: 'Is what I *am* doing now what I *should be* doing now?' If you are in a meeting about something that doesn't involve you and that you know too little about to contribute effectively, then the answer has to be a resounding: 'NO!'.

Having said that, if you become aware of a meeting you feel you should attend but to which you haven't been invited, ask if there is any way in which you could contribute. You might have misunderstood the purpose, or the organiser might have assumed you would be too busy or not sufficiently interested to attend.

Identify any pre-meeting reading or preparation that would help things along

It is a waste of everyone's time to start a meeting with a session where you either all sit and read briefing materials or have them read to you. (The exception would be when the information is hot off the press and so could not have been circulated beforehand.) Send out whatever you can in advance and ask people to prepare; you can cut the time of your meeting considerably if everyone is briefed before they sit down around the table.

If you have invited anyone with specialist knowledge to your meeting, particularly if it is someone from outside your own department, or indeed, the organisation, make sure they are fully briefed on anything other attendees will be aware of by virtue of being in the department/organisation.

Create an agenda, with timings

Timekeeping is one of the biggest problems when it comes to meetings, and one of the ways in which you can combat problems with time is to have an agenda. An agenda need not be long or complicated, but should be the road map of the meeting, with milestones. List the topics to be covered, by whom, and how long you expect them to take. If you have specialists attending for just a couple of topics, time it so they can attend only that part of the meeting that is relevant to them. It will then be up to the Chair (who may or may not be you) to see that things run to time.

Below is an example.

Meeting to plan website enhancement initiative to be held at 3pm in the boardroom		
3.00	Greeting and introductions	BG – 5 mins
3.05	The current website – an overview	DL – 10 mins
3.15	Customer feedback summary	GK – 15 mins
3.30	Proposed enhancements	DL – 15 mins
3.45	Open discussion on proposed enhancements	BG to lead – 20 mins
4.05	Next steps	BG – 10 mins
4.15	Close	

Send out all relevant information in a pack to invitees

Gather everything together and send it in one go – do not send things in dribs and drabs unless it is completely unavoidable due to availability. People will soon get fed up if they have a one hour meeting in their diary for which they receive three separate lots of information that they are expected to read.

Book a room and order refreshments if necessary

A word here about the environment: book somewhere appropriate. Having three people around a boardroom table the size of a rugby pitch can feel as uncomfortable as cramming ten people into a broom cupboard. Make sure the temperature can be regulated (being able to open a window on a hot day will do the trick, provided the noise from outside won't prove distracting). Having drinks for people as they arrive can help build rapport and – should the meeting be a long one – you might consider providing biscuits and/or lunch.

Step 2: What to do during the meeting

Whenever you attend a meeting, you should be consciously and actively involved and engaged. You have been invited and have chosen to attend because you have something worthwhile to contribute, so make sure you take the opportunity to do so.

Meeting roles

There are a number of roles, any one of which you might fulfil in a meeting, and which include:

- chair;
- facilitator;
- project manager;
- worker;
- expert; and,
- administrator.

We are going to look at the role of the chair in more detail shortly, but first, let's take a look at what behaviours are desirable, irrespective of the role you play.

Desirable behaviours

The sorts of behaviours that are desirable include:

- controlling;
- guiding;
- facilitating;
- challenging;
- supporting;
- hypothesising;
- questioning;
- listening; and,
- suggesting.

Your aim should be to help the meeting group to the best of your ability to achieve the objective.

Undesirable behaviours

For all sorts of reasons, people can behave in unhelpful ways in meetings. Some of these include:

- they have an axe to grind;
- they are 'empire building';
- there are issues of alliances and politics at play;
- they are 'points scoring' against a rival;
- they want to discredit someone, either present or not; or
- they want to please.

You may find it difficult, even impossible to influence someone else's behaviour if they are determined to follow a certain path, but what you must not do is be drawn into behaving badly yourself, either by alliance or opposition.

If you yourself are an effective chair and you find yourself in a meeting with someone doing a not so good job, it can be tempting to take over. Try your best to resist that, while still prodding things along in the right direction. Also, if people are ignoring the chair, particularly if the chair is someone junior, try acknowledging the chair by referring things back to her and perhaps making suggestions that support her position.

Chairing a meeting

The chair has a number of functions to fulfil, including:

- keeping to time and managing the agenda;
- involving all attendees, by controlling chatterboxes and encouraging the quiet ones;
- keeping discussion on track;
- facilitating, not dominating; and,
- ensuring notes are taken and distributed promptly.

As we know, meetings can be minefields. However, by following a basic formula and having a few simple rules, the ones you chair should run according to plan.

First and foremost, always, but always start your meetings on time. Also, when latecomers do arrive, then I would suggest that you DO NOT recap for them. If you always delay and recap as a matter of routine, then you are giving the message that it is okay for people to be late and you are also setting yourself up to fail with regard to the timings on your agenda. If you have people coming in for specific items only, then you will be wasting their time, too.

I appreciate organisational culture can be an issue; I once worked for an organisation where managers would be deliberately late for meetings in order to show how busy they were. That kind of behaviour should not be encouraged. It is rude to others who are sufficiently well organised to be on time and is the kind of game playing that ought not to happen.

Make some introductions, both people (it's surprising how many people work for the same organisation for years and yet don't talk face to face) and topic, just to emphasise the objective of the meeting.

If appropriate, run through the notes from the last meeting. Don't simply read them through, however; that is a waste of time. Instead, concentrate on action points and check that they have all been fulfilled.

Initiate the business of the meeting. This should be agenda-driven and controlled. Use tactics to keep people to the point and, if you feel a topic is descending into waffle, try giving each person two minutes or one statement in which they must express their opinion.

Close by summing up, including telling people when to expect meeting notes, and set a time for the next meeting if there is to be one. Always end on time. You and others have allocated an amount of time for the meeting and may well have further appointments. If people are thinking about how late they are for their next meeting, then they are not concentrating on this one.

I was once asked by my then boss to deputise for him at a meeting about a new qualification that was to be introduced. He gave me very little information beforehand, so in the early part of the meeting I was gathering information so that whatever contribution I could make was relevant. The chair was good: she noticed I had yet to speak and so drew me into the discussion with a direct question. I explained I was still getting to grips with the idea behind the qualification and asked if she could tell me why a student would choose the proposed new one over a similar, established one. I expected a practised, concise answer because to me this was key and should have been identified either at or even before the first meeting. Instead, I was met with a blank expression, and then she said: 'Well, that's a good question and not one I feel I can answer'. It was opened to debate, and the ensuing discussion took pretty much the remainder of the time allotted for the meeting. I was shocked: if they didn't know why they were doing it several meetings in, then what a colossal waste of time and money!

Step 3: Tasks to complete after the meeting

Okay, so now your meeting has gone according to plan, you have achieved what you set out to achieve and you have waved off a group of happy attendees, each of whom feels that they have spent their time wisely and got a good return on their investment. So that's it, right? Now you get to gather up your papers, sit back and relax for a moment and look forward to the glowing reports that will go back to your manager.

Wrong! Now we embark on the next stage of the process of ensuring productive meetings: producing accurate and effective records.

Effective records

Every meeting should be recorded in some way or other; if it isn't, how can you be sure that everyone will remember what they agreed to do, and how will you be sure that you can check to see it has all been done? Different organisations may well have their own methods and templates with which you may have to comply, but as a general guide, I would suggest the following things are recorded:

- when and where the meeting took place;
- what it was about;
- who attended;
- who was invited, but did not attend – and I would split this into 'apologies' for those who had the courtesy to let you know beforehand and 'absent' for those who simply failed to show up: they may protest at first, but they ought to behave better in future;
- what happened, with initials to show who did or said what;
- what actions were agreed, with initials and deadlines; and,
- what will happen next.

It is important that these are created and distributed as quickly as possible; if a group of people come out of a meeting all fired up to get on with a project, you need to give them the impetus to continue. They, like you, very probably have many things competing for their attention; make sure your project is at the forefront of everyone's mind.

Conclusion

If you spend just one day a week either attending or travelling to and from meetings, then after just five years, you have devoted a whole year of your working life to meetings. Consequently it makes eminent good sense to have a recipe for success. Stick to the basics and you will succeed – remember that a clear objective plus a good, well-timed agenda plus the right attendees plus an effective chair should do the trick every time.

Ensuring productive meetings checklist

- I only call a meeting when that is the best course of action to take.

- I know that a meeting must have a clear objective.

- I invite people who can contribute to meeting the defined objective.

- I do not automatically attend meetings just because I have been invited.

- I prepare thoroughly, reading all relevant information provided to me and providing relevant information including a timed agenda to others.

- During a meeting, I take care to behave in a manner that is helpful and supportive.

- I do my best to ensure meetings run to time.

- I get notes with action points out promptly.

- I complete my own action points and follow up to see that others complete theirs.

Case notes: Nicola's to-do list

Nicola has a range of options with regard to dealing with the issues on her to-do list; it's just a question of choosing the right one in each case. They could actually all be dealt with by holding meetings, but that isn't necessarily the best way.

Item 1 – the new system. This is important but not urgent; there will be a lot of tasks arising: plans to be made, training to be organised and so on, but not today. What is urgent today is that she gets the message to her team leaders before they hear from elsewhere and start banging on her door demanding information. Nicola has a regular weekly meeting with her team leaders every Wednesday. She decides to email them with the news today and ask them to come to the Wednesday meeting prepared to discuss the matter fully.

Item 2 – the monthly performance figures. How Nicola handles this depends largely on the figures. If there are no major anomalies or surprises, she can email the report to her boss and offer to discuss it further before the management meeting if her boss feels that is necessary. Further discussion may otherwise wait until the scheduled Friday catch-up. If there are surprises, however, then it is likely that Nicola needs to meet with her boss to talk them through.

Item 3 – the website project. Nicola can either bite the bullet and simply find the time, putting in extra hours if necessary, or she can delegate it to the team leader who expressed an interest. This would be a useful development opportunity and would allow Nicola to focus on the new system, which she sees as her main priority. If she is to delegate the website project involvement, she will have to meet with her team leader as soon as possible so that she can hand over the pile of information that has to be read in preparation for the project meeting.

Further reading

In print:

- Making Meetings Work, Julie-Ann Amos, How To Books Ltd (2000)

- How to Manage Meetings, Alan Barker, Kogan Page (2002)

- How to Conduct Productive Meetings, Donald L. Kirkpatrick, ASTD Press (2006)

- Running Meetings: Expert Solutions to Everyday Challenges (Pocket Mentor Series), Harvard Business School Press (2006)

- Meetings That Work!: A Practical Guide to Shorter and More Productive Meetings, Richard Y. Yang & Kevin R. Kehoe, Jossey Bass (1999)

Online:

- http://www.mindtools.com/CommSkll/RunningMeetings.htm – 'Running effective meetings' on the Mind Tools website.

- http://humanresources.about.com/od/meetingmanagement/a/meetings_work.htm – tips for meetings management on the About.com website.

- http://www.socialmediatoday.com/SMC/147410 – useful article on the Social Media Today website.

- http://www.elpnet.nct/documents/PositiveandProductiveMeetings .pdf – 'Positive and productive meetings' workbook from Sanderson, Balfour, Cunningham and George.

- http://www.prismleadership.org/inc/Lcading_a_Productive_Staff _Meeting.doc – notes on leading a productive staff meeting from Prism Leadership.

Chapter 4.6
Effective negotiation

NVQ Application:

This chapter is relevant to the following NVQ in Management Units:

- D12 Participate in meetings
- D17 Build and sustain collaborative relationships with other organisations
- E1 Manage a budget
- E15 Procure supplies
- F19 Sell products/services to customers

Linked chapters:

The information in this chapter is related to information in the following chapters:

- 1.2 Clear communication
- 4.2 Establishing and managing relationships
- 4.5 Ensuring productive meetings
- 5.2 Setting and working with budgets
- 5.3 Managing resources
- 5.4 Working with suppliers
- 6.2 Marketing and selling
- 6.5 Problem solving and decision-making

Introduction

Negotiation is something we all participate in, every day, without even giving it much thought. It is largely about give and take: giving ground on some issues whilst taking what is offered elsewhere. Sound negotiation skills are essential to your progress and development in your career. You must negotiate with a wide range of people at all levels in order to achieve your objectives, whether business or personal. Within this framework, negotiation can be thought of as a process of bargaining to achieve a mutually acceptable outcome.

Objectives

The aim of this chapter is to introduce a structured approach to negotiation. It will help you to:

- use a framework for negotiation;
- understand BATNA (Best Alternative To a Negotiated Agreement);
- be familiar with the two main approaches to negotiation;
- know how to handle an aggressive negotiator; and,
- know how to get the best out of an expert negotiator.

Factors in negotiation

Negotiation is all about the relationship between the parties involved. Many factors come into play, including:

- whether the relationship is valued: if neither party needs or values the relationship, then the motivation to reach agreement will be very low as either or both could simply walk away; when one party values the relationship more than the other, that gives an advantage to the person who values it less as for them there is less at stake if the process fails;
- who holds the power: we considered a range of power bases uncovered by French and Raven's research in chapter 4.2, Establishing and managing relationships, and negotiation is one

of the places when the balance of power in a relationship comes most strongly to the fore;

- skill at communication: quite simply, you need to be able to understand the message the other party is giving and be able to get your own message across clearly, and if one or more parties do not communicate well, the process will be tortuous for all concerned; and,

- experience and confidence: whilst confidence might go some way to making up for a lack of experience, and experience is likely to boost confidence, if there is a noticeable imbalance then the party with the greatest experience and/or confidence will have the advantage.

Consider the following conversations between Detective Constable Newman and Fingers Bob: Bob has been picked up because he fits the description of one of two men who robbed a jewellery store in town. It wouldn't be the first time: Fingers Bob has form. In this first conversation, Bob is confident that DC Newman has no evidence. He was gloved and masked the whole time. He might be on the security tapes, but there is no way to prove that either of the men robbing the store was him.

DC N: You were there, I know it. Who was the other man?

FB: You know nothing. I was nowhere near the place – ask my wife, we were watching telly!

DC N: Don't lie. Just tell me who it was.

FB: I'm telling you nothing – I know nothing!

DC N: I know it was you. Do you want to take the rap on your own? You'll do time for this one.

FB: You've got no proof. Now let me go!

Now imagine that Fingers Bob took his gloves off briefly and in the confusion he forgot to wipe his prints:

DC N: You were there, I know it. Who was the other man?

FB: You know nothing. I was nowhere near the place – ask my wife, we were watching telly!

DC N: Don't lie. Your fingerprints were found at the scene. You're going down for a long time for this one.

FB: I'm not a grass!

DC N: Do you want to take the rap on your own? Don't be stupid, man. Help me and you'll be helping yourself.

FB: I need an assurance…

DC N: You've got it.

FB: It was…

The difference was caused by the shift in the balance of power. In the first scenario, Bob was confident he was safe. In the second, he knew that DC Newman held the upper hand.

Scope for agreement

Scope for agreement exists in the crossover of the area of your wants and needs and the wants and needs of the other party. The area may be large or small, depending upon the overlap, and can be illustrated as a simple Venn diagram:

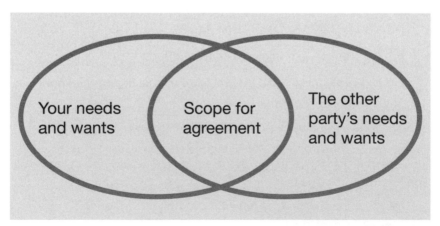

Scope for agreement in negotiations

Consider the following example:

> Chef 1: *Where's that lemon? I need it for the cake I'm making.*
>
> Chef 2: *I've got it – I need the juice for my curry.*
>
> Chef 1: *Just the juice?*
>
> Chef 2: *Yes.*
>
> Chef 1: *Well, I only need the zest.*
>
> Chef 2: *Okay, I'll let you have the rind when I've juiced it.*

Here we have a win-win situation, because discussion revealed the needs and wants of both parties and there was scope for agreement. If Chef 1 had wanted both zest and juice for his cake, then things might have gone differently. It is here that the factors in negotiation that we looked at earlier can come into play. If there was a power imbalance, for example, one chef might pull rank or the other appeal to a higher authority. As it is, the chefs found common ground and both went away happy.

Case study: IT matters

Customer Services manager Ian has just arranged to meet with the IT manager to discuss serious problems that have been experienced over the past six weeks or so with regard to the computer billing system and the IT network. The problems have interrupted the department sporadically for the best part of a year, but lately have become more severe.

As a direct result of the IT issues, Customer Services have missed deadlines and targets and Ian was taken to task about this by his manager.

Traditionally, relationships and dependencies between departments have operated on a 'goodwill' basis. Ian strongly feels that he needs to put the relationship on a more formal footing and thinks that putting in place a Service Level Agreement is the way forward.

What preparation must Ian undertake?

We'll come back to Ian later.

Stages of negotiation

There are five distinct stages to the negotiation process:

- Preparation.

- Debate.

- Proposal.

- Bargaining.

- Agreement.

You can use the mnemonic 'Please Don't Pick Bitter Apples' to help you remember the stages in order. Let's look at each of them in more detail.

Preparation

Preparation is key to your success in most things and negotiation is no exception to the rule. Your preparation should:

- gather information about the other party;

- specify your own objectives;

- be clear as to your minimum requirements, below which you will walk away; and,

- know your BATNA.

There are some circumstances in which the other party will have more information and knowledge than you: when dealing with funders and lenders, for example; but you should still research thoroughly prior to any but the most basic initial contact. Try not to get too caught up in second-guessing the other party's aims and objectives, but do consider – in broad strokes – what they might wish to achieve.

BATNA

Your BATNA is your Best Alternative To a Negotiated Agreement. This is not the same as the absolute minimum requirement, below which you will walk away, but rather it is your best option outside of the negotiation. It is an alternative and it effectively removes a slavish dependency on arriving at an agreement at any cost. If you cannot negotiate a better deal than your BATNA represents, then the negotiation is not viable.

Say you are looking for a property to develop, you have the cash to pay for it, and the market is slow: you have a strong BATNA when negotiating with any seller or agent because there are many properties available and any one of them might suit your needs just as well as any of the others. If the market is brisk and you need a mortgage, your BATNA is weaker.

Debate

When you come face to face (or talk on the phone) then once the niceties have been observed, you will embark upon a debate relating to the matter in hand. Your aim (and theirs) is to establish the aims and objectives of the other party and to make your own opening position known. Based on your preparation and what you learn here, you will be able to move on to the next step and formulate a proposal.

Proposal

At this stage nothing is set in stone; you are still getting the lie of the land. Do not make your initial proposal either too generous or insulting: it is an opening gambit. You are unlikely to gain agreement immediately, you are simply moving the debate onto more formal ground.

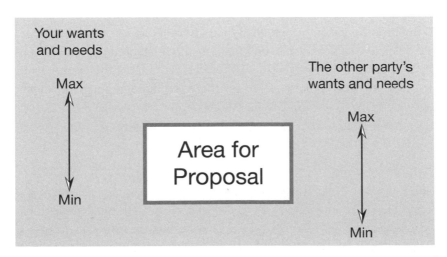

Area for proposal

Bargaining

By now you are on much firmer ground with regard to each knowing what the other is looking for and so achieving mutually satisfactory consensus. You have discussed requirements, exchanged information, and made proposals that indicate opening positions. Now you can move on to make a firmer offer, although again your opening offer might not be where you eventually settle. If it is you making the offer, be clear about the fact that it is an offer and also about what it includes. If you are in receipt of an offer, seek clarification and be sure that you fully understand what is on the table. Without clear understanding at this point, subsequent negotiating will be flawed. As the discussion moves forward and you near completion, offer concessions that cost you little but have value to the other party and aim to trade them for items that have value for you.

Try to keep things flexible for the duration of the bargaining stage; if you hit a brick wall over one particular aspect of the negotiation, agree to set it aside for now and move on. You can return to it once other issues have been agreed upon, by which time it may be less of a stumbling block.

Agreement

By the time you reach this stage, all parties should be confident of where they stand. It is a good idea to summarise what has been agreed; if there are any misunderstandings, you can clear them up now rather than having to sort them out later, after the paperwork has been drawn up. Be sure to get the minutes of the meeting typed up promptly for the same reason – should there be any misperceptions or misunderstandings, you will identify them sooner rather than later. If there are no minutes, then send a letter detailing the main points of the agreement so that you have more than just a handshake on which to base your deal.

Approaches to negotiation

Whilst there are arguably a number of styles of negotiation – such as factual or intuitive, for example – there are two main approaches. These are collaborative and competitive. Whist different industries may demand different approaches, I would assert that in the majority of cases the best approach to use is a collaborative one. The following questions should help you assess whether the situation is likely to have a collaborative or a competitive approach:

- Are all parties equally committed to the relationship?
- Have you established clear objectives?
- Are all parties equally experienced and confident negotiators?
- Are all parties communicating openly?
- Will the negotiation be given sufficient time?

The more 'no' answers to these questions, the more likely the negotiation will be competitive. Being aware of that will allow you to prepare for the situation.

Collaborative negotiation

A collaborative negotiation is one that seeks to achieve an outcome that benefits both parties. There will be give and take, concessions will be offered and accepted (or not, as is appropriate) and the aim will be to meet as many objectives as possible for both parties. Collaborative negotiations leave the door open to do business again in the future, even if on this occasion it is not possible to reach consensus and no deal is struck.

Competitive negotiation

A competitive negotiation is in many ways a destructive one. By its very nature, it guarantees a winner and a loser and that in itself makes exploring further business deals a highly unlikely option.

Competitive	Collaborative
Sarcastic	Pleasant
Overloads with information and/or questions	Communicates in a clear manner
Divulges as little information about aims and objectives as possible	Exchanges information
Makes insulting offers	Makes realistic offers
Sneers at concessions and proposals	Acknowledges and accepts where appropriate concessions and proposals
Springs surprises	Pre-warns about information

Assertion vs. aggression

Whichever style you use, you will be best served by taking an assertive stance. This simply means that you stand up for your own rights without violating the rights of others. It is about being fair minded, confident and constructive.

What to do when faced with aggression

- Refuse to be drawn in.

- Keep your temper.

- Suggest that you negotiate with someone else from that organisation instead.

- Suggest a break and either reconvene later the same day or on another day.

- Be clear as to what you will and will not tolerate.

- Walk away if necessary.

Using an expert in negotiation

There are likely to be times when you would benefit from using an expert or advocate to handle negotiations on your behalf. For example, if initiating or defending legal action, you would generally be wise to use a solicitor. Whilst you are in your advocate's hands during the negotiation, you must brief that person fully beforehand and monitor closely the proceedings, as you retain responsibility for the outcome.

If employing someone in this capacity, first be sure to check their credentials so you are confident they can do what they claim. Also, set a budget: charges for experts can run away if you are not careful. Gather as much information as you can so that you boost your own knowledge in the area concerned, and learn from the experience, so that you are better prepared and informed should you face a similar situation in the future.

Conclusion

Negotiation can be straightforward or it can be tricky, collaborative or competitive, short and sweet or protracted and convoluted. Whatever situation you face, using the framework to help you prepare and progress through the stages will help. Always set objectives beforehand and establish your BATNA, as some deals might be just too costly for you to accept.

Exercise: IT matters

Earlier in the chapter we took a look at Ian and the problems IT were causing Customer Services. Ian has booked a meeting with the IT manager with the aim of negotiating a Service Level Agreement and we asked:

What preparation must Ian undertake?

In the light of what you have learned since, use the space below to answer that question. There are some suggestions at the end of the chapter.

_____

_____

_____

_____

_____

_____

_____

Effective negotiation checklist

- Negotiation is all about the relationship between the parties involved.

- Scope for agreement exists in the area between the wants and needs of the negotiating parties.

- Within the negotiation framework, there are five distinct stages: preparation; debate; proposal; bargaining; and, agreement.

- The BATNA is the Best Alternative To a Negotiated Agreement. A strong BATNA gives you the upper hand in a negotiation.

- Negotiation may be either competitive or collaborative.

- Sometimes it pays to use an advocate: if you choose to do so, be sure to check their credentials carefully and stay as closely involved with the negotiation process as possible.

Case notes: IT matters

Ian will have his work cut out. The chances are he's not the only manager experiencing problems with IT, and if the IT manager agrees to one SLA, then other departments are likely to seek one, too

Ian has two things to negotiate. The first is simply to get the green light for the SLA. Then he must go on to negotiate the terms.

To get his SLA, Ian needs information. He needs a record of when the system has failed and what impact that had on Customer Services' performance. It will do no harm to know what effect systems problems have had on other departments, and it may be that pressure from a number of managers will be needed to gain agreement to the SLA route, so Ian needs to sound out allies. Unusually, Ian doesn't have a BATNA: because this is a negotiation between colleagues and the systems used are in-house, there is no alternative provider.

Further reading

In print:

- The Perfect Negotiation, Gavin Kennedy, Random House Business Books (1992)

- Negotiate to Succeed, Julie Lewthwaite, Thorogood (2000)

- The Secrets of Successful Negotiation: Effective Strategies for Enhancing Your Negotiating Power, Juliet Nierenberg & Irene S. Ross, Duncan Baird Publishers (2003)

- Bare Knuckle Negotiation: Knockout Negotiation Tactics They Won't Teach You at Business School, Simon Hazeldine, Lean Market Press (2006)

- Getting to Yes: Negotiating an Agreement Without Giving In, Roger Fisher & William Ury, Random House Business Books (2003)

Online:

- http://work911.com/articles/negotiate.htm – information on negotiation from The Work911 Workplace website.

- http://academicearth.org/lectures/what-is-effective-negotiation – lecture by Stan Christenson on the Academic Earth website.

- http://www.mindtools.com/CommSkll/NegotiationSkills.htm – article on 'win-win negotiation' on the Mind Tools website.

- http://www.e-myth.com/cs/user/print/post/10-steps-to-effective-negotiation – article on the e-myth website.

- http://www.ebsglobal.net/programmes/negotiation-quiz – quiz to help identify your negotiating style from Edinburgh Business School.

Part 5
Managing resources

Chapter 5.1
Financial planning, management and control

NVQ Application:

This chapter is relevant to the following NVQ in Management Units:

- E1 Manage a budget
- E2 Manage finance for your area of responsibility
- E3 Obtain finance for the organisation

Linked chapters:

The information in this chapter is related to information in the following chapters:

- 2.2 Strategic management and business planning
- 4.6 Effective negotiation
- 5.2 Setting and working with budgets

Introduction

Many of us find that, despite our not having a background in finance or even necessarily an aptitude for figures, we are required to make sense of financial information and to use it to inform our management decisions. The chances are that whatever the position you hold within an organisation, it would be of benefit to you to be able to have at least a rudimentary grasp of the meaning of the available financial data.

Objectives

The aim of this chapter is to explain, in simple terms, the essential elements of financial planning and control. It will help you to:

- understand the three main financial statements and the relationship between them;

- know how to use financial ratios to establish business performance;

- understand costing and pricing, and break-even analysis;

- be aware of different sources of finance and funding; and,

- know how money flows within the business.

Financial statements

There are three main financial statements:

- the Profit and Loss Account, which shows revenue, expenditure and overall profitability over a period of time;

- the Cash Flow Statement, which shows cash in and cash out of the business over a period of time; and,

- the Balance Sheet, which is a snapshot of the business at a point in time.

These statements may be prepared historically or as forecasts over any chosen period to show how a business is – or is expected to be – performing. They will each be prepared at least annually.

Profit and Loss Account

The Profit and Loss Account (P&L) is prepared over a specific period of time, and at least annually; the P&L is a requirement of a business's accounting process.

The P&L shows:

- **Revenue.** This is generally the proceeds from sales of products or services (but may include, for example, sales of fixed assets). The sales figure, which excludes VAT, will generally not tally with the cash flow, as payment for sales may be made in advance or in arrears.

- **Expenditure.** Shows 'cost of sales'; that is, the direct costs of the goods and services you have actually sold, not the cost of raw materials etc. purchased during the period.

- **Profit/Loss figure.** The P&L ultimately shows the outcome of trading; i.e. whether, over the period of time covered by the account (generally one year) the business has made or lost money. This figure is useful in deriving ratios, which we will look at shortly.

Cash Flow Statement

The cash flow statement shows exactly that – the flow of cash in real terms into and out of the business over the period of time for which the statement has been prepared (usually one year). Whilst the P&L shows *invoiced* sales and expenditure, the cash flow statement shows the *actual* movement of money, so money in may include pre-payments, current period payments and late payments, whereas the P&L relates only to transactions applying to the calendar period it covers.

Balance Sheet

Again, there is a requirement for businesses to produce an annual balance sheet. The balance sheet shows the business at a frozen point in time. It is a snapshot, whereas the P&L and cash flow cover periods of time. It illustrates the summary of the balances of the assets and liabilities of the business, showing:

- how much money is in the business (business assets);
- where it came from (sources of finance and amount of debt);
- how easily it may be accessed (liquidity); and,
- how safe it is (solvency).

The balance sheet has two columns: assets and liabilities. Assets, which is the column on the left, shows what you have done with the money in the business:

- Fixed assets: generally have a life of more than one year and would include equipment and buildings.

- Current assets: have a life of less than one year and would include stock, work in progress (WIP), debtors and cash at bank.

- Investments: perhaps shares or bonds bought by the business.

Tangible fixed assets are depreciated over their lifetime. Consequently you might buy a piece of machinery for £10,000 that after one year is valued at £7,000, after two years, £5,000 and so on, until it has no value on the balance sheet at all.

Liabilities, which is the column on the right, shows where the money in the business came from:

- Share capital or equity introduced by the owners.

- Loan capital and borrowings from the bank or creditors.

- Reserves and retained earnings (i.e. profit made but not paid/drawn out).

The two columns have to balance: the source of funds (the liabilities) always equals the application of funds (the assets). To put it another way, what you own equals what you owe.

Information from the balance sheet can be used to compare the performance of the same business at different times, allowing you to spot seasonal trends and changes in the market.

N.B. If at any time you are not sure as to what the figures are telling you, ask an expert.

Ratio analysis

There are a number of ratios that can be derived from financial statements to show how the business is performing. These include:

- gearing;

- earnings per share;

- current ratio;

- quick ratio; and,

- payback.

Gearing

This is the ratio between the amount borrowed and the capital assets owned and it is an indication of solvency.

$$\frac{\text{Total borrowing}}{\text{Equity + total borrowing}} = \text{gearing}$$

Ideally the figure would be no greater than 50 per cent: low gearing is preferable; high gearing is high risk.

Earnings per share

$$\frac{\text{Net earnings}}{\text{Outstanding shares}} = \text{earnings per share}$$

This can be used to compare performances of similar companies or the same company at different periods of time.

Current ratio

Also known as the working capital ratio.

$$\frac{\text{Current assets}}{\text{Current liabilities}} = \text{current ratio}$$

This is a quick measure of the ability of a business to pay debts on a day-to-day basis.

Quick ratio

Also known as the acid test ratio.

$$\frac{\text{Liquid assets}}{\text{Current liabilities}} = \text{quick ratio}$$

Ideally, the outcome should be at least 1, which shows that liabilities are covered by 'quick', that is, easily accessed, assets.

Both the current and quick ratios are indicators of liquidity.

Payback

Payback shows how long it takes to earn back your investment in a project or scheme. It is a quick calculation, easy to understand, and effective. For example, if you are planning a sales promotion that will cost £80,000 that you expect will increase profits by £4,000 per month, then the payback is:

$$\frac{80,000}{4,000} = 20 \text{ months}$$

Alternatively, if a new website for online sales will cost £60,000, but based on research you are confident that the new business it brings in will boost profits by £10,000 per month, then the payback is:

$$\frac{60,000}{10,000} = \text{six months}$$

If you were deciding which of the two projects to pursue first, then these figures would help in making that decision. (As a general rule, the shorter the payback, the more attractive the proposition.)

Financing the business

Generally speaking, there are three sources of funding for a business:

- loan finance;

- equity (either shareholder capital or equity introduced by the owners); and,

- grants.

The decision as to which source of funding to pursue would be based on availability and relative cost. It is always worth exploring whether there is a grant or award available for a project you are undertaking. When interest rates are high, it may be advantageous to borrow money if you can do so at a favourable rate even if you have the funds available, as you will earn more in interest on the money in the bank than the loan would cost you. If interest rates are low, it will generally be cheaper to use money in the bank if you have it rather than borrow.

Whatever the source of your funding, read the contract carefully and take expert advice if necessary to avoid committing to something that turns out to be more costly in the long run. Grants may have specific conditions attached and loans may include penalty clauses. Be sure you know what you are committing to!

If you need to prepare a bid or proposal, then first of all be sure that you understand what information must be provided. A small amount of additional information is unlikely to harm your bid and may possibly help; insufficient information, or information submitted in a different format to that required, may result in disqualification.

Bids and proposals tend to have their own language and there may be a considerable amount of information available to you from previous bids that have been prepared. Seek this out, it can save you a lot of time. (It can be a good idea to make copies of previous bids accessible to all via the computer network. Time spent duplicating work is time wasted.)

Costing and pricing

In simple terms, there are two types of cost a business must meet:

- direct costs: those costs directly attributable to the product or service being sold; and,

- overheads: everything else, including wages, rent, rates, insurance, marketing, warehousing and distribution.

A quick calculation to help you arrive at a price for your product or service that takes into account all the costs and allows for a profit is as follows:

- estimate sales for one year;

- calculate the direct costs;

- calculate the overhead costs;

- add these figures together and divide by the number of units you expect to sell;

- add your profit margin; then,

- add VAT if necessary.

Now consider whether this is a price that people will pay. Look at your competitors: what are they charging? Can you charge a wee bit more than your calculated figure or do you have to squeeze your costs and your profit margin to get your price down? Is your estimated sales figure achievable? What happens if you sell either more or less than this figure? What is your break-even point?

Break-even analysis

Once you have completed your costing and pricing estimate, you can work out the volume you must sell to cover all costs – in other words, to break even.

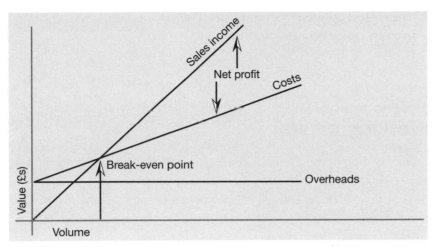

Break-even analysis

The unit price affects the break-even point, allowing you to experiment with different prices and see what difference that makes. The information can then be used to set sales targets and to prepare financial forecasts for the coming year.

Cash flow

We have already established that cash flow is exactly that: the money flowing into and out of the business. Cash flow is the lifeblood of a business and must be monitored and protected. For example, if you always pay your suppliers on time but allow your customers to take longer than agreed terms to pay you, then money will flow out of the business faster than it flows in and you could have a negative cash flow. Conversely, if you take payment for goods and services at point of sale or in advance but pay your creditors in arrears, then given regular customers and stock turnover, you will have a positive cash flow.

There is a difference between 'cash' and 'profit'. As we saw earlier, the cash flow statement shows the actual movement of cash in real terms, whereas the P&L shows the invoiced amounts per calendar period. Consequently, you can have a business that is profitable and yet short of cash, or that even, in extreme cases, becomes insolvent.

Working capital

Money tied up in the production process is known as 'working capital'. You order raw materials from your suppliers and have to be confident you can pay them on time. You sell finished goods to your customers and have to be confident they will pay you on time. This process is funded by your working capital. In simple terms, it looks like this:

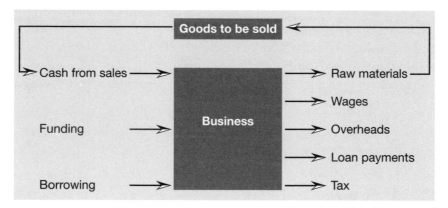

The flow of working capital

The money going out must be less than the money coming in for the business to be viable. You can get a rough idea of the working capital required by multiplying one month's sales by the number of months it takes to get paid by your customers. Accepting a big order from a customer or planning for rapid expansion are both dangerous and the risk should be calculated carefully. Remember to take into account the payback.

Credit management and control

Good credit management and control procedures are vital to good cash flow. You should always credit check your customers, especially if the terms to be extended to them are generous and represent great risk to the business. Ask for references from other firms that extend them credit, too, to see how promptly they pay. If in doubt, put them on prepayment terms for a period of time before extending credit.

Aged debtors

Keep a close eye on your aged debt analysis: if your terms are 30 days, then the majority of your customers should be in this bracket. Accounts should only be at periods greater than this if there are queries or problems: in other words, genuine reasons for withholding payment.

Below is a simple example of an aged debtors report. As you will see, the overall debt outstanding is less this month than last and some of the older debt has been cleared – although £800 that had been outstanding for 60 days last month remains outstanding and shows in the 90 days column this month. No customer has exceeded his credit limit, although Jasper's is getting pretty close.

	Current	30 days	60 days	90 days	90 days +	Total	
This month	9,000	7,100	2,550	800	0	19,450	
Last month	9,500	5,400	1,850	0	450	17,200	

Analysis of debtors

Debtors	Current	30 days	60 days	90 days	90 days +	Total	Credit limit
Bead Box	1,750	1,400	400			3,550	5,000
Marr, K		200	100			300	1,000
Potts, R	1,000		50			1,050	2,000
Jasper's	6,250	5,500	2,000	800		14,550	15,000
	9,000	7,100	2,550	800	0	19,450	

Aged creditors

For the sake of your cash flow, you also need to monitor your aged creditors; if your organisation is currently withholding payment of a large bill, then when the money does go out, it will impact on cash flow. Don't be caught out!

	Current	30 days	60 days	90 days	90 days +	Total	
This month	11,550	9,900	1,250	0	0	22,700	
Last month	14,000	8,500	2,000			24,500	

Top ten creditors

Creditors	Current	30 days	60 days	90 days	90 days +	Total	Credit limit
Crinson, J	800		750			1,550	5,000
PR Pro	4,500	3,000	500			8,000	10,000
Allan's	250	900				1,150	3,000
Barfly	6,000	6,000				12,000	15,000
Total	11,550	9,900	1,250	0	0	22,700	

Overall things look pretty good. The organisation is paying its bills more or less on time and not exceeding credit limits. You should maximise your credit terms with suppliers as, if you receive goods but do not pay for them immediately, that is in effect a free loan. Any extension to your normal credit period that you can negotiate will boost cash flow, but similarly, if you fail to pay on time and have your credit terms reduced or removed, then cash flow will be adversely affected.

Credit control

When chasing debt, remember that the 80/20 rule applies and go for the bigger amounts first. If a company consistently pays late, consider moving them to a pre-payment account.

Credit control checklist:

- Invoice promptly.

- Get the paperwork right first time – don't give people a reason to pay late due to carelessness.

- Remind and ring late payers soon after the due date has passed.

- Remember the 80/20 rule – go after the bigger amounts first.

- Handle queries swiftly and efficiently.

- Don't be afraid to use sanctions, even legal action.

- Do not say you will do anything you are not prepared to do.

Conclusion

Understanding the figures does not come easily to all of us. Despite that, many of us have to be able to make sense of them. I hope this information will help you to do that and would urge you to talk to others in your organisation whose understanding is greater than your own. Perhaps choose such a person as a mentor, even if only for a short period of time.

The last word here goes to serial entrepreneur Sir Tom Cowie and is taken from 'Sir Tom Cowie – A True Entrepreneur', Denise Robertson, The University of Sunderland Press (2004):

'I wanted regular breakdowns of all aspects of the business. Financial information is the compass of a business, just as in a ship. If the business meets with disaster then the compass... the accountancy... is gravely at fault.'

Quiz

The following questions are based on the information in the chapter. Refer back to fill in any gaps you have after your first stab at it, but see how many you can answer without looking back – or forward! The checklist will prove useful and the answers follow it.

1. What are the three main financial statements called?

2. What is the difference between what they show?

3. What three things does the P&L statement show?

4. Name two types of financial asset.

5. Name two types of financial liability.

6. What does the quick ratio show?

7. June aims to introduce a new design of t-shirt to her range. It will cost £9,000 to get the shirt to market, it will retail for £20 with a profit margin of 75 per cent and she is confident that she can sell 200 garments a month. What is the payback?

8. What is working capital?

9. How can you get a rough idea of how much working capital your business requires?

10. What is the difference between 'debtors' and 'creditors'?

Financial planning, management and control checklist

- The three main financial statements are the Profit and Loss Account, The Cash Flow Statement and the Balance Sheet.

- Whilst the P&L and the Cash Flow Statement show performance over a period of time, the Balance Sheet is a snapshot.

- Ratios can be used to indicate business performance.

- There are three main sources of funding for a business: loans, equity and grants.

- There are two types of cost that must be met: direct and overhead.

- Break-even analysis shows how much must be sold to cover all costs.

- Working capital is the term for money tied up in the production process.

- Aged debtors owe money to the organisation.

- Aged creditors are owed money by the organisation.

Quiz answers

1. Profit and Loss (P&L); Cash Flow Statement, Balance Sheet.

2. The P&L and Cash Flow show what happened over a period of time, whereas the Balance Sheet is a snapshot.

3. Revenue, expenditure and the profit or loss figure.

4. Financial assets include: fixed assets, current assets and investments.

5. Financial liabilities include: share capital and equity, loan capital and borrowings, reserves and retained earnings.

6. The quick ratio shows whether liabilities are fully covered by easily accessed assets.

7. $\dfrac{9,000}{3,000}$ = 3 months payback.

8. Working capital is money tied up in the production process.

9. One month's sales multiplied by the number of month's credit taken by customers gives a rough idea of the working capital required.

10. Debtors owe you money, creditors are owed money by you.

Further reading

In print:

- Understanding Company Financial Statements (6th edition), R.H. Parker, Penguin Books (2007)

- Management Accounting for Decision Makers, Graham Mott, Pitman Publishing (1991)

- Budgeting and Finance, Peter H. Engel, The McGraw-Hill Companies Inc. (1996)

- Finance for Non-financial Managers in a Week, Roger Mason, The Institute of Management Foundation (1993)

- Guide to Financial Management, John Tennent, Economist Books (2008)

Online:

- http://managementhelp.org/finance/fp_fnce/fp_fnce.htm – 'Basic guide to financial management in for-profits' from the Free Management Library.

- http://www.bized.co.uk/virtual/bank/business/planning/financial/index.htm – article on financial planning from the biz/ed website.

- http://en.wikipedia.org/wiki/Income_statement – information about and examples of profit and loss statements.

- http://www.businesslink.gov.uk/bdotg/action/layer?topicId=1073 858944 – information on financial planning from the Business Link website.

- http://moneyterms.co.uk/profit_and_loss/ – information on the profit and loss statement, with links to information on the other financial statements from the Moneyterms website.

- http://www.voa.gov.uk/business.rates/index.htm – information on business rates chargeable.

Chapter 5.2
Setting and working with budgets

NVQ Application:

This chapter is relevant to the following NVQ in Management Units:

- E1 Manage a budget

- E2 Manage finance for your area of responsibility

- E15 Procure supplies

- F1 Manage a project

- F4 Develop and implement marketing plans for your area of responsibility

Linked chapters:

The information in this chapter is related to information in the following chapters:

- 5.1 Financial planning, management and control

- 5.3 Managing resources

- 5.4 Working with suppliers

- 6.1 Marketing and selling

- 6.4 Project planning and management

Introduction

Of all the things we need to grasp as managers, it seems to be the financial elements that cause the most distress; and yet, an understanding of the information provided can help us greatly in achieving our objectives. Here we are going to take a look at budgeting; the process, the reasoning behind it and the management of it.

Budgeting is not a skill that we have never used before. It is fair to say that any of us who aim to live within our means are already skilled at both setting and abiding by a personal budget. Whether budgeting for personal or business purposes, the principles remain the same: spend no more than you have to, or can afford.

Objectives

The aim of this chapter is to explain budgets and how they can aid you as a manager. It will help you to:

- understand the benefits of budgeting;
- know what to include when setting a budget;
- understand different methods of budgeting; and,
- know how to record information accurately and effectively.

So what is a budget?

A budget may be thought of as a plan, a set of targets, or as a business management tool. It is also a promise; when you commit to a budget, you are promising to operate within budgetary constraints and you might be making that promise to your line manager, your bank manager or your partner, depending upon the type of budget you are dealing with. Whoever it is, you may be sure that to break your promise will require explanation and justification, and will possibly generate repercussions. Also, while you may get away with it once, maybe twice at a push, to continue to break that promise will very definitely have consequences.

Budgeting does not have to be overly complicated; on a personal level, it can be as simple as working out what's left after the bills are paid and some money has been set aside for contingencies, then spending no more than that on yourself for the month. Spending more than that, or not ensuring that the essentials are covered before you shop for treats, will have consequences. These may come in the form of bank charges for direct debits that could not be paid or for going overdrawn; your mobile could be cut off or you could receive an eviction notice. Setting an adequate, workable budget and sticking to it is a good idea!

When you are setting a budget there are a number of questions you can ask yourself:

- How much will I have?

- How much will I need?

- How can I reconcile those two amounts?

- Has this been done before?

- If so, what happened last time?

There is an old saying: You cut your coat according to your cloth; so it is with budgeting. When times are good, you might have enough for a frock coat; when times are tough, you might be lucky to manage a bomber jacket.

You must also look at the overall picture, take into account what is happening elsewhere in the business and work out what that means to you. For example, say you are the customer services manager and you find out that the marketing department is going to have a big promotion to attract new customers. What that means for you is that your staff will have more to do. You need to know when the promotion will take place and how many new customers they aim to attract; then you can work out if you need additional resources and by when they need to be in place.

We'll return to Jane and her budget later.

Stages of budgeting

There are five main stages your budget planning and management will go through:

- gather information;

- draft your budget;

- gain authorisation;

- implement the plan; and,

- monitor and evaluate progress.

Let's take a look at each of those in turn.

Gather information

There are three main types of information that you are likely to use: historical, current, and 'educated guess'.

Perhaps the easiest information to acquire will be historical, in the form of what happened last time. Last year's budget figures along with how the department (or organisation, depending upon your level of responsibility) performed against it ought to be readily available.

In so far as current information is concerned, you are likely to require answers to the following questions:

- What is being planned elsewhere? You must find out what is planned in any areas that may impact on yours: will those plans cause you more or less work?

- What will your staff costs be? You will need to know what the projected salary increase and any bonus will be.

- What will supplies and materials cost you? Seek quotes from suppliers and details of fixed costs that you must meet.

Some of the costs you have to deal with will have no statistical information attached to them and it is in these cases that you will have to make an educated guess. Your estimates should be based on either what has happened in similar situations or rudimentary calculations rather than be figures you simply pull out of the air, but it is arguably these figures that will be monitored most closely.

Draft your budget

When you have pulled together all the relevant information you can draft your budget. Once you've had a first stab at it, spend some time going through the figures: what went wrong (if anything) last time? Where can you make savings if you have to? How can you improve things? If your budget is for a project, then it may help to talk things through with other project managers and to learn from their experience.

What comes first, the budget or the plan, is a bit chicken and egg. Say you are updating the company website. You will start with your objectives, as until you know what you must achieve you cannot do anything. After that your budget and your plan are liable to grow organically and in tandem. The one supports the other. Without sound budgeting, the plan – no matter how good in itself – is unachievable as the resources you need will be unavailable. Without sound planning, the budget is worthless and you might as well set fire to the money.

Remember that your budget will shape your next year. Get it right and you have a success on your hands; get it wrong and you have a year of misery ahead.

Present your information in whatever way your organisation requires. Ideally, there will be a standard template available to all to ensure uniformity and all departments will use it to prepare their budgetary information. This ensures that when the various departmental or project budgets are pulled together to form the master budget, reading the figures is relatively straightforward.

Gain authorisation

Once all the departmental budgets have been prepared, they need to be consolidated centrally. Each budget must be reviewed in the light of the others and the overarching aims and objectives must be seen to be congruent.

If you have done your research thoroughly and prepared well, gaining authorisation for your budget should be a formality. If not, or if plans exist elsewhere that you could not have known about but that will impact on you, you may need to do further work on your budget until it is accepted. You may also find that you have changes forced upon you because of issues affecting the business; if so, look at what your allocated budget is and redraw your plans as best you can.

Having been pulled together and validated or amended as required, the individual budgets are pulled apart again and returned to their point of origin. Costs are best controlled at the point at which they are incurred: for example, the best person to control the marketing budget is the marketing manager. When budgets are handled in this way, the various departments are known as 'budget centres' or 'cost centres'.

Implement the plan

Once everything has been agreed, you get the green light to go ahead and implement your plan. You may have been working toward this already, or this may be the time your project team meets for the first time; whichever, you need to make sure that everyone knows what is expected of them so that you don't deviate from the plan or from the budget.

Monitor and evaluate progress

Make sure that you have systems and procedures in place to monitor progress against budget on a regular basis. If you find any discrepancies, you must address them immediately. If you are able to adjust the way you spend your budget to get back on track, all well and good – but do it quickly and let the relevant people know. If you will run out of money, then you must raise this with your manager promptly. Before you meet to discuss the matter, however, do spend time creating a workable plan that shows with what help you can still achieve what you set out to do. Aim never to just show up with a problem, but always to have a solution to offer, too.

Different types of budget

There are a number of budgets that are generally set, including the following:

Sales budget

Calculated by value and quantity and also, perhaps, by factors such as product, area, client or seasonal factors.

Production budget

This looks at costs of machine time expressed in standard hours.

The sales and production budgets should be mutually supportive: production needs to be able to provide the number of units that sales aim to sell. Following on from that, the production costs budget takes into account raw materials and parts, direct labour costs and overheads.

Personnel budget

This looks at the organisation's total labour requirements and feeds into departmental and project budgets.

Operating and service department budget

This takes into account areas such as administration, finance, warehousing, transport and marketing.

Capital expenditure budget

This is a supplementary budget and is generally prepared over a longer term than just one year. It takes into account such things as land, buildings, machinery and furniture.

Types of budgeting

There are two main methods used when setting budgets: incremental and zero-base.

Incremental budgeting

Incremental budgeting boils down to looking at what happened last year and adding a bit on for inflation – or perhaps taking a bit off due to recession, as you are required to manage with less. It is widely used because it is the quickest and easiest way to arrive at a final budget, but it has its drawbacks; reusing the figures means that last year's problems will very likely also be the coming year's problems. Yes, there are times when it is acceptable to budget incrementally, but you should not use this method without being acutely aware of its limitations.

Zero-base budgeting

Zero-base budgeting has, as its benchmark, the 'minimum survival level' of a department and all expenditure above this must be justified. Everything is challenged: planning and costing start from scratch; nothing simply carries on. This makes it a much more time-consuming and complicated process, but it is far better to invest time in planning than in fire fighting to rescue a flawed plan that you are struggling to implement.

Master budget forecasts

Just as there are three main financial statements, there are three main master budget forecasts that can be prepared using the figures:

- **Profit and Loss forecast:** summarises everything in the various budgets and shows, in terms of costs vs. income, whether the business is expected to make a profit or a loss for the period.

- **Cash budget:** looks at the balance between cash in and cash out and indicates whether the business will always have sufficient funds to operate or if it might be necessary to source additional finance, perhaps short-term to ride out a temporary cash-flow shortage.

- **Balance sheet:** which again shows the big picture using projected figures.

Conclusion

Budgeting is all about balance. To put it in its simplest terms: provided money out does not exceed money in, then you have a successful budget.

Budgets are also dynamic. The bigger the organisation, the more complex the budget and no matter how carefully you research and draw up your budgetary plan, there are things that can impact upon it over which you simply have no control. These include the actions of competitors, changes in the global economy, and the reaction of the board or other managers to external threats. However, even under those circumstances, the fact that your starting point is a sound, workable budget backed up by good planning will make it easier for you to adapt and respond to whatever challenges may arise.

Exercise: Costly Christmas

Earlier in the chapter we took a look at Jane and her Christmas budget. At that time, we asked:

How can Jane avoid repeating last year's mistakes?

In the light of what you have learned since, use the space below to answer that question. There are some suggestions at the end of the chapter.

_____

_____

_____

_____

_____

Setting and working with budgets checklist

- I understand the basic principle of budgeting: live within your means.

- I take into account both historical and current information when drafting my budget, and where there is no statistical data, use an educated guess to arrive at the figures.

- I am familiar with the five main stages of budgeting: gather information; draft your budget; gain authorisation; implement the plan; and, monitor and evaluate progress.

- I am familiar with the various different types of budget that might be prepared.

- I am familiar with the advantages and shortcomings of both incremental and zero-base budgeting.

- I am familiar with budgeting forecasts.

Case notes: Costly Christmas

Jane would be advised to take a methodical, painstaking approach to her Christmas planning. First, she must decide how much she can afford to spend. Next, she must write down everything she needs to buy. Having done that, she should put a realistic figure next to each item on her list. Finally, she must add up the figures and see what they come to.

If the final figure is higher than her budget, she must decide whether she is prepared to dig a little deeper or if she must look for places where costs may be cut. Shopping around, or shopping online, may enable her to make savings.

Jane also needs to work out where the money will come from. Will she put an amount aside each month between now and Christmas? Will all or part be charged to a credit card? If so, what will the estimated interest be? She will also need to resist the temptation to impulse buy in the shops, perhaps by buying as much as possible online or in advance. What is essential is that having set her budget, she sticks to it. There are no repercussions if she manages to save a little here and there, but if she overspends she will pay the price, both in additional interest charges and by missing out in the New Year.

Further reading

In print:

- Budgeting and Finance, Peter H. Engel, McGraw-Hill (1996)

- A Guide to Setting Budgets and Managing Cashflows for Small to Medium Size Business, Jennifer Rhodes, Emerald Publishing (2010)

- Manage Budgets and Financial Plans, Ana Anandarajah, Al Aseervatham & Howard Reid, Pearson Education Australia (2009)

- Budgeting for Non-financial Managers, Iain Maitland, Financial Times/Prentice Hall (1999)

- Beyond Budgeting: How Managers Can Break Free from the Annual Performance Trap, Jeremy Hope & Robin Fraser, Harvard Business School Press (2003)

Online:

- http://www.businesslink.gov.uk/bdotg/action/layer?topicId=1074 416511 – information on budgeting and business planning from the Business Link website.

- http://www.bizhelp24.com/accounting/budget-preparing.html – information on preparing a budget from the bizhelp24 website.

- http://www.sba.gov/idc/groups/public/documents/sba_homepage /pub_fm8.pdf – U.S. Small Business Administration paper on 'Budgeting for the Small Business'.

- http://www.dwmbeancounter.com/budgeting.html – useful tutorial on budgeting and forecasting from the Bean Counter website.

- http://www.flyingsolo.com.au/p272164469_FAQs-on-small-business-budgeting.html – useful information on budgeting from the Flying Solo website.

Chapter 5.3
Managing resources

NVQ Application:

This chapter is relevant to the following NVQ in Management Units:

- D5 Allocate and check work in your team
- D6 Allocate and monitor the progress and quality of work in your area of responsibility
- E4 Promote the use of technology within your organisation
- E8 Manage physical resources
- E11 Communicate information and knowledge
- E12 Manage knowledge in your area of responsibility
- E13 Promote knowledge management in your organisation

Linked chapters:

The information in this chapter is related to information in the following chapters:

- 1.1 Planning and managing your own professional development
- 1.2 Clear communication
- 1.3 Managing your time
- 1.4 Managing information and developing networks
- 2.2 Strategic management and business planning
- 2.3 Operating within the law.
- 4.1 Employing people
- 4.3 Building and leading the team

Introduction

Managing resources requires a wide range of skills and is closely linked both to the development and management of the buyer-supplier relationship and the control and storage of stock. It has links into many other areas, too, including time management, recruitment and budgeting, for example. The decisions required are two-fold: how will resources be allocated and, once allocated, how will they be deployed?

Objectives

The aim of this chapter is to get the right results from your management and use of resources. It will help you to:

- understand what is meant by 'resources';

- implement systems to manage them effectively;

- monitor and evaluate usage; and,

- be aware of management information systems.

What are resources?

Resources are those things we have at our disposal to help us achieve our objectives in a timely and satisfactory manner. Some are tangible, like machinery, and some are intangible, such as time. The behaviour of some is predictable, like systems, and the behaviour of others is not, as is the case with people.

There are eight main areas that we need to focus on:

- people;

- money;

- materials;

- systems;

- time;

- plant and machinery;

- equipment; and,

- premises.

Let's take a closer look at those.

People

If we accept as our management definition 'the ability to achieve results through the efforts of others', then managing people can be seen to be a key skill. This is not just about having the right people doing the right things in the best way, it is also about giving up responsibility for processes whilst retaining responsibility for results. It is about trust, dealing fairly and honestly with people, and acting with integrity at all times.

How well you and your team communicate: with each other, with other teams in the same organisation, with suppliers and specialists in other organisations, is key to your success here. We know we cannot do everything ourselves: managing people effectively is how we achieve the desired results.

Allocating work on one or more projects across a team can be quite complicated: you need to ensure that everyone is fully occupied without being swamped and that the whole thing doesn't fall apart if someone wants a day off or falls ill, and estimating workloads during a time of growth or change can be especially tricky.

There are ways to approach the task that can help. One such is to enter onto a spreadsheet tasks and individuals to show how many days per month will be spent by each worker on each task. For example:

TASKS	TOTAL	Pete	Ann	Fred
Research	12	4	4	4
Website maintenance	12	2	8	2
Customer care	13	9	2	2
Project work	20	4	5	11
TOTAL	57	19	19	19

The example allows 19 workdays per month per individual and is shared between their main tasks. (Nineteen days per month averaged over the year allows for some holiday and sickness; however, depending upon the holiday allowance and average sickness, you might want to use fewer days in your estimates.) Adding in new tasks or changing the split between tasks and/or individuals should be easy using a spreadsheet and you will see the results immediately, which will help with the planning process.

Key skills:

- *planning*
- *communication*
- *delegation*
- *appraisal*
- *project planning and management*

See also chapter 4.3, Building and leading the team.

Money

The money at your disposal has undoubtedly been calculated, negotiated and then allocated with the achievement of specific objectives in mind. Every purchase must be considered and justified, otherwise you will run out of money before the budget period is up or the project completed.

Key skills:

- *budgeting*
- *financial planning, management and control*
- *project planning and management*

See also chapter 5.2, Setting and working with budgets.

Materials

There are many different types of materials, for example, raw materials for the production process; stationery; marketing materials; training room supplies. Management of them impacts directly on the bottom line, either favourably or adversely. Overstocking is expensive as money is tied up in stored materials, whereas running out of materials can result in loss of production.

Key skills:

- *budgeting*
- *production planning and management*
- *stock control*
- *managing suppliers*

See also chapter 5.4, Working with suppliers.

Systems

Systems and procedures are what we use to get things done. They are used and operated by people, but still need to be sound and robust and help rather than hinder the efforts of the team to get results. Simple requests from customers should be able to be dealt with swiftly and without fuss; your systems and procedures will either allow this or not.

The best people to feed back on the usefulness of systems and procedures are the people using them on a daily basis. Consider having regular system reviews, perhaps backed up with a quality improvement 'suggestion box' scheme that also rewards those whose ideas result in improvement.

Key skills:

- *organisation*
- *Total Quality Management*
- *monitoring/evaluation/review*
- *managing change*
- *staff development*
- *communication*

See also chapter 6.6, Implementing and managing quality systems and procedures.

Time

Time is finite: it cannot be earned, saved up or put by for another day. We must make good use of each day, because once it is over, it is lost. Managing time effectively is liberating, as it frees us from the drudgery of chasing deadlines and feeling overburdened, and having to work extra hours just to get by.

If you have people whose time is charged to projects, then you will very likely also have some system in place to record how they spend their time, whether on paper or on computer. People are generally the most costly element of managing both a business and a project. It is a good idea to agree with them beforehand how much time their contribution will take and to allocate them that number of hours plus a small contingency in case of complications. Without that control, you are working in the dark. This should be one of your key factors to monitor as it will tell you if your budgeting is accurate and whether you will complete the project within the time allocated.

Key skills:

- *organisation*
- *planning*
- *negotiation*
- *budgeting*
- *project planning and management*
- *communication*

See also chapter 1.3, Managing your time.

Plant and machinery

Plant and machinery is expensive, and also costs money when it stands idle. If manufacturing machines are not operating, then nothing is being made so there is nothing to sell. Organise shifts to keep machines running at optimum levels whilst allowing for planned maintenance. If there is spare capacity, investigate the possibility of either introducing new products or taking on manufacturing work for another company. Unless it is unavoidable, do not have either machines or the people that operate them doing nothing.

Key skills:

- *organisation*
- *time management*
- *planning*

See also chapter 2.2, Strategic management and business planning.

Equipment

I am including here such things as computers, photocopiers, telephone systems and so on. When you purchase such items, make sure they are fit for purpose. Yes, you need to get the most for your money that you can, but that will not always mean buying the least expensive. Make sure that equipment is regularly maintained and that you have some sort of contingency or back up for equipment that is critical to the business. Make sure also that what you have is sufficient for your needs, whether that be computers, telephone lines or anything else.

It is also a good idea to keep an eye on technological developments. There are many gadgets and devices that can aid communication, enable people to work more effectively while on the move, and save time, for example. You may have to resist being seduced by the hype, but if something genuinely is a benefit to the business and not just a shiny new toy, consider investing some money in technology.

Key skills:

- *planning*
- *negotiation*
- *budgeting*

See also chapter 2.2, Strategic management and business planning.

Premises

Premises need to be suitable in terms of size, lighting and heating, layout and number of rooms and so on. If you are in premises that are larger than you need or that you hope to 'grow into', can you rent out the extra space? Depending upon your circumstances, it might make good sense to do so.

It is a good idea to find out what grants may be available for improvement. Keep on top of maintenance and make sure that you are up to date with fire checks, health and safety training, risk assessments and so on.

Key skills:

- *organisation*
- *supplier management*

See also chapter 2.3, Operating within the law.

Case study: Joe's challenge

Joe has been asked to do something about the state of the stockroom. He has been told that it must be sorted out by the end of the month. The stockroom is huge and contains a wide range of supplies, some inexpensive, some high value, some with a rapid turnover, and others with a slower one.

Where on earth should Joe start?

We'll come back to Joe later.

Securing resources

When deciding what you need, be sure to include the team in the process. Base decisions on past experience, industry and company knowledge and awareness, trends and so on, and start with a blank sheet. Draw up a list of your requirements.

Your next step should be to undertake an audit of what resources are currently available to you and to look at how they are being used. You need to be confident that they are organised, deployed and employed in such a way as to support your strategic objectives. This should reduce your list of needs quite considerably, although you may still need to request additional resources to meet shortfalls or to plug gaps.

When requesting resources, have a budget backed up with justification as to why this is the best way to meet the needs of the project or department. Be clear about any assumptions you have made with regard to (for example) trends or planned business activity. Be prepared to negotiate and perhaps to amend your plans, as necessary. Remember to talk in benefits – you are selling your ideas and plans.

Always monitor usage of resources and compare it to the plan; be sure to investigate any variances. If errors in the original plan come to light as a result of your investigation, take corrective action swiftly. If you identify any planning errors, gather as much information as possible and then make your decision as to what to do based on the following questions:

- Can I live with it?

- Can I economise elsewhere and manage on the existing budget?

- Can I renegotiate to boost my budget?

Knowledge management

Knowledge management is an increasingly hot topic, and indeed, knowledge might be argued to be a company's greatest resource in the twenty-first century. Generally two types of knowledge are recognised: explicit, which is recorded in the form of brochures, price lists, quality procedures and so on and which is easy to pass on, and tacit, which might be thought of as 'know-how' and which is very difficult to pass on.

Organisations must actively seek to record tacit knowledge and turn it into explicit knowledge. Say, for example, that the widget-processor jams every so often and when it does the only way to get it going again is to hit it with a mallet in a certain place, and only Freda knows where and how hard. That is Freda's tacit knowledge, but what if the widget-processor jams on the first day of Freda's summer holiday?

It is essential that people share what they know. You cannot risk having only one person in possession of the knowledge of how to do any particular job. If you do, then should that person leave, be dismissed or have some sort of accident, your organisation will suffer disproportionately.

It is essential to have systems in place to make sure that people share information routinely so that tacit knowledge may be converted into explicit knowledge. Arguably the easiest ways this can be achieved are through observation and interview. In the case of observation, an expert can be shadowed, take an 'apprentice', or be given a task that he or she works through as a training exercise with a group of learners. With interview, you would do just that. The results could be written up as procedures or guidelines, reported via the intranet, whatever you deem to be the appropriate way to record and share the knowledge.

Management information systems

A management information system is simply any organised system that collects, processes, presents and stores information with the aim of facilitating good decision-making. Information is what keeps businesses moving in the right direction, and whilst you will collect a lot of data, it is only when this is processed into usable information and provided to the right people that it benefits the business.

The majority of systems nowadays will be computer-based and thus easy to access for the majority of people – although you might want to restrict access to key people or make it read only in some cases.

It is necessary to consider what information is available and from where, and to actively seek out that which is deemed to be useful. Look for patterns in the data. Combining data and identifying patterns, asking 'What if...?' and 'What does that mean for me...?' converts information into useful knowledge.

It is important to remember that information management has no intrinsic value; it might simply be thought of as another form of tidying up. Where the value arises lies in what you can do with that information.

Conclusion

Resource planning and management is based on a series of questions:

- What are my strategic objectives?
- What resources are available to me?
- What additional resources will I require?
- Where can I get those resources from?
- How much will they cost?
- How will I allocate and use those resources?
- How will I monitor quantity and quality of output?

Managing resources draws on key management skills: budgeting, project planning, managing people, for example, and it underpins all strategy and planning. You must also put in place controls, so that you can be confident resources are being used wisely. No doubt you can think of more elements to the process besides these, but what it shows is that having a structured approach – a framework within which to operate – gives us the best chance of success.

Exercise: Joe's challenge

Earlier in the chapter we took a look at Joe. At that time, we asked:

Where on earth should Joe start?

In the light of what you have learned since, use the space below to answer that question. There are some suggestions at the end of the chapter.

_____

_____

_____

_____

_____

_____

Managing resources checklist

- The eight main areas to take into account are: people, money, materials, systems, time, plant and machinery, equipment, and premises.

- Some resources are tangible (like machinery) and some are intangible (like time).

- When considering what resources must be secured, the first step is to take an audit of what we already have.

- Use of resources should be carefully monitored and variances from the plan thoroughly investigated.

- Knowledge is an increasingly valuable business resource.

- A Management Information System is an organised system that facilitates decision-making by turning data into usable information.

Case notes: Joe's challenge

Joe should start, as always, by talking to people and collecting information. Joe has a deadline but no clear objectives. Just what is it about the stockroom that must be sorted out? Do any other issues (such as pilfering or poor stocks, for example) link in? Is this a task he is expected to handle on his own or can he call on other help and resources? Must he fit it in alongside his existing responsibilities or will he be excused other duties until this has been completed?

Once Joe has the information he requires, he should first consider his objectives: has he got everything he needs to meet them? If not, then he must identify what he needs, how much and for how long, and why he needs it: he can then approach his manager and negotiate additional resources.

If he has all he needs and/or knows what extra resources he can have, he can go on to draw up a plan. This should show if the deadline is realistic. He then needs to implement his plan, monitor progress along the way, and, when the project is complete, evaluate and report on the outcome.

Further reading

In print:

- Managing Resources Effectively, Jill Mordaunt, T. O'Sullivan & R. Paton, Open University Worldwide (2007)

- Management Information Systems, Terry Lucey, Thomson (2005)

- Managing Financial Resources, Mick Broadbent & John Cullen, Butterworth-Heinemann (2003)

- Managing Resources and Information: Competence Approach to Supervisory Management, Roger Cartwright, George Green, Anita Candy & Michael Collins, WileyBlackell (1998)

- Strategy and Human Resource Management, Peter Boxall & John Purcell, Palgrave Macmillan (2007)

Online:

- http://www.financehub.org.uk/managing_money_and_resources/default.aspa – useful article on the financehub website.

- http://management.about.com/cs/projectmanagement/a/PM101.htm – project management article focusing on managing resources on the About.com website.

- http://www.shell-livewire.org/business-library/management/Resource-Management-Managing-Resources/ – resource management information from the Shell Livewire website.

- http://www.humanresourcemanagement.co.uk/ – human resource management website offering information for both employees and employers.

- http://managementhelp.org/hr_mgmnt/hr_mgmnt.htm – human resource management article on the Free Management Library website.

Chapter 5.4
Working with suppliers

Introduction

Years ago when I worked as a retail manager, the general consensus was that when sales representatives came into the shop, they should be treated like second-class citizens: make them wait, don't try too hard to be polite, keep them in their place. I quickly decided that was wrong and set out to develop good working relationships with the people who came into my store. That was a decision that paid off in spades as instead of merely trying to sell me as much as possible, they worked with me to keep my stocks right and support my promotions in a way that benefited us both. I also got the best of the giveaways and special offers!

I chose the title for this chapter quite deliberately: 'Working *with* suppliers'. If you take the time and trouble to forge good working relationships with your suppliers, you are in a good position to get the best deals and prices available and – should you have an urgent need for something – they will be more likely to put themselves out for you than if you treat them with indifference.

Remember too that your suppliers are very likely suppliers to your competitors. Add suppliers to your network of contacts and some very useful snippets of information may well come your way.

Objectives

The aim of this chapter is to take a look at the big picture when it comes to working with suppliers. It will help you to:

- establish supplier selection systems;
- monitor and evaluate supplier performance;
- operate effective purchasing systems, and,
- operate effective stock control systems.

The purchasing function

In manufacturing especially, purchasing is a crucial function and the profit achievable is directly related to its efficiency. The objectives of the purchasing function are to provide everything needed:

- in sufficient *quantity*;
- at the right *quality*;
- *on time*; and,
- at the *optimum price*.

Cheapest is not always best, but no more than is necessary should be paid for anything.

Control

As with all other areas of a business, it is unlikely that just one person will be able to do everything required to purchase everything needed, although one person – or a team that communicates well – should ideally have overall responsibility. If ten departments each independently buy ten widgets every month, you will miss out on the available discount for buying one hundred widgets. Having centralised ordering systems will remedy that.

Purchasing procedures will help greatly, both at departmental level and in the purchasing function itself. Requests for purchases should be dealt with swiftly; discuss and negotiate with both the originator of the request and the potential suppliers of the goods, and make sure that there is a link to both stores and stock control.

Economic purchasing

An equation can be used to determine the most cost-effective quantity to purchase:

$$EOQ = \sqrt{\frac{200 \times U \times O}{H \times C}}$$

EOQ = Economic Order Quantity

U = annual usage

O = cost of ordering

H = holding cost

C = cost per unit.

Whilst this should be used for guidance only, it can be a useful tool.

Look for discounts, but be conscious of the cost of tying up working capital and be sure it is not higher than the amount you save by purchasing in bulk. Investigate whether it is possible to get a better price if you commit to a supplier for a fixed period of time. Say you currently buy from half a dozen stationery suppliers: if you start to buy everything from just two, so putting more business their way, will this result in a better deal overall?

Review and renegotiate on a regular basis, bargain and be prepared to change supplier in order to get a better deal. Loyalty, sadly, is not always rewarded, as evidenced by the number of price comparison websites and the fact that if you shop around and change supplier, you can save a great deal of money on things such as insurance and power.

Case study: Going cuckoo

Kenny works for a business that manufactures cuckoo clocks. The business operates for 48 weeks of the year, closing for two weeks in the summer and two weeks at Christmas. He is on a mission to get the best possible deal from all suppliers and is currently looking at the cost of cuckoos.

The business normally buys 100 hand-painted wooden cuckoos every two weeks at a unit cost of £2. Kenny has discovered that if he buys a minimum of 450 cuckoos, he can receive a 20% discount. The bigger quantity will mean using space in the garage where the accountant, who comes in twice a week, parks her car. The cost of parking outside the garage will be £10 per week.

To get the best price, how often, and in what quantities, should Kenny order cuckoos?

We'll come back to Kenny later.

Buying technology

The purchase of technology warrants a particular mention, as it is very much a specialist function: a generalist is unlikely to be able to keep up to date with change and development in this area. Also, remember that we are not just talking about hardware here; software must be kept up to date – and be properly licensed – in order that the business can get the most from the technology at its disposal. As always, monitor and evaluate purchases carefully and make sure that they are:

- fit for purpose;
- 'future-proof'; and,
- industry 'compliant' (e.g. PC vs. Mac).

Where possible, tie in any necessary training and maintenance contracts, which ought to help ensure that the organisation gets the best out of any investment.

The buyer-supplier relationship

We have already discussed the 'human' aspect of the buyer-supplier relationship, but it is worth mentioning that it is also covered by legislation aimed to protect both parties. Scotland has similar protection to England, Wales and Northern Ireland, where the main Acts that come into play are:

- The Sale of Goods Act 1979;

- The Unfair Contract Terms Act 1977;

- Consumer Protection from Unfair Trading Regulations 2008; and,

- Business Protection from Misleading Marketing Regulations 2008.

Choosing a supplier

When choosing a supplier, you are looking for a balance between price and service: there is no point in getting the lowest prices if the service is poor, and no point to the best service if the price is high. In our personal lives we may choose to pay a premium price for something because it fulfils a need: to feel good, to have the latest 'in' thing; to appear to be stylish and successful. In business, however, paying a premium 'just because' is rarely an option. The money in a business has to work hard, especially when times are tough.

It is a good idea to define the requirements a supplier must meet: you may require all suppliers to have achieved ISO 9000 accreditation, for example. In fairness, many relationships are based on trading history; you may also take less trouble over a supplier with whom you spend a moderate amount once or twice a year than one with whom you are likely to be placing frequent high value orders.

When you approach a supplier, remember that they will seek credit references before accepting you as a customer; by the same token, it is quite acceptable for you to seek information about them. Ask for testimonials from their existing client base and if it is possible for you to speak directly to one or more clients to get more detailed feedback, be sure to do so.

It is useful to have a list of approved suppliers so that you know whom you may contact. Your purchasing procedures should take care of this requirement.

Even with such a list, you may receive one-off requests for purchases of goods that none of your regular or approved suppliers can provide. If this happens, you will need to find someone new. Start by looking at your network: can anyone recommend a suitable supplier, or perhaps even supply the goods themselves? Next stop would be trade journals, directories and/or the Internet. With certain purchases, whether 'specials' or regular requirements, it may be prudent to provide a specification so that the supplier knows exactly what it is that you want.

Seeking tenders/quotations

When you are seeking quotations or putting work out for tender, you must take care to ensure that you get the information you need in the format in which you want it. You should:

- be very specific about what you want people to quote for;

- tell them how you want their bids: whether in the form of a written quotation, a presentation, or perhaps written in the first instance, with a presentation to be given by those companies that are short listed;

- when you make a decision, let people know promptly;

- consider getting acceptance of the work from your chosen supplier before turning down the others; and,

- even if you don't use a supplier on this occasion, if they were good enough to be short listed you will most likely want to keep the door open for possible future business.

Contracts

Be sure to read all contracts thoroughly and carefully. It can be easy to be caught up in the spirit of goodwill that is often generated when new business is being done, but that is no excuse not to check the small print.

Something that doesn't seem to matter so much when everyone is optimistic about a deal may suddenly become a big issue some months down the line when reality bites and things become difficult. If there is anything of which you are unsure, seek further advice before signing.

Evaluating supplier performance

Monitor supplier performance on such criteria as:

- promptness of delivery;
- suitability of packaging;
- price and terms; and,
- service.

If a supplier consistently fails to meet the required standards or if performance begins to slip, discuss this with them on an informal basis initially and see if there is a way forward. If things do not improve, escalate your complaint to put it on a formal footing and check the contract to see what redress that might give you. Whilst it may be a last resort, if you feel that you have to cancel a contract or stop using a supplier, then do: the important thing is that your organisation does not suffer because of misplaced loyalty. (Equally, you should not stop using a good supplier based on your personal opinion of their current representative!) The measure of a company is often how it deals with things that go wrong. Particularly if you have an established relationship with a supplier, you may feel it only fair that you give them the chance to show how good they can be under pressure.

Stock control

When you are aiming to control the stock you carry, there are three decisions you must make:

- What will you monitor?
- How often will you check it?
- How much will you order?

Decisions regarding whom to buy from and in what quantities may well have been taken elsewhere, based on available discounts and economic ordering quantities, but here we are looking at storing and maintaining required levels of stocks.

The stocks you hold will generally fall into the following categories:

- consumables, such as paper, toner cartridges or machine oil;

- raw materials and components, for the production process;

- work in progress, which is the term for any goods that are tied up in the production process; and,

- finished goods, ready for sale.

Stock represents a big chunk of working capital and both holding too much stock or running out of essentials can be very costly for a business. When deciding what to monitor, focus on key components. Remember the 80/20 rule and focus on the 20 per cent of stock that equates to 80 per cent of the value. (You may also wish to keep an eye on low value but essential items. For example, jump rings cost pennies, but to a jewellery manufacturer specialising in traditional charm bracelets are likely to be essential stock that it would be costly to run out of.)

There are two main methods of controlling stock. The first is to make regular stock checks and order whatever is needed to top stocks up to the optimum (or maximum) level. This might mean checking stocks in an entire warehouse every week and ordering a range of items to top levels up across the board. The second is to designate a minimum stock holding level and to reorder as soon as that level is reached. This might mean whoever removes the critical stock item flagging up that just that item must be ordered now.

Factors to take into account when considering what quantities to order in and when include:

- lead times, which is how long it takes a supplier to respond to a request for goods;

- discounts; and,

- fluctuations in demand, which might perhaps be seasonal.

Other factors to consider are the holding period (how long stock will be on the shelf) and stock turnover (using the oldest first). These factors are critical in the case of perishable goods.

Just In Time

Just In Time ordering, or JIT, is the practise of cutting stock to a minimum and relying on a supplier's ability to deliver what is needed just as it is needed. It cuts the cost of stockholding drastically, but is a potentially high-risk strategy with a huge dependency on the supplier.

Conclusion

Investing time in the buyer-supplier relationship and treating suppliers as an important part of your network of contacts can pay off in spades. Add to that good stock control methods and your working capital should work very hard indeed, for the benefit of the business.

Exercise: Going cuckoo

Earlier in the chapter we took a look at Kenny and his dilemma regarding ordering and storage of hand-painted wooden cuckoos. At that time, the following question was asked:

To get the best price, how often, and in what quantities, should Kenny order cuckoos?

Use the space below to make some notes. There is a suggestion at the end of the chapter.

_____

_____

_____

_____

Working with suppliers checklist

- I understand the objectives of the purchasing function.

- I know how to work out economic ordering quantities.

- I take particular care when buying technology, due to the particular consideration it warrants.

- I know what regulates the buyer-supplier relationship.

- I appreciate the value of that relationship and incorporate suppliers into my wider network of contacts.

- I have procedures for choosing suppliers and ensure they are followed.

- When I put work out to tender, I am very specific about the requirements.

- I regularly review and evaluate supplier performance and price.

- I take care to adequately control stock.

Case notes: Going cuckoo

Using the EOQ equation, Kenny works out the economic order quantity as follows:

The square root of 200 x 2400 (the annual usage) x 3840 (the annual discounted cost in £s) ÷ 480 (the cost in £s of parking) x 1.6 (unit cost per cuckoo) = approximately 500 cuckoos.

Kenny decides to place quarterly orders for batches of 600 cuckoos. Taking into account the cost of the parking, Kenny's strategy will save the business almost £1500.

Further reading

In print:

- Excellence in Supplier Management, Stuart Emmett & Barry Crocker, Cambridge Academic (2009)

- Collaborative Advantage: How Organizations Win by Working Together, Elizabeth Lank, Palgrave Macmillan (2005)

- The Supply-Based Advantage: How to Link Suppliers to Your Organization's Corporate Strategy, Stephen Rogers, Amacom (2009)

- Guide to Supply Chain Management: How Getting it Right Boosts Corporate Performance, David Jacoby, Economist Books (2009)

- The Power of Two: How Smart Companies Create Win:Win Customer-Supplier Partnerships That Outperform the Competition, Carlos Cordon & Thomas E. Vollmann, Palgrave Macmillan (2008)

Online:

- http://www.tradingstandards.gov.uk/ – website of the UK Trading Standards Institute.

- http://www.smallbusinessjourney.com/documents/Suppliers.pdf – useful information with case studies from the Small Business Journey website.

- http://www.businesslink.gov.uk/bdotg/action/layer?topicId=1074 404815 – information on dealing with suppliers from the Business Link website.

- http://www.ictknowledgebase.org.uk/projectworkingwithsuppliers – useful information from the website of the London Advice Services Alliance.

- http://www.shell-livewire.org/home/business-library/management/ Resource-Management-Working-with-Suppliers/ – information on resource management/working with suppliers from the Shell Livewire website.

Part 6
Managing progress

Chapter 6.1
Market research

Introduction

Market research is simply research that finds out information about the various elements of the market you are doing business in: what people want, what they think of what they can get, who else is operating in it, and so on. It might be about existing or potential customers, products or services, competitors, what they offer and how they deliver it – any aspect of the market in which your organisation operates. You can collect data yourself, commission a specialist firm to gather it or utilise published reports. In practice, a combination of methods is most likely to yield useful, cost-effective information.

Without good market research, it is nigh on impossible to know in what direction the business should be headed or where new opportunities or threats might lie. Market research costs money, but properly conducted, evaluated and utilised can impact directly – and positively – on the bottom line.

Objectives

The aim of this chapter is to focus on what market research is and what it can do for a business. It will help you to:

- understand both primary and secondary market research;
- understand market forces and SWOT analysis;
- know how to conduct market research for your business;
- analyse the data generated; and,
- use that to influence and inform business strategy.

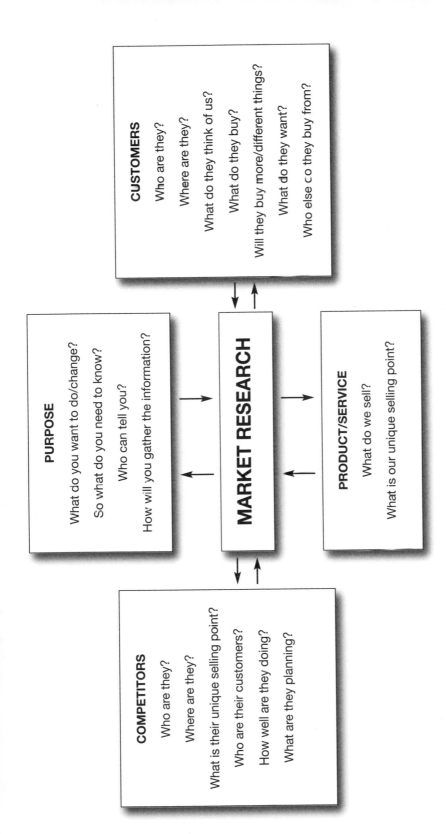

PURPOSE

What do you want to do/change?

So what do you need to know?

Who can tell you?

How will you gather the information?

CUSTOMERS

Who are they?

Where are they?

What do they think of us?

What do they buy?

Will they buy more/different things?

What do they want?

Who else co they buy from?

MARKET RESEARCH

COMPETITORS

Who are they?

Where are they?

What is their unique selling point?

Who are their customers?

How well are they doing?

What are they planning?

PRODUCT/SERVICE

What do we sell?

What is our unique selling point?

WHAT NOW ???

What do you need to know?

The diagram gives an idea of what market research is likely to help you to find out, about your customers, your competitors, your product(s) and/or service(s), and even about the purpose of your organisation. Once you are clear as to what you need to know, you can give some thought as to how you can find out.

Gathering data

There are two principle types of research you can call on: secondary, which is research that has been carried out by others and published, for example national statistics or BRAD (British Rate and Data, a comprehensive media database); and primary research, which is bespoke research which you either commission or conduct yourself. Before we consider those in more detail, let's take a look at some of the other elements that can come into play and affect the market.

Market forces

Market forces are external events that bring pressure to bear upon the business. They are commonly defined as PESTLE, which stands for the type of forces to be taken into account:

- Political;
- Economic;
- Socio-cultural;
- Technological;
- Legal; and,
- Environmental.

This is covered in more depth in chapter 2.2, Strategic management and business planning.

SWOT analysis

To conduct a SWOT analysis simply means to consider the business in a certain context and to identify what strengths, weaknesses, opportunities and threats exist. Suppose a footwear manufacturer was considering whether to add handbags to their product list: their business analysis and market research might lead them to draw up a SWOT analysis as follows:

Should we add handbags to the products we offer?

Strengths	Weaknesses
We already have the capability and the capacity to manufacture them We have the shops to sell them in Shoes and handbags go together	We're not known for handbag manufacture Customers think of us as a traditional footwear specialist We lack experience
Opportunities	**Threats**
It maximises use of our machines and people We could build a brand and a reputation	Many competitors already sell handbags Competitors know the market better than we do

That is admittedly a simplistic example, but you get the gist, I'm sure.

Product/market matrix

A product/market matrix is a table showing products or needs in the rows and potential customer groups or markets in columns. The example indicates the approach a manufacturer of footwear might take.

MARKET

PRODUCT	Women	Men	Children
Trainers	✓	✓	✓
Wellingtons	✓	✓	✓
Brogues		✓	
Mules	✓		

Looking at your products and markets in this way will help you to focus both your research and your marketing activity to get the best response.

Customer profile

Having looked at your markets in this broad way, you can move on to more accurately profile your customers. For example, what age of children are your shoes aimed at? Are you aiming your adult shoes at the fashion market or are they more traditional in style? Considering your market in this way should enable you to be more specific about the segment you are operating in. For example:

- We provide training shoes for children aged six and over.

- We provide fashion shoes for women aged between 18 and 35.

- We provide Wellington boots for people of all ages.

Planning your research

The first thing to determine is why you are conducting research in the first place: what do you hope to achieve as a result of the exercise? This should lead quite naturally to enabling you to define what it is that you need to know. There is a vast amount of information available and if research is conducted without purpose, it can collect a whole load of data that means very little in business terms. The four main subjects upon which you can gather data are:

- customers, both current and prospective;

- competitors, both current and potential, if you plan to move into new areas;

- your business, in terms of what it can and cannot deliver; and,

- the market, in terms of how it looks now and how it might change.

The sorts of things you are likely to want to know might include:

Customers:

- What is my average customer profile in terms of gender, age, income, etc?
- What do they watch, listen to and read?
- What are their needs?

Competitors:

- What is their product range and what do they charge?
- How good are they?
- Are there any gaps in the market?

Ourselves:

- Have we got our charging structure right?
- If we get more business, can we cope with it logistically?
- What additional products or services could we offer?

The market:

- What is the size of the market?
- Is the market static, rapidly changing, or seasonal?
- What effect are changes in the economy having on the market?

Secondary research

Secondary research relates to published data that is already available. Again, the problem is likely to be getting just the data you want without getting bogged down or distracted by the wealth of information that is available. Sources of information include:

- The Internet: nowadays the first port of call for most things, the caveat being that you have to be confident that the information you gather is from a trusted source.

- The library: libraries allow access to reference books and trade directories that might otherwise be unavailable. You will be able to gather information here that you cannot get online, so do treat it as a source of information in its own right. If you can also gain access to your local university's library, then so much the better.

- Business Link: free business support and advice service available through local advisers or accessible online (web address in the 'further reading' section).

- Trade publications: specialist publications on your sector can provide information on market trends and activity. You may well glean information about competitors and other organisations.

- British Chambers of Commerce: The British Chambers of Commerce (BCC) is, in its own words, 'the national body for a powerful and influential Network of Accredited Chambers of Commerce across the UK; a Network that directly serves not only its member businesses but the wider business community.' The BCC provides information, training and the opportunity to network. Its web address is included at the end of the chapter.

Primary research

Published information is useful for getting a general feel for the market, but to get specialist or tailored information you will need to conduct your own research. You may choose to commission a specialist organisation, undertake it yourself, or perhaps employ a mix of the two.

Arguably the most important information relates to customers, both existing and prospective. The best way to find out what they think and what they need is to ask them, and this may be done in a number of ways:

- face to face – by conducting interviews, perhaps in shopping precincts or at fairs and events, or focus groups;

- over the telephone – which can give you a greater geographical spread of respondents;

- by post – which gives people more time to consider their answers; and,

- via the Internet – either by email or with a survey for website visitors to complete.

Designing customer surveys

Begin by thinking what it is you want to find out as a result of conducting the survey. Once you have a list of subjects that you want information about, you can design questions that will get at that information for you. Keep questions simple: simply-worded and addressing just one aspect at a time. For example:

Q. Which of these magazines do you read regularly:

- Classic Rock

- SFX

- Uncut

- None of the above

Q. Do you buy a newspaper every day?

- yes/no

Multiple choice and closed questions are useful for collecting data that can be compiled and compared, but you might want to put one or more open questions into the survey, as this might bring up issues you and your team hadn't considered.

If you are looking for personal or sensitive data such as age, income or house value, use bands that people can choose from. For example:

Q. What age are you?

- 16-25

- 25-35

- 36-45

- etc.

Before you launch your survey on the wider world, it is a good idea to get some feedback as to how your questionnaire reads. Use colleagues or a small sample of friendly customers.

Focus groups

A focus group is simply a group of actual or potential customers who come together to discuss your product or service. They can be very useful when discussing potential new products or services, too, and the information they give can prove very valuable, if acted upon.

Levi Strauss ignored to their cost customer feedback that suggested their plans to start making suits would fail, as the brand was too strongly connected to jeans and casual clothing. They went ahead anyway – and their suits failed to sell.

Competitor scans

The more information you have about your competitors, the stronger your position when it comes to strategic planning. The sorts of things you might want to know include:

- who they are;
- where they are located;
- what is their product range;
- what is their price/discount structure;
- what are their ordering and delivery procedures;
- what are their terms and conditions; and,
- who are their customers.

There are many ways to find out information, including:

- brochures and price lists;
- company reports;
- news reports and trade magazines;

- the Internet; and,

- your network of contacts.

Test marketing

It makes sense to have a trial run before you invest huge amounts of capital into a new product or service. Multiple retailers typically trial new lines in a handful of stores, only stocking in all stores those that prove to be successful in the trial. Manufacturers make prototypes before committing to wide scale production. It limits your exposure and reduces the cost of failure.

Analysing information

Your research is likely to collect a great deal of data for you. It increases greatly in value once it has been analysed and turned into information, which in turn assists the decision making process. Your customer survey, after analysis, might tell you that forty per cent of respondents read Classic Rock magazine. Had you been debating whether Classic Rock was a good place to advertise, this factual information would help you to make an informed decision.

Sales forecasts and targets

These should be prepared for each product and service your organisation offers. As with budgeting, you can use zero-base or incremental techniques. Unlike budgeting, incremental techniques, based on available historical data, can be more reliable, although if you are forecasting for a new market offer, you will have to start from zero. The sorts of factors you have to take into account include:

- competitors and their plans, if known;

- the economic climate; and,

- planned marketing activity.

Conclusion

Market research is not just an exercise that is conducted in isolation. Sound market research informs business decisions and helps to shape strategic planning, as you exploit opportunities and address identified weaknesses. Above all, market research is an ongoing activity. The nature of the data is that as soon as it is collected, it is out of date, especially in swift-moving markets. Keep on top of your research and your market and you will see the difference in the bottom line.

Market research checklist

- Market research is the means by which you find out about the economic environment in which your organisation operates.

- The main areas for attention are customers, competitors, how your organisation is viewed and what is the market like overall.

- Factors that impact upon the business may be internal or external.

- Conducting a PESTLE analysis may identify external forces that could impact upon the business.

- SWOT analysis is a valuable technique that allows you to consider the business in a particular context.

- Sources of information are many and varied and include the library, the Internet, customers, and the press.

- If you want to know what customers think, ask them.

Exercise: Surveying customers

How did you get on? You could try your survey out on some colleagues to see what they think of it, and perhaps discuss with your manager the possibility or value of implementing the survey.

Further reading

In print:

- An Introduction to Market and Social Research: Planning and Using Research Tools and Techniques, Karen Adams & Ian Brace, Kogan Page Ltd. (2006)

- Market Research in Practice: A Guide to the Basics, Paul N. Hague & Nicholas Hague, Kogan Page (2004)

- Marketing Research: An Integrated Approach, Alan Wilson, Financial Times/Prentice Hall (2006)

- The Market Research Toolbox: A Concise Guide for Beginners, Professor Edward F. McQuarrie, Sage Publications Inc. (2005)

- Consumer Behaviour and Marketing Strategy, J. Paul Peter & Jerry C. Olson, McGraw-Hill Higher Education (2007)

Online:

- http://www.marketresearchworld.net/ – website of Market Research World, offering extensive resources for anyone with an interest in market research.

- http://www.businesslink.gov.uk/bdotg/action/layer?topicId=1073 901910 – information on market research and market reports on the Business Link website.

- http://www.britishchambers.org.uk/ – the website of the British Chambers of Commerce.

- http://managementhelp.org/mrktng/mk_rsrch/mk_rsrch.htm – information on market research from the Free Management Library.

- http://tutor2u.net/business/presentations/marketing/marketresearch methods/default.html – information on market research from the tutor2u website.

Chapter 6.2
Marketing and selling

Introduction

Marketing and selling – often lumped into one by people who don't waste their time on such trivial pursuits – are frequently given a bad press. This hasn't been helped over the years by the sometimes outrageous claims of advertisers and events such as the scandal of double-glazing sales people refusing to leave people's homes without a signed order, and sometimes staying until gone midnight, back in the 1990s. Douglas Adams had fun at the expense of marketers in 'The Restaurant at the End of the Universe' (they were struggling with the concept of the wheel as they didn't know what colour it should be) and comedian Bill Hicks advised anyone involved in sales and marketing to: '…kill yourself'. Mocked and in some cases reviled the world over, it seems, marketers and sales people carry on regardless. And thank goodness they do, because without them and the money they bring in, there would be no jobs, no business, no economy.

Marketing and selling products and services is arguably the most important function of any business. It's all very well making the finest widgets the world has ever seen, but if no-one knows about them or how to acquire them, what good will it do you?

Objectives

The aim of this chapter is to give an overview of the twin processes of marketing and selling products and services. It will help you to:

- define marketing and sales objectives;
- know the purpose of a marketing plan and how to prepare one;
- be aware of the psychology of buying;
- know how to structure a sales presentation; and,
- understand advertising methods and media.

What is it all about?

In simple terms, marketing involves telling people about your product or service, and selling is the act of exchanging it for money.

In practice, of course, it is more complicated than this. The Chartered Institute of Marketing defines marketing as: 'The management process responsible for identifying, anticipating and satisfying customer requirements profitably'. A sale, on the other hand, is 'an agreement by which one of the contracting parties, called the seller, gives a thing and passes the title to it, in exchange for a certain price in current money, to the other party, who is called the buyer or purchaser, who, on his part, agrees to pay such price' (www.lectlaw.com).

Both marketing and selling begin with a sound understanding of the product or service being provided. Once that is fully understood, it is possible to move on and formulate a plan that takes it to the right people at the right time, place and price. Marketing is increasingly being acknowledged as a science, which seems only fair, bearing in mind the blend of psychology and economics – to name but two elements – that combine to inform the practice.

The marketing plan

When pulling together a marketing plan, there are six core elements to cover. They are:

- a full explanation of how the requirements of each element of the marketing mix will be satisfied;
- a thorough definition of the target customers;
- marketing objectives;
- an assessment of the resources required;
- a budget; and,
- a summary with timetable for action.

Let's take a closer look at each of those elements in turn.

The marketing mix

Professor Neil Borden of Harvard Business School identified the marketing mix, also known as the four Ps, in the early 1960s. He believed that each of these four elements, product, price, placement and promotion, could influence a buying decision.

- **Product:** a full description of what the business is offering, including details of features and benefits, the unique selling point, added value and guarantees/warranties. Features and benefits are a useful way of defining your product or service. Features tell what a product or service is, in terms of size, colour, power, duration and so on, whereas benefits tell what a product or service does for the customer, in terms of, for example, style, economy, prestige. Features appeal to the logical left-brain, whereas benefits speak to the emotional right hemisphere. As we shall see when we look at sales, both are equally important when helping a customer to make a buying decision.

- **Price:** when establishing a price for your product or service, you need to balance what the market will bear against what it costs you to provide the product or service. Costs are a result of your purchasing policies, wage rates and suchlike; price relates back to your market research.

- **Placement:** the distribution strategy for the product or service, taking into account that customers may have preconceptions about where or how they buy certain products or services.

- **Promotion:** arguably the heart of your marketing strategy is how you will broadcast the message to your target market. For the process to be effective, you need to know that market thoroughly and to use a range of methods of communicating with it, such as print, television, radio and Internet advertising; website; exhibitions; telesales and so on, and also an appropriate style. Goods and services aimed at teenagers will be promoted in a different way to those aimed at the retirement market. Information conveyed in terms of benefits is especially powerful, as potential customers can understand what is in it for them.

As a direct result of the rapid growth of service industries, a further three Ps have been added to the mix:

- **Process:** the processes that are in place to deal with customer orders, from initial enquiry, through sales and into after-sales activity.

- **Physical evidence:** things such as sales brochures and websites that people are provided with or can access for further information.

- **People:** this includes all people who will come into contact with customers and have an influence on the transaction.

Increasingly, all seven Ps are now applied to all businesses, whether supplying products or services.

The target customers

You must be able to define with some accuracy your target customers and say why they will choose your products and services over those of any competitors. It may help you to segment your market. This involves starting with a broad statement describing the market you are in: for example; 'we manufacture and sell shoes'. That is fine as far as a description of the business goes, but it doesn't tell you anything about what sort of shoes, how many ranges, and to whom you might sell them. Are they safety shoes? Fashion shoes? Women's, men's or children's shoes? Are they at the luxury end of the market or the economy end? Asking questions like this helps you to understand your product, its position in the market place and, as a consequence, the potential customers for each of your products. This in turn helps you with marketing plans and objectives; the products are all shoes, but you would market safety shoes quite differently to the way you would market men's dress shoes, women's fashion boots or kids' trainers.

Armed with your understanding of your product/service and potential customers, you can move on to consider and set your marketing objectives.

Setting marketing objectives

Marketing objectives typically cover areas such as volume of sales, profitability and market share. They should, as with all objectives, be SMART: specific, measurable, achievable, realistic and time-bound. For example:

- Achieve annual sales turnover of £1.5 million.

- Achieve profitability of 33 per cent return on sales over the year.

- Increase market share by 5 per cent by the end of the year.

The resource requirement

This should be carefully assessed and recorded in terms of the main resources at your disposal:

- People: staff and whatever specialists might be required.

- Systems: the systems and procedures through which you will make things happen.

- Time: how long will campaigns and activities take?

- Materials: those necessary for the running of the department and the planned promotional activity.

- Premises: the cost of the office space and any storage facilities for promotional materials.

- Equipment, or plant and machinery: that is needed to support the planned activity.

- Costs: all of the above, plus any relevant others, need to be carefully and accurately costed so that the marketing budget may be pulled together.

The budget

Using the figures above, you should be able to draw up a marketing budget. Don't forget to include everything, and aim to be prudent but not miserly. Well-targeted marketing activity should pay for itself over time. (It may help to consider payback, which is covered in chapter 5.1: Financial planning, management and control.) You might want to break down further costs relating to, for example, print advertising or online promotion, but do be careful not to overlook anything. If you are called upon to justify your budget, the more information you have at your disposal, the easier that will be.

The summary

Summarise all elements of the plan and include a timetable. Gantt charts lend themselves particularly well to at-a-glance overviews of activities. (See chapter 6.4, Project planning and management.)

Exercise: The marketing mix

Pick a product or service that your organisation offers and with which you are reasonably familiar. Look at the grid below: with that product/ service in mind, try to make at least three entries below each heading, where relevant.

Product/Service:	
Price:	Placement:
Promotion:	Process:
Physical evidence:	People:

Can you think of any opportunities that are not currently being exploited?

What can you do about those?

Selling

The information from your marketing plan will very much inform your sales strategy. Your sales targets, for example, will be a direct result of the plan. In amongst all this talk of selling and sales targets, however, let's just think about what it is that people buy.

Nothing happens until someone buys something. Just looking around my working environment here, I can see very many things that I have bought: there's a CD player, CD towers filled with CDs, there are books, a lamp, a desk, a laptop on which I am working, a printer; there are also, since I have my desk in the spare bedroom, a wardrobe and two chests of drawers; there are both blinds and curtains at the window, there are pictures and a clock on the walls. But that's just a list of stuff. That doesn't even begin to indicate how I chose those particular things out of all the similar items on offer or what it is that they might mean to me.

Let's take my CD player. It's a Denon, quite compact and with 'bookshelf' speakers. On a logical level, I bought it because Denon is a brand with which I am familiar, Denon gear gets consistently good reviews and that particular set up is a good size for the room I am using it in. I really bought it because I think it looks great and, for the size, the speakers can really belt it out. The set up in my living room is quite different and consists of an amp, 5.1 surround sound speakers, and two floor speakers so I can listen to music in stereo. Linked in, I have a CD player, a DVD player, a tape deck and a turntable. Each item was bought after careful consideration and with easily explained logic: but really, I bought my amp because it kicks ass, my speakers because they can handle pretty much anything I put through them and my turntable because it just looks so neat!

Most of my purchases were based on emotion – I could have had a cheaper set-up that sounded very similar indeed – but I can back them up with logic: I got goods built to a high standard, the reputation of the manufacturers is excellent, the reviews are very favourable. Price was also not the primary consideration: when I went to the shop where I bought my main gear, I walked in with a budget and came out with a hole in my credit card. (I can even justify that: it's not like I go out as much as I used to, I don't have a 'shoe' habit like (insert name of chosen friend here), it'll all last me for years.) Think about some of your own purchases and I'm confident you'll see the same sort of pattern emerging.

Right there is one of the most important things you'll ever learn as a sales-person: we buy with emotion and justify with logic. That's why features and benefits are so important. The feature, the logical element to a purchase, is all about solving problems. You buy a watch because you need to know what time it is. The benefit, which appeals to us emotionally, is something that makes us feel good. You buy a particular make because it's currently popular, all your friends have one, and it conveys prestige. Most of us have an area where we are most easily parted from our cash, too; I've mentioned shoes already. For me, it's books and music, for another friend, it's pens.

Here's another key point: people don't like to be sold to, but they love to be helped to buy. You've probably gathered from what you've just read that I have a love of music and I like to hear it to best effect. That being the case, when I went to get my sound system, I didn't need to be 'sold' to in the traditional understanding of that word. But I got a lot of help to make the right decision as to what to buy. That is so important for customers: they feel in charge of the transaction, they are making a considered purchase that is tailored to their needs, not just being railroaded into shelling out for whatever has been over-ordered and is filling up the stockroom.

Which leads me to another key point: this kind of involvement helps avoid post-purchase remorse, that awful sinking feeling you experience when you get something home, unpack it and wonder why on earth you parted with cash for it in the first place. If you make people feel good about what they buy, the chances of the goods coming back are hugely reduced whereas the chances of the people coming back are hugely increased.

Six steps to successful sales

There are six key elements to take into account when selling:

- You need someone to sell to.

- You need information about what you are selling.

- You must remember to ask for the business.

- You must be prepared to negotiate to seal the deal.

- You must provide the goods and services you have sold.

- You must follow up on the transaction.

You need someone to sell to

That's not quite as daft as it might sound. It's all very well having wonderful products and services, but you need someone to take an interest in them, and you will have to do some work to find that person. As part of the process of developing the marketing plan for the business, customers will have been profiled. Now you need to get at those customers and persuade them to let you tell them more.

There are four main ways of getting your message to customers:

- Write to them.

- Telephone them.

- Place advertising where they will see it.

- Make face to face contact.

Sales leads may come from a variety of sources:

- *From your advertising.* Consider using a code in each advert and tracking to see which adverts are the most successful.

- *From old customer records.* Follow up on people who haven't purchased from you in a while; they might be in the market again when you call.

- *From referrals.* Ask your current customers if they know of anyone who might be interested in your products or services; consider some sort of incentive if the referral results in a purchase.

- *From a bought list.* Lists of contact data are available for sale and may be customised to your company's requirements, so saving time by focusing effort more sharply on the target market you have identified. It is also possible to use a telesales company to call the list for you and to make appointments for your sales people to call. That way, your sales people's time is made best use of.

You need information about what you are selling

This may take various forms:

- Brochures and leaflets.

- Point of sale posters and promotional material.

- Presentations.

- Briefing notes.

Some of this information is aimed directly at the prospective customer, some is provided for the benefit of the sales people to allow them to speak knowledgeably about what it is they are selling. Make the effort to know your product or service inside out and practise your presentation until it is second nature.

When you are making a presentation to a customer, whether face to face or over the telephone, remember that it is a conversation you are having. Yes, you are telling them about your current offering, but ask questions, too. Find out about their needs and wants, use this information to tie in features and benefits, involve the customer and get things on a personal level; it is very easy to say 'no' to someone who has just talked at you for two solid minutes without drawing breath, far more difficult when you have been chatting with them for longer and can see the benefit to you of what they are offering.

You must remember to ask for the business

The best and most persuasive sales presentation in the world will fail if you do not ask for the business at the end of it. In fact, asking for the business is the logical next step; it lets the prospect know that you have given all of the information necessary for them to make a decision and it is what is required to keep the transaction moving forward. People expect to be asked, so don't be shy – ask them to buy!

You must be prepared to negotiate to seal the deal

People will often assume that the first price you give them is your opening gambit and heralds the start of negotiating what they will eventually pay. Even if you are selling in a retail outlet, you may be asked if there is discount for cash or money off if more than one unit is bought. Be prepared for this. Don't go straight in at your 'best' price, know what authority you have to offer price reductions and/or discounts, and if you drop your price, do so incrementally.

Wherever possible, offer something that is worth more to the customer than it costs you to deliver: an extra six-month's warranty, a year's technical support.

Remember also to 'sell up'; in the same way as someone buying a lettuce from a greengrocer should be offered tomatoes, cucumber, celery, radishes and so on, and a customer buying boots should be offered cleaning materials, a matching handbag, shoe trees etc, remember that part of the negotiation process is to sell related products and services. This may or may not be linked to any discounts you offer, but don't miss the opportunity to introduce additional products into the conversation.

You must provide the goods and services you have sold

On time and in perfect condition.

You must follow up on the transaction

At the very least, make a phone call to check all is well. This also gives you the opportunity to develop the relationship with the customer and to make further sales in the future. People who have bought from the business once will, provided all went well, be open to buying again. They have confidence in the business and they know what to expect.

If you have a regular client base whom you contact, be sure to make notes as to birthdays, anniversaries and so on and give a call or send an email on those occasions to keep the relationship going, even if no sales are currently likely. Also, if you come across any information that might be of interest to them, let them know. Keep yourself in the customer's mind in a positive way and when goods and services are required, you will be the first person they think of.

Conclusion

Marketing and selling are an art. Not everyone can do these things well. Perhaps the most important things needed are the ability to connect with people, combined with tenacity; you should never give up. By all means learn from your experiences and adapt your strategy and approach as a consequence, but keep at it. If you don't try, you can't sell.

Marketing and selling checklist

- I know what marketing and selling entail and appreciate both the differences and the synergy between them.

- I understand the marketing mix; that is, the traditional four Ps (Product, Price, Placement, Promotion) and the more recently added ones (Process, Physical evidence, People).

- I can define target customers accurately.

- I can set sound and achievable marketing and sales objectives.

- I understand how to draw up budgets for marketing and sales.

- I understand that people buy with emotion and justify with logic.

- I know how to generate sales leads.

- I appreciate the importance of establishing rapport and building a relationship with prospects and customers.

Exercise notes: The marketing mix

There is no wrong or right answer here, although if you are struggling you might want to become more familiar with the products and services your organisation offers and/or talk things through with your manager or mentor.

If you identified some opportunities that aren't currently being exploited, can you raise them with your manager or with the marketing department, or is there a suggestion scheme through which you can put them forward? It's a shame for good ideas to go to waste, and whilst there might be a good reason why those avenues aren't being explored, you may have just come up with something that others haven't yet considered.

Further reading

In print:

- How to Win Customers and Keep Them for Life, Michael LeBoeuf, Judy Piatkus (Publishers) Ltd (1987)

- How to Market Your Business: A Practical Guide to Advertising, PR, Selling Direct and Online Marketing, Dave Patten, Kogan Page Ltd. (2008)

- Brilliant Marketing: What the Best Marketers Know, Do and Say, Richard Hall, Prentice Hall (2009)

- Guerrilla Marketing: Easy and Inexpensive Strategies for Making Big Profits from Your Small Business (4th revised edition), Jay Conrad Levinson, Piatkus Books (2007)

- The New Rules of Marketing and PR: How to Use News Releases, Blogs, Podcasting, Viral Marketing and Online Media to Reach Buyers Directly, David Meerman Scott, John Wiley & Sons (2008)

Online:

- http://www.ismm.co.uk/ – The Institute of Sales and Marketing Management, which is the only professional body for salespeople.

- http://www.cim.co.uk/ – The Chartered Institute of Marketing, the world's biggest community of professional marketers.

- http://www.themarketer.co.uk/ – The magazine produced by the CIM.

- http://www.freelanceuk.com/marketing/index.shtml – information on sales and marketing from the freelance:uk website.

- http://www.1000ventures.com/business_guide/marketing_main.html – information on marketing and selling from e-COACH.

Chapter 6.3
Customer service

NVQ Application:

This chapter is relevant to the following NVQ in Management Units:

- B3 Develop a strategic plan for your organisation
- F5 Resolve customer service problems
- F6 Monitor and solve customer service problems
- F7 Support customer service improvements
- F8 Work with others to improve customer care
- F10 Develop a customer focused organisation
- F11 Manage the achievement of customer satisfaction
- F17 Manage the delivery of customer service in your area of responsibility

Linked chapters:

The information in this chapter is related to information in the following chapters:

- 1.2 Clear communication
- 2.2 Strategic management and business planning
- 4.2 Establishing and managing relationships
- 6.1 Market research
- 6.2 Marketing and selling
- 6.5 Problem solving and decision-making
- 6.6 Implementing and managing quality systems and procedures

Introduction

Ask anyone for a time when a company let them down and they'll probably have to think about it before answering. Not to come up with an instance, just to come up with their 'best' or, rather, most appalling example. Just since I moved into the flat I currently live in, less than a year ago at the time of writing, I have amassed a whole new batch of horror stories, some of which I'll share with you during the course of the chapter. I have far fewer tales of when companies have met or exceeded my expectations, but cheerfully I have some of those to share with you, too.

Talking to friends and family, I know I am not simply unlucky; everyone seems to be in the same boat. But how is it, in an age when companies are more aware than ever of the need for good customer service, that so many of them still get it so wrong, so often?

Objectives

The aim of this chapter is to raise awareness of the fact that 'customer service' applies to all people, in all walks of life. Standards and principles of good service are expected from everyone, whether doctors, dustmen or dress designers. It will help you to:

- recognise what constitutes good service;
- be aware of the danger areas in your business;
- know how to handle complaints so that they don't come back;
- have a strategy for dealing with angry customers; and,
- understand how to integrate principles of customer service into your business strategy.

Who are your customers?

All of us – from the moment we wake up to the moment we go to sleep – are customers. If we are awoken by an alarm, from whom did we buy it? Who sold us the bed and the sheets that we sleep in? Who will provide our breakfast? How will we travel to work? When we get there, from whom will we need information, support or advice?

In our world, being a customer is a way of life, something we don't generally even think about – until something goes wrong. Curiously we expect more from an organisation that has failed us, notice their capability more, talk about them more to family, friends and colleagues, than we do a company that jogs along causing us no problems whatsoever. When it comes to recommending a company when we are asked, however, it is the latter that get a mention.

It is important to remember that people can be your customers without any money changing hands. Most people nowadays are both familiar and comfortable with the idea of internal customers – your colleagues, and external customers – your paying clients. If you work for an organisation that provides support and advice that is free at the point of contact, those people who use the service are also customers. No matter who your customers are or how much, if anything, they pay you, they are deserving of the same levels of care and consideration.

So what is 'good customer service'?

Third time lucky

When I was furnishing my flat, I ordered a buffet table from a shop in town. I got a phone call on the delivery day to say the table had come into the shop but was damaged, so had been sent back and re-ordered: I would have to wait another week. A week later, my table duly turned up. We pulled some of the packaging off outside the building to make it easier to manoeuvre up stairs and around corners – and saw a crack in one of the granite inlays. Back it went again.

The third time proved to be lucky. My table was carried into the flat and carefully placed exactly where I wanted it. The delivery men (the father and son of the shop owner, as this was a family business) refused a tip, but presented me with a set of six very attractive wine glasses by way of apology for the problems suffered. Bearing in mind that the problems were not of their making, I was especially delighted.

Bad connection

When I arranged to have the landline connected I was twice left waiting for engineers who didn't turn up. I was working for someone else at the time, so this cost me precious holiday. When – finally – the line was connected, the engineer who did it did not even require access to the flat. In addition, the service had been provided to the property and cabled into each flat at the expense of the developer and all that was required was, in effect, for a switch to be flipped to 'on'. Despite this, the company in question tried to make a full connection charge of over one hundred pounds to each flat. When I queried this, the woman I was speaking to halved the cost at a stroke. I still felt robbed.

What made the difference?

In each of the above examples although I ended up with what I wanted, something went wrong with the transaction. In the first instance I was delighted and went on both to buy more things from that shop and recommend it to friends. In the second, I was left feeling angry and cheated, and my heart sinks if ever I have to contact that organisation. What made the difference?

Good customer service is maddeningly intangible. Although we all know it when we experience it, it means different things to different people, expectations may be coloured by prior knowledge, and even the same person on a different day can perceive service differently.

Even so, if we wish to define service, we can do so quite simply: good service meets people's needs and makes them feel good. The skill of the service giver – and I include sales people here – is in identifying those needs in the first place.

Moments of truth

Every time you interact with a customer face to face, on the telephone or in writing, you make an impression, whether good or bad. These interactions are 'moments of truth' and they give the opportunity to provide a memorable experience for the customer.

'It's not my counter!'

Have you ever picked up something you wished to buy, headed for a till and been met with those words? Have you then put the item down and walked out without it? I certainly have, more than once. Every bit as bad is: 'It's not my counter, but I'll serve you anyway'. All a customer needs is to be treated courteously and served promptly; and if it is your job to serve customers, then it doesn't matter whether it's your counter or not, that is what you should do – and without sounding as though you are doing people a favour!

'It's not my counter' is an attitude and may also be demonstrated by 'It's not my telephone', '...my department', '...my problem'. If you are the one dealing with the customer, then it is very much your responsibility and you must deal with it accordingly.

People who deal with customers directly have a great deal of power: the power to gain or lose customers for the company, the power to make their own, their colleagues' and their customers' lives easier or more difficult. It is all about personal choice: you chose your job and you choose your behaviour; in a service job, you should drop your problems at the door.

Some time ago I worked with a woman who in the previous year had suffered both a nasty car crash and the death of her mother, to whom she was very close. She then had to deal with the break-up of her long-term relationship, something she didn't want to happen, and the subsequent loss of her home as she could not afford to keep the house on her own. To top it all off, she took a personal phone call from her estranged partner who rang her while she was at work, was overheard by a manager and received a written warning for being on a personal call during work time. (Yes, sadly such organisations still exist.)

You would never have known any of this to hear her on the phone to her customers. She treated them exactly the same as she always had, was cheerful and helpful and got on with the job she was paid to do. Professional to the last, she refused to let her personal situation affect her business performance. Needless to say, I was hugely impressed.

A word about customers...

They don't need you, you need them.

Without customers, you don't have a job; so far from being an unnecessary inconvenience or an interruption to your day, they are the purpose of your day.

Nobody ever won an argument with a customer.

If you treat a customer well, they'll tell a few people about it; if you treat a customer badly, they'll tell EVERYONE about it!!!

Whoever your customer may be, there is one thing they all have in common: their behaviour is generally a direct response to your – or your organisation's – treatment of them.

Danger areas

There are a number of areas that pose particular danger when dealing with customers. Let's consider some of them.

People can't get an answer when they ring you

This is something that people seem universally to hate. The problem is compounded when an unanswered telephone doesn't trip over to an answering machine, or if messages left prompt no response.

Ideally a telephone should be answered within three rings. With each additional ring, tension starts to build.

Perhaps the most hated telephone systems of all are those that require callers to press a series of buttons before – if they are lucky – they are allowed to speak to a person. We all know that they have their uses, but they are incredibly frustrating, especially when they send the caller round in ever decreasing circles or interrupt a caller on hold every twenty seconds or so with a pointless and patronising message about how important their call is. If you must have such a system, call it yourself on a regular basis and see how easy it is to get to where you want to be. If you start to get annoyed, then imagine how your customers feel.

Letters and emails go unanswered

Written communications should be dealt with promptly. Emails should ideally be at least acknowledged within 24 hours, letters within two days.

People stand and wait, unacknowledged by staff

There is absolutely no excuse for this – it is appallingly rude. At the very least, your frontline people should give a nod and a smile to the next in line. If you want to see how a professional does it, watch a good bartender.

Appointments aren't kept

We have probably all taken time off work and waited in for people who simply do not turn up. This is a massive source of irritation for people and shows tremendous arrogance and disrespect on behalf of the company concerned. Companies who treat their customers like this simply do not deserve to have them; if you find you cannot keep a pre-arranged appointment, let your customer know as soon as possible.

Promises aren't kept

There may be reasons outside of your control that mean you cannot keep a promise made to a customer. If so, then let the customer know as soon as you can, explain the situation, and make alternative arrangements that you stick to no matter what. It is a good idea to 'underpromise and overdeliver'. In other words, if you think you can resolve a problem in two days but know it could take three, tell the customer it will take three days; they will then be happy if it takes the full three days and delighted if it only takes two.

Staff blame one another for problems

Any business should present a united front when dealing with customers. I don't mean 'close ranks' by this, I mean that they should operate as a single unit. As soon as a finger is pointed in blame ('That'll be our accounts department – they always get it wrong!') or eyes are rolled, credibility is lost. If your staff don't respect or trust one another, then why on earth should a customer respect or trust your company?

Staff don't care

Apathy is fatal for business. If this is a problem in your organisation, then you need to get to the bottom of it promptly. Don't just punish people, find out what the root cause of the problem is. What is the attitude that cascades form senior management? How well do the staff believe they are treated or valued? If they feel that no one cares or nothing matters, then they will pass that message on to others.

Systems are unhelpful or ridiculous

I suspect we've all been at the mercy of 'computer says "no"' at some point, although the most ridiculous example I have encountered so far is when I wanted to change the name on a telecoms account from mine to that of my (then) husband. The only thing to be changed was the given name: the surname, address and bank account the bill was to be paid out of were to remain exactly the same. However, I was told 'The computer won't let me' and that the only way in which this could be done was if the account in my name was cancelled, which would attract a penalty charge as the 12-month contract period was not up. The line would then have to be disconnected, although we were told it should be reconnected within 14 days with a new number once my husband had been accepted as a new customer. Finally a new contract would have to be agreed and a new direct debit set up, after which we might be able to have our old phone number back. Everyone I spoke to while trying to sort this out was apathetic and unhelpful. I dislike intensely having to deal with that particular organisation, as their staff seem to be almost universally ill-informed, they so very rarely do what they say they will, and their systems appear to be designed to hinder, rather than help the customer.

Even when in the grip of systems that hinder rather than help, however, remember that you choose your behaviour. It is also a good idea to lobby for change if processes or equipment that persistently cause problems exist.

Top ten golden rules for great service

1. Be available – don't keep customers waiting unnecessarily.

2. Don't blame others in the organisation for problems, operate as a single unit.

3. Treat all your customers courteously and with respect.

4. Keep your promises wherever possible.

5. If you cannot keep a promise, contact the customer as soon as you can and make alternative arrangements.

6. Underpromise and overdeliver.

7. Know your products, services and systems thoroughly.

8. Avoid apathy at all costs.

9. No matter how you feel or what you are coping with, you should not take it out on your customers.

10. Make sure that your 'moments of truth' provide positive, memorable experiences for your customers.

We'll come back to Lynne in a little while.

Complaints

An organisation often gets its best chance to shine when something goes wrong: that is the true test of the boasts made about customer service and the importance of customers. There are many reasons why good service – and good complaint handling skills and procedures – are beneficial, including:

- no problems, or satisfactorily resolved problems, keep the money coming in as there is no valid reason for a customer to withhold payment;

- customers are confident enough in the company and its products/ services to offer repeat and/or additional business, and recommend you to others; and,

- if a problem does arise, good systems, procedures and standards of service mean it can be resolved swiftly and cost-effectively.

If a customer is taking the trouble to complain, they either still wish to be your customer or they have no choice in the matter. Monopoly still exists in some areas.

Six point plan for effective complaint handling

We can use the mnemonic Good Customers Make Pay Days Possible to remember the steps to follow when handling complaints. The steps are:

1. Get the facts
2. Check your understanding
3. Make sure information is accurate
4. Propose a course of action
5. Do what you said you would
6. Pursue progress to completion

Let's look at those in more detail.

Get the facts

Ask open questions and listen to the answers. Don't assume anything – the customer might have a problem that is similar to something that has cropped up before, but the detail might be different. Take your time to be sure you have all the facts relating to this particular issue.

Check your understanding

Go through things as you understand them with the customer. If your understanding is complete you can move on, if not, you can correct where necessary. By the end of this stage your customer should be feeling reassured that you know what the situation is.

Make sure information is accurate

Where necessary, check details with colleagues. If you find any discrepancies, go back to the customer. If it turns out that the fault lies with the customer, not the company, you must tell them without making them feel stupid. Be polite and show respect. Don't say 'You don't understand' or 'You got it wrong'; instead focus on the facts and simply explain the situation.

Propose a course of action

Based on what you have found out and your own knowledge and experience, propose a course of action and make sure the customer understands what will happen and by when.

Do what you said you would

It goes without saying, but make sure you initiate action on the issue. As mentioned earlier, always keep your customer informed and if there is a genuine reason why something will not happen as described, get in touch and tell them.

Pursue progress to completion

If you are relying on others to do things for you, keep tabs on them and chase them up if necessary. Keep your customer informed and when all action is completed, check that they are satisfied.

Some dos and don'ts to bear in mind...

DO:

- Look for trends

- Take personal responsibility

- Learn from it

- Make it easy for customers to complain to you

DON'T:

- Conceal levels of dissatisfaction

- Take it out on staff

- Point the finger elsewhere

A complaint is a form of feedback on a company's performance. Your complaints system is a form of ongoing appraisal system. Always distinguish between attack and appraisal. Always look for the kernel of truth.

Angry customers

Customers who are angry are feeling very emotional, and it is as vital that you deal with the emotion effectively as it is that you get the facts and resolve the problem.

- Stay cool, but acknowledge the emotion. Smiles are normally helpful to communication, but not when a customer is angry – it will make it look as if you are laughing at him.

- Let the customer get it out of their system.

- Empathise. Nod, use phrases like 'I understand', let them know it's okay to be angry (but not to be aggressive). Beware of nodding too much. A contact of mine was sitting in on a meeting and was, in his opinion, empathising with a client who was angry by nodding his understanding only to have her exclaim 'Who are you? Noddy? Are you trying to be funny?'

- Focus on the facts. Once the emotion has been acknowledged, it needs to be put aside. Focusing on the facts will help you to achieve this.

- Apologise if necessary, but only when both you and the customer know what the apology is for.

Customer service strategy

In order that customer service is kept at the forefront of an organisation's culture, it is a good idea to develop a specific customer service strategy. This should be an integral part of the overall business strategy, recorded, and communicated to everyone who needs to know.

A good place to start is to find out where you stand in the eyes of your customers. Initiate a customer satisfaction survey to find out what they want and what they think of your performance so far. Use this information to inform your training strategy and set performance standards. It can be a good idea to develop a mission statement. Keep it short, simple and memorable.

Don't conduct a survey as a one-off activity; collect this information on a regular basis. You should also measure performance against standards and reward success.

Some organisations employ 'mystery shoppers' to randomly sample goods and services to see how they measure up. If this is something you are interested in, there are specialist agencies that can handle the procedure for you.

It can be helpful to know how you measure up against the competition; contact a competitor and make a slightly tricky request at a difficult time (lunchtime or closing time, for example) and see how they cope. Then do the same thing with your own company to see how you compare.

Make sure that staff are empowered – within limits – to take decisions and actions without always having to refer to a manager for permission. This allows them to deal with routine issues more quickly and avoids bumping up outstanding query levels.

Regulation

You should also be aware that in some industries, for example financial services, complaint handling policies and procedures might be dictated or influenced by external regulation (e.g. the Financial Services and Markets Act). This may outline requirements such as timescales for handling complaints, or customers' options if they remain dissatisfied.

Unresolved complaints handled by certain types of businesses may also ultimately be referred to an independent ombudsman service for adjudication, such as Energywatch, the Financial Ombudsman Service or Otelo (Office of the Telecommunications Ombudsman). Even if the Ombudsman's final ruling is made in favour of the company, a 'case fee' is often charged, which means it makes sound financial sense to resolve complaints amicably with your customers, rather than let things get that far.

Conclusion

The quality of your customer service is a key way in which you can gain competitive advantage, resulting in a bigger share of the available market. It takes time and dedication to get policies and procedures in place and to train your staff, but the costs incurred ought to pay off in spades.

Exercise: Lynne's lunchtime encounter

Earlier in the chapter we took a look at Lynne who was just getting back to work after popping out for a sandwich when a customer started telling her all about her woes. At that time, we asked:

What should Lynne do?

In the light of what you have learned, use the space below to answer that question. There are some suggestions at the end of the chapter.

_____

_____

_____

_____

_____

_____

Customer service checklist

- I am conscious of moments of truth and take care to handle them carefully.

- I own the problem.

- I do not point the finger of blame at others.

- I am conscious of danger areas and take action to minimise adverse effects.

- I am aware of the impact of staff morale on the standard of service offered to customers and do what I can to keep morale up.

- I know how to handle complaints so that they don't come back.

- I welcome complaints as a means of feedback that allows me to improve the performance of the business.

- I know how to handle angry customers.

Case notes: Lynne's lunchtime encounter

It's a no-brainer, isn't it? Lynne must take responsibility for dealing with the customer's problem. She can delegate the tasks needed to resolve the situation and she may well need to speak to the advertising manager to agree on compensation, but even though the encounter was a chance one, it is now up to Lynne to take the problem on.

Further reading

In print:

- Incredible Customer Service: The Final Test; David Freemantle; McGraw-Hill Book Company (1992)

- A Complaint is a Gift; Janelle Barlow and Claus Moller, Berrett-Koehler Publishers (1996)

- Beyond the Next Wave: Imagining the Next Generation of Customers; Glen Peters, Pitman Publishing (1996)

- How to Win Customers and Keep Them for Life; Michael LeBoeuf, Judy Piatkus (Publishers) Ltd (1987)

- Customer First: A Strategy for Quality Service; Denis Walker, Gower (1990)

- Effective Customer Care, Amanda Knight, The Directory of Social Change (1999)

Online:

- http://www.instituteofcustomerservice.com/ – the website of the Institute of Customer Service.

- http://www.ukcsi.com/ – The UK Customer Satisfaction Index website.

- http://www.thewowawards.com/ – Customer Service Awards site.

- http://www.businessballs.com/customer_service.htm – information on customer service for the businessballs website.

- http://managementhelp.org/customer/service.htm – information on customer service from the Free Management Library website.

Chapter 6.4
Project planning and management

NVQ Application:

This chapter is relevant to the following NVQ in Management Units:

- C4 Lead change
- C5 Plan change
- C6 Implement change
- D9 Build and manage teams
- E1 Manage a budget
- F1 Manage a project
- F2 Manage a programme of complementary projects

Linked chapters:

The information in this chapter is related to information in the following chapters:

- 1.2 Clear communication
- 1.3 Managing your time
- 3.1 Managing and implementing change
- 4.1 Employing people
- 4.2 Establishing and managing relationships
- 4.3 Building and leading the team
- 4.4 Developing and motivating others

- 4.5 Ensuring productive meetings

- 4.6 Effective negotiation

- 5.1 Financial planning, management and control

- 5.2 Setting and working with budgets

- 5.3 Managing resources

- 5.4 Working with suppliers

- 6.5 Problem solving and decision-making

Introduction

The ability to effectively plan and manage projects is a requirement of all businesses, large and small. Some may be wide-ranging, complicated and high budget, others may be small-scale, simple and low budget. Some, such as a product launch, may be one-off events; others, such as building a website, may be repeated time and again for different clients with minor – or major – adjustments to the process, and the customer might be internal or external. Whichever of the above criteria apply, the same approach to planning and management should help to ensure success.

Objectives

The aim of this chapter is to provide a framework that enables you to plan and manage projects effectively. It will help you to:

- be aware of a variety of project planning techniques and choose to use the most appropriate for your needs;

- devise and implement a plan for your project;

- monitor progress against the plan; and,

- evaluate and report on the outcome.

What is a 'project'?

Work is generally described as a 'project' when something has a precisely defined outcome and definite start and end dates. For some organisations, such as consultancies, projects are the basis of all work; for others, projects run alongside regular tasks. As a general rule, a project:

- is a one-off event;

- is time-bound;

- involves change of some sort;

- has clearly defined, measurable and achievable objectives that are easy to understand; and,

- has a specific outcome.

Advantages of project planning

There are a number of advantages to taking a planned and strategic approach to your projects, including:

- it ensures nothing is overlooked;

- tasks may be completed in a logical order;

- the project timeline can be clearly seen;

- it highlights points where there may be too much or too little for the team to complete;

- dependencies and potential bottlenecks are identified; and,

- it becomes much easier to identify the resources required.

Project stages of progression

As with most things, a step-by-step approach to projects pays dividends and ensures you keep control. The main stages a project goes through are as follows:

- Agree the scope of the project and set objectives.
- Develop the project plan.
- Secure resources.
- Define roles and responsibilities.
- Control and monitor progress.
- Close, evaluate and report.

Agree scope and set objectives

Defining and refining the specification and scope of a project begins with the initial enquiry or instruction. The required outcomes must be clearly understood from the outset; if you do not know exactly what it is that you need to achieve, you cannot identify the steps necessary to get results. It's like developing a recipe: until you know how you want the finished product to look, feel and taste, you cannot decide upon the ingredients, preparation and cooking processes involved.

The outcome will be agreed with the customer, who may be your manager or a paying client, and the deadline will very likely also be set at this point.

Develop the project plan

Once you are clear as to the purpose and nature of the project, you can begin to plan to achieve that. The nature of 'how' will depend upon many things: the culture of your organisation, the pool of skills and knowledge you may draw from, and your own preferences and experience.

The project plan for this book was relatively simple: the purpose, outline content and deadline were agreed with the publisher in advance and, armed with that information, I prepared a plan that showed:

- how much time would be spent on research, how much on writing, and finally how much on review, proof-reading and editing; and,

- what tasks had to be completed, on a week-by-week basis, to ensure the deadline was met.

I prepared a Gantt chart to keep tabs on progress – it was easy for me (or anyone else with an interest) to see at a glance where I was supposed to be with the project and to then compare that with where I was.

Writing the book was especially straightforward to plan because to create the first draft, I had only my own activity to take into account. This isn't always the case, however.

In a previous job, working within customer services, I was struck by how many times staff couldn't find the right bit of information, or came across something for the first time that stumped them. I took it upon myself to conduct an informal survey as to the kind of things they would like to have at their fingertips, then prepared a proposal for the creation of the customer services desk aid, an *aide memoire* that sat on the desktop and was easy to flip through to find information. (These days it would all be on computer!) I got the go-ahead and a budget and completed the project, which was deemed to be a huge success. As a consequence, I was asked to manage a project to provide desk aids for each of the various departments that fell under the operations umbrella.

I had two choices. On the one hand, I could handle the project entirely myself, spending time in each department conducting the same type of survey and then gathering all the relevant information to create the desk aid. This would have been time consuming and I was concerned that I would miss the small details that make the big difference, knowledge of which comes from experience. Alternatively I could form a project team by asking managers for a representative from each department who would then create a desk aid for their area of expertise. I plumped for the latter; those people had specific experience and specialist knowledge that would add immense value to the finished product, and also boost ownership and acceptance. Also, a great deal of time was saved and we were able to have a 'launch', as all departments got their desk aids together.

The steps followed were:

- define scope and outcomes and set deadline;

- bring together the team, brief them fully and set a timetable for completion of work;

- hold regular meetings – and one-to-one support sessions – so that we could monitor progress;

- deliver the finished product to each department on schedule; and,

- evaluate, report – and celebrate our success.

Project work like this may be seen as the essence of management: getting things done through other people.

Secure resources

Perhaps the first thing you need to identify and secure are the members of the core project team, who need to be engaged and enthused about the project as early as possible. In addition to your core team, you will most likely need admin support and perhaps temporary staff and/or contractors/specialists.

You will also need to secure finance and to work out how your budget will be spent. If it appears to be insufficient, you must renegotiate and try to get your budget raised; if this cannot be done, then you must see if it is possible to cut costs somewhere.

Securing finance and appointing your core project team is a chicken and egg scenario. People will very likely be your biggest cost, and without an idea of budget, it can be difficult to know whom you can afford. Tricky as this can be, you must negotiate and move your plans forward.

Define roles and responsibilities

Once you have your team and you know what you must achieve, it is time to break down the project into tasks and to assign those tasks, and specific roles, to individuals within the team. Some tasks and role responsibilities will be obvious; if you have one or more 'experts' in your team, for example. Others might take a bit more negotiation.

Project work is a great way to help develop staff, to challenge their 'comfort zones' and to allow them to take on extra responsibility. Don't be afraid to try this; just be sure you have adequate support and reporting procedures in place should anyone need help.

Control and monitor progress

The key to control is to break the project down into tasks and, where necessary, break down the task into smaller, more manageable units of activity. It is a good idea to set milestones, because they:

- represent specific stages with regard to achievement;
- show progress at a glance to all; and,
- focus overall attention on results.

Milestones must be set for progress points that are readily verifiable so that there is no doubt whatsoever when a milestone has been reached.

Whilst you will choose what to monitor and how often, much of your monitoring will be dictated by the requirements of the funder, client or senior management team. Useful activities include:

- regular team meetings;
- critical checks; and
- management reports.

Things that we monitor and control include:

- time;
- cost; and,
- quality.

These are arguably the key indicators as to success. When choosing specific things to monitor, remember the Pareto principle and aim to monitor at least the 20 per cent of things that affect 80 per cent of the outcome.

Reporting should be easy to complete and regular. Consider a monthly (or weekly, depending upon your timescale) form or checklist. Be always alert to potential improvements and never be afraid to tweak things – or even, if necessary, change them radically – if it will improve working or reporting practices. Flexibility is key: it is better to bend than to break and we would be foolish if we didn't put into action what we learn from our experiences.

Dealing with failure

Arguably the most important step to getting back on track if things have gone awry is to admit that there is problem. Once you have acknowledged that it exists, you need to be able to define it as clearly as possible and work out the implications. Try the following steps:

- identify exactly what has gone wrong and be careful to define it in terms of the cause of the problem, not the symptoms;
- investigate why this happened;
- calculate what it will cost you (in terms of time and money) to get back on track;
- agree amendments with stakeholders;
- document and record changes; and,
- add whatever is necessary to the monitoring process to prevent it happening again.

Close, evaluate and report

Once the project work has been completed, there are some final tasks to carry out. These include:

- Cut off cost centres – set a date after which no more charges to the project will be accepted. Allow a little time for final invoices and time sheets to come in, but you must have a cut-off point, not least so that you can report on how you performed against budget.

- Write your final report, indicating how you performed against such things as time, quality and budget.

- Finally, don't forget to celebrate your successes!

Project planning techniques

Project management is dependent upon the project manager having a clear understanding not only of what the desired outcome of the project is, but also of the available resources, individual tasks, milestones and final deadline upon which that outcome is dependent. Detailed and accurate scheduling and monitoring is essential and whilst hand-drawn charts are better than none at all, it is a good idea to use computer based information that ideally can be shared by network with all members of the team (although you may have to restrict who has the authority to amend documents).

A number of project planning techniques exist, including:

- flow charting;
- task analysis charts;
- Gantt charts;
- histograms;
- critical path analysis;
- event scheduling; and,
- PRINCE2.

Flow charting

A flow chart represents a process in a graphical model. It makes it easy to identify the (often sequential) steps required to complete a task and can both help people understand the process better and identify areas that are potentially problematic.

The following is a simple flow chart prepared by a training manager to cover the design and delivery of a customer services workshop.

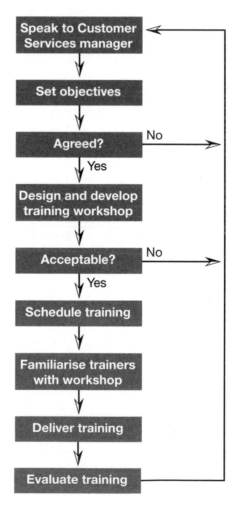

Example flow chart

Well-drawn flow charts can help with the preparation of both task analysis and Gantt charts and can also facilitate the identification of the critical path.

Task analysis charts

Having created a flow chart and numbered tasks in the order in which they must be completed, it is a straightforward matter to then devise a task analysis chart.

The chart below expands on the flow chart example above. For ease, I have included only people in the resources section.

Task no.	Task description	Dependency	Deadline	Resources
1	Speak to CS manager		Week 1	Training manager CS manager
2	Set objectives	Task 1	Week 1	Training manager CS manager
3	Design and develop workshop	Tasks 1 & 2	Week 3	Training manager Training admin
4	Schedule training	Tasks 2 & 3	Week 4	Training admin CS supervisor
5	Train the trainers	Task 3	Week 4	Training manager Trainers
6	Deliver training	Tasks 3 & 5	Week 7	Trainers
7	Evaluate	Task 5	Week 8	Training manager Training admin CS manager

Example task analysis chart

Gantt charts

Devised by and named after Henry Gantt in around 1910, the Gantt chart is a powerful tool for project managers and schedulers. It is a horizontal bar chart that provides an at-a-glance overview of a project, highlighting dependencies and milestones and showing how long each task requires – or has available to it – for completion.

The following example continues the theme of our customer services training workshop.

Task Week →	1	2	3	4	5	6	7	8
Meet CS manager	█							
Set objectives	█							
Design/develop workshop	█	█	█					
Schedule training			█	█				
Train the trainers			█	█				
Deliver training				█	█	█	█	
Evaluate							█	█

Example Gantt chart

I use Gantts a lot and find them very useful indeed. For more complex projects, however, a Gantt chart might be used in conjunction with a resources histogram. The benefit of this is that whilst a Gantt is easy to read, it does not give an indication of the magnitude of any particular task, merely the time in which it is to be completed. A resources histogram will show the magnitude as well as the duration of a task.

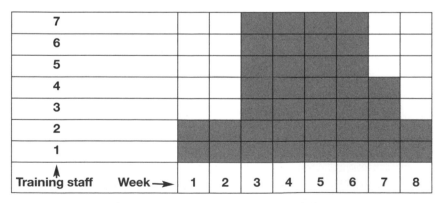

Example resources histogram

Critical path analysis

The critical path of a project may be shown by tracing a line through those tasks on the dependency network that have no slack; this is the path where, if slippage occurs, the end date will also slip.

Event scheduling

Event scheduling is used when it is necessary to prepare a detailed plan for a specific and distinct activity: perhaps a launch day or a press conference. Planning for such an event is likely to begin well in advance. If it is an annual event, then planning for the next year might begin in the aftermath of the current year's event in order that lessons learned aren't lost or forgotten.

You should aim to list each step in the process and to break each one down into tasks. 'Secure a venue' might break down as follows:

- research possible venues online;

- speak to my network and ask for recommendations and warnings;

- draw up a long list and contact each for price and availability;

- arrange to visit those that fit the bill;

- prepare a shortlist and present to senior management; and,

- contract with selected venue.

PRINCE2

The acronym is derived as follows: **PR**ojects **IN** **C**ontrolled Environments. PRINCE2 is a process-based project management method that was developed and is used extensively by the UK government. The method developed and grew over a number of years and whilst it was initially intended for use with IT based projects, by the launch of the current version in 1996, the IT terminology had been taken out. It is recognised widely in the private sector, both nationally and internationally, and the method is freely available to all. There are training courses you can attend and doing so might give you additional insights – as well as something to put on your

CV – but you are free to access and follow the guidelines without doing that. The 'Further reading' section contains information that will help you to find out more about PRINCE2, if you should so wish.

Conclusion

Having a framework within which to operate makes even complicated projects easier to plan, manage and control. Within a business, no project exists in isolation. To use a cliché – but one that is also an accurate analogy – it's all about keeping your plates spinning. Keeping on top of not only all the elements of your project (or projects), but the elements of others that impact on it and that it in turn impacts upon. Taking a step-by-step methodical approach helps massively in that process.

Exercise: Induction update

Earlier in the chapter we took a look at your manager's request that you review and update the telephone skills course used on the induction programme. At that time, the following questions were raised:

Who do you talk to?

What questions do you ask?

What are your first steps?

In the light of what you have learned since, use the space below to answer those questions. There are some suggestions at the end of the chapter.

_____

_____

_____

_____

Project planning and management checklist

- A project generally has definite start and end dates and a defined outcome.

- Addressing the tasks within a framework increases the chances of success.

- The main stages a project goes through are as follows:
  - Agree the scope of the project and set objectives;
  - Develop the project plan;
  - Secure resources;
  - Define roles and responsibilities;
  - Control and monitor progress; and,
  - Close, evaluate and report.

- A number of project planning techniques exist to help with planning and monitoring, including flow charts, Gantt charts, and resources histograms.

Case notes: Induction update

Whether you personally have training experience or not, don't let that put you off – this is simply a project like any other and your approach would be the same. Your first steps are to agree the scope of the project and set objectives.

You need to know:

- what the deadline is;
- if the whole induction is being revamped or just this workshop;
- if the time allotted for the workshop has changed;
- if the objectives of the workshop have changed; and,
- if the current workshop meets the needs of trainees and managers.

You will get some of this information from your manager, but you may also need to speak with other managers whose staff undertake the induction programme to see if they have any insights. You will very likely wish to speak with your colleagues to get their thoughts and perhaps to some of the people who have been through the course to see how useful it was, what they found most or least useful and so on.

Once you have all the necessary information, you can move on to draw up your plan.

Further reading

In print:

- Project Management, Phil Baguley, Teach Yourself (2008)

- The Essentials of Project Management, Dennis Locke, Gower (1988)

- Successful Project Management in a Week (2nd edition), Mark Brown, Hodder and Stoughton (1998)

- PRINCE2 for Dummies, Nick Graham, John Wiley & Sons Ltd (2008)

- Managing Projects Large and Small: The Fundamental Skills for Delivering on Budget and on Time, Harvard Business School Press (2004)

Online:

- http://www.prince2.com/ – PRINCE2 project management resource website.

- http://managementhelp.org/plan_dec/project/project.htm – information on project management from the Free Business Library.

- http://www.businessballs.com/project.htm – information on project management from the businessballs website.

- http://www.projectsmart.co.uk/project-planning-step-by-step. html – guide to project planning on the Project Smart website.

- http://www.mindtools.com/pages/main/newMN_PPM.htm – information on project management tools on the Mind Tools website.

Chapter 6.5
Problem solving and decision-making

NVQ Application:

This chapter is relevant to the following NVQ in Management Units:

- B3 Develop a strategic plan for your business

- C4 Lead change

- E10 Take effective decisions

- F1 Manage a project

- F2 Manage a programme of complementary projects

- F5 Resolve customer service problems

- F6 Monitor and solve customer service problems

Linked chapters:

The information in this chapter is related to information in the following chapters:

- 1.2 Clear communication

- 2.2 Strategic management and business planning

- 2.3 Operating within the law

- 3.1 Managing and implementing change

- 3.2 Innovation and creativity

- 4.6 Effective negotiation

- 6.3 Customer service

- 6.4 Project planning and management

Introduction

We all face problems to be solved and decisions to be made on a daily basis, in work and in life. Some are simple, relatively straightforward and safe, whilst others may be complicated, difficult and involve a degree of risk.

The Kepner-Tregoe method of rational decision-making draws a distinction between:

- problems, which are deviances from the norm;

- plans, which are the means of dealing with potential problems; and,

- decisions, which are choices between alternatives.

They see problem analysis as being concerned with identifying the cause of a situation whereas decision-making is about taking corrective action.

Whatever we may face, there are tried and tested methods and techniques that we can call on to help us so that the decisions we make and the way in which we implement them are less risky – or at least, so that the risks they pose are calculated ones.

Objectives

The aim of this chapter is to acquaint you with some of the various methods and approaches available to you when you are faced with issues that require resolution. It will help you to:

- understand the problem solving process;

- be familiar with the different types of decision you might be called upon to make;

- know when it is most appropriate to involve others in the process;

- use creativity in problem solving and decision-making;

- gain the commitment and backing you need to implement even unpopular or difficult decisions; and,

- evaluate effectiveness.

The problem solving process

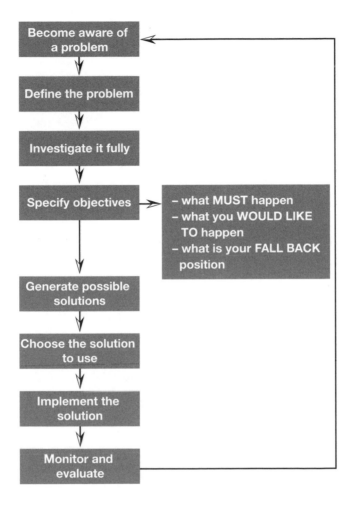

If we accept the premise that a problem is the difference between what *is* happening and what you *would like to be* happening, and a decision is a considered response to remedy that situation, then the above diagram gives us a framework within which we may operate.

We'll return to Dawn and her dilemma later. First, let's move on to take a step-by-step look at the problem solving process.

Become aware of a problem

It sounds obvious, but until we become aware of a problem, it effectively does not exist for us. There are a number of ways we can become aware of problems:

- catastrophic event;
- regular reporting;
- shop floor whispers and rumours;
- tip-offs from your network; and,
- the news.

Catastrophic event

There are two ways in which this could happen:

- Sudden and unavoidable, such as a severe storm that blows up and rips the roof off your house. In business terms, this might be a major technological change that sees your market rapidly eroded, a product your company makes that has sudden and serious bad press, a fault in a product that causes recall for health and safety reasons, even the sudden death of a senior figure or supporter.

  Gerald Ratner famously made a speech at the Institute of Directors in 1991 in which he described his company's products as 'crap'. The fallout from that speech resulted in the near collapse of his previously very popular and successful company. His defence was that he was speaking at a private function and did not expect his words, which he insists were in jest, to be reported. Nevertheless, they were, and the result was catastrophic.

- As the result of something of which you were unaware, but that had been going on for some time, such as a leaking pipe under the upstairs bathroom floor that eventually results in the kitchen ceiling coming down. In business terms, this might mean an ongoing incidence of fraud or a fault in a manufacturing process.

  Between 1992 and 1995, Barings Bank trader Nick Leeson hid losses from his employer that ended up totalling £827 million and caused the collapse of the bank. Perhaps ironically, the final straw was the Kobe earthquake, which had a devastating effect on the Asian financial markets.

Regular reporting

If you are monitoring key figures on a regular basis, then variances will alert you to any changes.

'Shop floor' whispers and rumours

You can be sure if there is anything untoward going on, the staff will know and will talk about it. You may or may not be approached directly, depending upon the seniority of the person concerned, how serious the issue is deemed to be, the culture of your company or some other reason, but if you talk to your staff and keep your ear to the ground you stand a good chance of finding out if there is something of which you should be aware.

Over the years, I have known people claim overtime for hours they didn't work, approach customers with a view to starting a business with poached clients, and steal. Then there are the rows, affairs, instances of bullying and favouritism that impact adversely on the staff and the business. It is these kinds of things you might find out about, along with faults in systems and procedures or an individual or team causing problems for others. Talk to people, keep in touch and be approachable.

A word to the wise here: whilst I would generally advocate that you do not take a problem to your manager without having first considered what the solution might be, and that you similarly would ask for recommendations from anyone who brings a problem to you, there are some problems that manifest themselves at a level where this is impossible. By all means encourage people to suggest solutions where appropriate, but do recognise that there are some that simply cannot be resolved, even in theory, by people with a particular level of knowledge, expertise and authority. Nor is resolving such problems their job: they have done their job in this instance by alerting you to the situation.

Tip-offs from your network

One of the major benefits of developing a network is that if one of your contacts gets a tip off, they will pass it on to you if it seems relevant (and of course you would return the favour). Don't under-estimate this source of information; if you and your contacts are all conscientious about developing your own networks, then your reach can be very long indeed.

The news

Keep an eye on the news as big problems may well first be hinted at here. Don't just take on board the basic story, think of what the implications of a happening may be. If one of your biggest customers collapses, then the problem is obvious; if, however, that company is reported as having removed contracts from or failed to renew them with one or more other suppliers, what caused their actions and where might you stand with them?

Define the problem

Once you are aware that something is not quite right, you should define it in clear, unambiguous terms so that you and any others involved are able to understand it easily.

Imagine you are the owner of a chain of coffee shops: one shop in particular is causing you a problem and is generating the majority of customer complaints. A number of issues are highlighted, but one thing comes up time and again: people do not like the coffee. You may go on to define your problem as follows: *the coffee being served in the High Street café is of substandard quality in terms of flavour and temperature*. You now know exactly what it is that you must address.

Investigate it fully

Get to the root of the problem and make sure that when you are seeking solutions, you are seeking to resolve the problem and not merely treat the symptoms. For example, if your problem is that you suffer from recurring headaches, you need to find the cause. Is it your eyesight, the amount of time you spend in front of a computer screen, or is your hat too tight? The problem is defined in the same terms in each case, but the cause is very different.

Fishbone diagrams

Fishbone diagrams, also known as 'cause-effect diagrams', were developed by Kaoru Ishikawa in the 1960s and are used to highlight the causes of events. The information they contain is generally drawn from six sources, as shown in the diagram below.

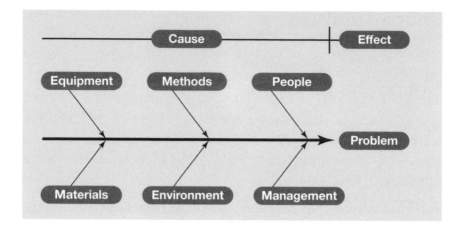

The coffee shop owner might investigate his problem and complete a diagram as follows:

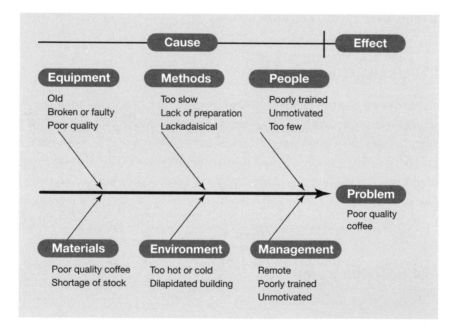

This gives a range of factors that need to be addressed and will lead on to decisions as to where to start and how to tackle the issues.

Specify objectives

In terms of:

- what MUST happen;

- what you WOULD LIKE TO happen; and,

- what is your FALL BACK position.

Force field analysis

Initially developed in the field of Social Science, force field analysis is a useful and simple technique for looking at those forces that are driving an issue forward alongside those that are hindering progress. Understanding the forces at play will help you to set realistic and achievable objectives. Force field analysis may also prove useful when breaking a problem down to get at the underlying cause.

A force field diagram prepared by our coffee shop owner might look like this:

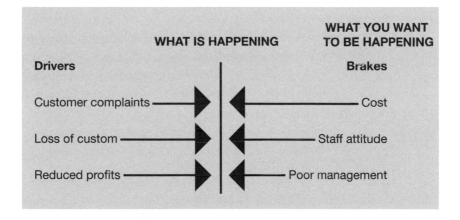

Generate possible solutions

When seeking a solution, your first decision is whether to work alone or to seek the input of a group of people. You might be better working with a group if:

- The scope of the problem is quite broad.

- A number of people are affected.

- Information is required from a range of areas and sources.

- There are likely to be a number of quite different ways to address the issue.

- Cross-function commitment will be required for successful implementation of the solution.

When the opposite is true and you face a basically straightforward issue affecting few people, then you are probably best working alone.

Problem solving groups

Despite the potential drawbacks – usually behavioural, such as political game-playing or grandstanding – working with a group of people to generate a solution has many advantages. You get to draw on a wealth of experience and knowledge, you make inroads into gaining commitment purely because a number of departments have a stake in the process, and you get the benefit of different viewpoints of the problem. Edward de Bono, the father of lateral thinking, asserts that to come up with a creative solution to a problem, you need to walk around it and view it from different angles; with the right members, your group can do that easily.

The most common technique used is brainstorming, which is a process of generating and recording ideas, no matter how crazy they may sound. Criticism is suspended for the ideas generation stage; evaluation begins only when you have a bunch of ideas to choose from. Consider using a warm-up exercise to get people in the right frame of mind: for example, see how many uses they can think of for a stapler, pencil sharpener or ruler. Don't forget to chip in your own ideas, too.

Choose the solution to use

Making and implementing a decision involves taking a risk; you cannot be completely certain of the outcome. Not making a decision, or making a decision and not acting upon it, will very likely involve a greater degree of risk; it is arguably always better to do something than to do nothing. Some would say doing *anything* is better than doing nothing.

Despite the inherent risk and the fear that may be attached to it, we must make management decisions or else stagnate. Consequently, we must try to choose those actions that give us the best chance of success, or where the inherent risk is understood.

There are several categories of decision:

- one best way decisions: these have one obvious right answer and are very rare;

- emergency decisions: decisions you have to take in a crisis where there is no time for wide research or discussion;

- intuitive decisions: where something just feels right or your 'gut instinct' urges you to take a particular decision;

- daring decisions: risky by nature, as you don't know what the outcome will be until you take action (I think it's the red wire – let's cut it!); and,

- double-edged decisions: where you solve the immediate problem, but at a cost (the hot air balloon is going to crash into the church steeple – but if we throw the dog out of the basket, we'll get enough lift to clear it).

Cooke and Slack, in 'Making Management Decisions', assert that three criteria should be borne in mind when considering options, those being:

- feasibility;

- acceptability; and,

- vulnerability.

When assessing possible solutions, especially if they were generated in a brainstorming session, first discard those that are not viable under any circumstances (for example, those that would be illegal or immoral). Then move on to the rest and use established criteria to evaluate them against your defined objectives. You might consider using:

- payback;

- cost/benefit analysis; and/or,

- lists of pros and cons.

Arguably the main barrier to your success when it comes to effective decision-making is the quality and reliability of the information available to you.

Courage may well be needed. Whilst not all decisions will be popular, that doesn't mean that from a business point of view they are 'bad'. Having the courage to take difficult, unpopular and risky decisions is one of the functions of management. Having said that, you must also be courageous enough to admit if a decision does turn out to be harmful, and to take the responsibility to put things right. Whatever happens, don't put off making a decision until it is too late; you might be forced down a route that is wholly inappropriate.

Once your decision has been made, you must let people know. If you have included payback or cost/benefit analysis as part of your decision-making criteria, then this information can be very useful to you now; talking in terms of benefits can be very persuasive.

Implement the solution

Your ability to make and act upon a decision depends upon a number of factors, including:

- your area of responsibility;

- your level of authority;

- the resources at your disposal; and,

- your own knowledge, skills and abilities.

Implementation may well involve preparing a project plan; this will also mean that you consider carefully the resources required and have a schedule for action and completion.

Monitor and evaluate

Monitor progress and take corrective action if required during the implementation stage. Once the project has been completed, evaluate not only the eventual outcome but also the efficacy of the various stages of the problem solving and decision-making process. This may lead you back into problem solving, depending on what your findings are.

Conclusion

Choosing solutions to problems can be straightforward or can be risky and worrying. Taking a step-by-step approach helps us to be sure we haven't overlooked anything and confident that our decisions are sound. Practice helps, as you become more adept at using the various tools and techniques available to you. Have courage, act boldly and learn from experience – both your own and that of colleagues and contacts.

Problem solving and decision-making checklist

- I understand the difference between problems and decisions.

- I am familiar with the problem solving process.

- I appreciate that there are a number of ways in which problems may be identified, including as a result of catastrophe, regular reporting, rumour, tip-offs, and the news.

- Once I become aware of a problem, I take time to define and investigate it.

- I specify objectives.

- I use techniques such as fishbone diagrams and brainstorming to help with the process.

- I know when it is best to involve others in the process.

- I use established criteria to help choose the best option to take.

- I inform the appropriate people.

- I implement solutions in a planned and methodical way.

- I monitor progress and evaluate the outcome.

Case notes: Dawn's dilemma

Before she decides anything, Dawn needs more information. Is Jenny planning to do anything special during her week off or would she be prepared to change it? How would the remaining three team leaders feel about managing between them for that week? If they agree to do it, will that be seen to have set a precedent? When is the training course to be held next? Could Rob and Phil agree between them as to which one should go this time? Would they both prefer to wait for a later course so they could attend together? If so, would one of the remaining team leaders like to go?

Once Dawn has all the facts, she can decide on her course of action. Her decision is important as it could affect staff morale, but not critical as it will not have an immediate and detrimental affect on the business. She does have to decide quickly, though, as there is a limited amount of time in which to operate.

Further reading

In print:

- How to be a Better Problem Solver, Michael Stevens, Kogan Page (1996)

- How to be a Better Decision Maker, Alan Barker, Kogan Page (1996)

- Making Management Decisions, S. Cooke and N. Slack, Prentice Hall (1990)

- The Rational Manager – a Systematic Approach to Problem Solving and Decision Making, Charles H. Kepner and Benjamin B. Tregoe, McGraw-Hill (1965)

- Serious Creativity, Edward de Bono, HarperCollins Publishing (1992)

- Creativity and Problem Solving at Work, Tudor Rickards, Gower Publishing Ltd (1997)

Online:

- http://www.businessballs.com/problemsolving.htm – information on problem solving and decision-making from the businessballs website.

- http://managementhelp.org/prsn_prd/prb_bsc.htm – 'Basic guidelines to problem solving and decision making' on the Free Management Library website.

- http://hbswk.hbs.edu/topics/decisionmaking.html – information on problem solving and decision making from the Harvard Business School's Working Knowledge website.

- http://training.fema.gov/EMIWeb/downloads/IS241.pdf – independent study of problem solving and decision making from the US Federal Emergency Management Agency.

- http://www.mindtools.com/pages/main/newMN_TED.htm – information on decision making techniques on the Mind Tools website.

Chapter 6.6
Implementing and managing quality systems and procedures

NVQ Application:

This chapter is relevant to the following NVQ in Management Units:

- F12 Improve organisational performance
- F13 Manage quality audits
- F14 Prepare for and participate in quality audits
- F15 Carry out quality audits

Linked chapters:

The information in this chapter is related to information in the following chapters:

- 1.2 Clear communication
- 1.3 Managing your time
- 2.2 Strategic management and business planning
- 2.3 Operating within the law
- 6.4 Project planning and management

Introduction

'Quality' is a term that has been bandied about a lot in recent decades. The concept has its roots much further back, in the changes brought about by the Industrial Revolution when, instead of a craftsman taking sole responsibility for producing something, the task was broken down into 'processes' with different people completing different ones. A requirement for some method of checking came about so that mistakes weren't perpetuated and standards were maintained. From that inauspicious beginning came the raft of procedure and legislation that exists today.

The concept, however, is a sound one. 'Quality' makes good business sense. It contributes directly to the viability, success and profitability of a business. Quality hits the bottom line.

Objectives

The aim of this chapter is to explain what 'quality' is and how it can benefit your organisation. It will help you to:

- understand the concept of Total Quality Management (TQM);

- know how to undertake a quality initiative;

- implement and maintain quality systems; and,

- carry out regular quality systems audits.

What do we mean by 'quality'?

The definition can be somewhat elusive. In this instance, for example, 'quality' does not necessarily mean 'expensive' or 'exclusive'. Nor can it be implied that a 'quality' item is made from top class materials or that ownership imparts a certain cachet to the owner. For our purposes we are going to accept that 'quality' means 'fit for purpose'; in other words, it does exactly what the purchaser requires and expects it to do. Consequently we can see that a plastic clothes peg can be as highly rated as an Aston Martin.

Quality inspection

Quality inspections are intended to weed out defective products. They can be beneficial in so far as they can stop a batch of defective parts reaching the production line, which would otherwise result in a whole batch of defective finished goods, but the shortcoming of the process is inherent in its nature.

Inspection of quality occurs after the event; the error has already been made and the costs incurred. Yes, more money can be saved in the long run by having quality inspections rather than not having them, but whilst quality inspection will prevent faulty parts from going any further in a production process and faulty goods from going out of the factory gate, it cannot stop the error from happening in the first place. (Although it ought to stop it from happening again.)

This is as true of inspections of widgets and car parts for defects as it is of sampling letters to customers for accuracy.

Quality assurance

Quality assurance goes further than quality inspection in that it takes a broader view of the concept of quality, looking not just at the end product but also at the processes involved in creating it. Whilst inspection aims for control but is costly in that it finds mistakes that have already been made, assurance strives for prevention and a situation of continuous improvement. Having said that, inspection alone is better than no check whatsoever: without either, or if systems fail, the results include returns, repairs, possible product recall, customer complaints, possible payments of compensation and loss of reputation. The more robust system is quality assurance, however, and we will return to it and examine it in more detail shortly.

Total Quality Management

Total Quality Management, or TQM, takes a holistic look at an organisation. The overarching objective is to meet the needs of customers and to do that all aspects of operation come under scrutiny: systems, processes, management, and people. Rather than a process like quality control or a system like quality assurance, TQM is a philosophy, one that is embraced by the entire workforce from top to bottom and embedded in the culture of the organisation.

ISO 9000

An internationally recognised standard for quality systems, awarded and regularly assessed by an independent body. The organisation responsible for maintaining the standard is the ISO itself, the International Organization for Standardization. Various other organisations can act as consultants or trainers to help with implementation if an organisation so chooses. The Standard is awarded following a successful assessment of systems by an Accredited Certification Body, any one of a number of such organisations that have been formed to audit applying organisations. Certificates issued are accepted worldwide.

Advantages of accreditation

Accreditation brings a whole range of advantages, including:

- it opens the doors to new business, as some people may insist on it as a pre-requisite of doing business;
- it is something to advertise and promote;
- it forces examination of processes and creation of procedures, which, done properly, will reduce waste and promote efficiency;
- it boosts employee engagement and motivation; and,
- it promotes international trade.

Issues to consider include:

- the cost, in terms of both time and money;

- the amount of paperwork that will be generated;

- there is an emphasis on documentation and compliance, not involvement and improvement;

- there is a lot of jargon and the process can be 'user-unfriendly'; and,

- there is a great danger that accreditation becomes an end in itself, rather than a means to improve the way things are done.

In this chapter we are going to look at quality assurance implementation, with or without accreditation. The principles are sound and the ISO itself advocates that quality systems can be successfully implemented without accreditation and yet still bring benefits to the business.

Case study: Alan's audit

Supervisor Alan has responsibility for 'quality' in the marketing department. Manager Hayley has told him that there will be a quality audit in a week's time. She has made it clear that she expects the department to 'pass' with flying colours.

The quality manual has not been updated in some years. Alan knows for a fact that Hayley has never opened it; in fact, she sees the whole 'quality' aspect of business as a paperwork exercise and a chore. He knows that the manual is full of procedures that may have been followed when it was written but that certainly aren't now – they are out of date and inaccurate. Alan strongly feels that this situation is wrong and knows from experience that they make things more difficult when someone new comes into the department. He sees that the audit has the potential to allow him to put things right – but knows it will be at the expense of his relationship with Hayley.

What should Alan do?

We'll return to Alan later.

Establishing quality assurance systems

When seeking to establish quality assurance systems, it pays to take a strategic approach. We are going to look now at a four step process that offers a framework for success.

Step one

Your first step, the one that will pave the way and set the direction for implementation, is to be very clear about why you are doing it. Take time over this as it will form the backbone of the message you give to staff and other stakeholders in order to gain their support and commitment. Set out first of all what it is that you want to achieve, and then list the perceived benefits. The first of those actions will give you your objectives for your implementation plan and the second your 'sales message' to gain support for the initiative. Talking in benefits is very persuasive; it helps people to see what is in it for them.

You should encapsulate this information in a policy statement. The policy statement should both take into account the needs of the customer and outline the way in which the business will operate.

Your implementation plan, based on sound project planning principles, should include the following information:

- the rationale for the initiative;
- the aims and objectives;
- the methodology;
- roles and responsibilities;
- resources required;
- timescale; and,
- monitoring and evaluation procedures.

Step two

Your next step is to get people involved. The support and commitment required to see a quality initiative through comes from the people affected by it, and the best way to gain it is through involvement and inclusion. There are a number of ways in which you can do this, including:

- gct as many people as is possible/practicable involved;
- appoint a quality manager;
- appoint a steering group; and,
- consider establishing quality circles.

Let's look at those in more detail.

Get people involved

The best way to promote ownership and improve your chances of gaining acceptance is to get as many people as is reasonable involved in analysing processes and developing procedures. The best procedures in the world will change nothing if people feel alienated and so refuse to use them.

Appoint a quality manager

This might be someone from within the organisation who has a passion for quality or a new appointee with relevant experience who can help with all aspects of implementation. (This can be especially useful if you are pursuing accreditation.) The purpose is twofold: firstly, it means that one person is dedicated to overseeing the entire operation and secondly, it provides the initiative with a figurehead. Having someone regularly report back on progress to all concerned can be a powerful tool and help keep the momentum going in the tricky middle section of implementation, when the buzz of launch has faded and yet the finish line is still some way off. The quality manager should be:

- an advocate for change;
- a promoter of quality issues;
- an effective communicator;
- a skilled analyst; and,
- a problem solver.

Appoint a steering group

The steering group – or Quality Improvement Forum – is the main body responsible for all decisions regarding quality management. A good steering group can make sure that no one loses sight of the original – and ultimate – destination. The purpose is not to have a bunch of managers who will carp and criticise, but to have the benefit of the experience and opinion of a diverse group of staff at all levels, with the possible addition of other stakeholders. Try to cover all functions; the steer will be more complete if the group can view the project from all angles. Whilst the purpose of the group is not to carp and criticise, it is equally not to back-slap and rubberstamp everything. Progress should be evaluated, deviances should be investigated and successes should be celebrated.

Consider establishing quality circles

Quality circles are voluntary groups that meet regularly in work time with the aim of identifying, analysing and finding solutions to work-related problems. Solutions are then presented as recommendations to management. Whilst the role does not commence until after quality implementation, deciding whether they are appropriate and scheduling in training for those involved is an integral part of the planning procedure.

Step three

Analyse the processes involved in delivering the products or services provided by the business. Having a step-by-step understanding of this allows you to determine how to measure quality levels and will allow you to develop procedures and write work instructions where necessary.

Procedures should offer a detailed definition of the activities performed and the responsibilities of the individual within each area of operation. Usually these are sufficient in themselves, but in the case of specialist or complicated activities, work instructions giving more detail may be required. If so, it is not necessary to repeat the information; simply use the procedure to refer to the work instruction.

When writing procedures and work instructions, stick to the following guidelines:

- use simple, clear, unambiguous language;

- keep it as brief as possible;

- be precise; and,

- stick to the facts.

All procedures and work instructions should be tested to check that they accurately reflect both the requirements of the task and the actual job done. Remember that someone who has never carried out a particular task before should be able to (unless there are, for example, specialist tools or machines to be used) complete the task by following the instructions. Creating these documents will take time but should cause little disruption; they are intended to formalise the working process, not to change it – unless of course, change is desirable.

The Quality Manual

The Quality Manual is the co-ordinating document for the quality system you are putting in place. It should contain the policy statement mentioned earlier, an organisation chart, and – if accreditation is to be sought – an indication of how the standards link to the procedures. Individual areas will have their own manuals containing procedures and work instructions.

Step four

If you have got this far, then you will be close to your implementation day. Celebrate the full launch of your quality programme. Plan at least a big event for staff and stakeholders, and issue press releases. This should be the start of an ongoing initiative where successes are publicised. Remember to talk in terms of benefits when you write about the success of the initiative, whether it's for the staff newsletter or a press release, the same guidelines apply: show people what it means for them.

Quality audits

Implementing your quality assurance system is only the first stage in the process; once you have your system in place, you must hold regular audits to ensure procedures are still relevant and are being followed. Audits are not just about checking that people are doing what the manual says they should, they are arguably more about checking that the documented process helps staff to do what they need to do. It is a means of confirming that the quality procedure is robust and effective, and initiating change if it is not.

It is advisable to schedule a series of planned audits throughout the year, supplemented by spot checks on targeted areas and procedures.

To further gather information and feedback from employees, consider having some sort of suggestion scheme, with a reward for good ideas that are introduced or implemented.

It is a good idea to tie your quality assurance scheme into customer care policies so that you can gather and benefit from feedback from customers.

Conclusion

If 'TQM' is a philosophy and 'quality' is a concept, how does that help the business? Well whilst there is no denying that in the initial stages there will be cost with little financial benefit as the system is established and introduced, over time a robust quality system should more than earn its keep. It is important that 'quality' is not seen as something to be endured: get the manuals written, gain accreditation, suffer the audits and hang on in there. Above all, promote the concept of continuous improvement; it is not a case of 'job done' when you have planned and implemented a quality assurance initiative: that is only the start.

Implementing and managing quality systems and procedures checklist

- I understand what the term 'quality' means in this instance.

- I appreciate both the benefits and shortcomings of quality inspections.

- I understand the differences between quality inspections and quality assurance.

- I understand that TQM is a philosophy.

- I know the best way to successfully introduce a quality initiative is to take a step-by-step approach.

- I appreciate what it is that quality audits aim to do.

Case notes: Alan's audit

Alan has a tough decision to make here, having to choose between what he knows is right and keeping a lazy manager happy.

The deciding factor is surely that having an out-of-date quality manual makes things more difficult when inducting new starters. The message it gives about the standards in the department is not a good one: if the manager and supervisor don't care about quality, then why on earth should the staff? Alan needs to find a way to persuade Hayley to allow him and the staff to work on updating the procedures. It is unacceptable of her to ask Alan to cover up – and anyway, a thorough audit ought to uncover the inaccuracies without him saying anything! If they can show the manual to be currently a 'work in progress' than that is surely better than 'failing' an inspection.

Further reading

In print:

- Total Quality Management, John S. Oakland, Heinemann (1989)

- Achieve Total Quality, David Hutchins, Director Books (1992)

- Take a Quality Ride: The Realities of Implementing a Quality Management System, Susan M. Hinkle, iUniverse.com (2006)

- Quality Management Demystified, Sid Kemp, McGraw-Hill Professional (2006)

- Quality Without Tears: The Art of Hassle-Free Management, Philip B. Crosby, McGraw-Hill Professional (1995)

Online:

- http://www.thecqi.org/ – the website of the Chartered Quality Institute.

- http://www.businessballs.com/dtiresources/quality_management _systems_QMS.pdf – information on quality management systems form the businessballs website.

- http://www.managementhelp.org/quality/quality.htm – information on quality management from the Free Management Library website.

- http://www.businesslink.gov.uk/bdotg/action/layer?topicId=1074 431977 – information on quality management standards on the Business Link website.

- http://www.quality.co.uk/ – the Quality Network website.

Last words

Towards the end of 2009, a Chartered Management Institute (CMI) survey showed that almost half of UK workers had left a job because of bad management. It isn't just the workers who are disenchanted: 68 per cent of managers said that they had fallen into the role by chance and 40 per cent admitted that they had not wanted the responsibility of managing people at all.

The CMI have launched a Manifesto for a Better Managed Britain. Ruth Spellman, Chief Executive of the CMI, asserts that 'We need a management and leadership revolution to meet the economic, social and political challenges facing Britain.'

Not all revolutions are born in blood and thunder. This one is most likely to be born in an attitude of quiet determination and application to the task in hand. And for many people, especially those who are pursuing planned personal development and have a clear idea of both where they are going and how long the journey will take, the process will be more evolutionary than revolutionary.

Having said that, great changes are needed in order that the UK keeps up with European neighbours. Planning your personal development and aiming to be the best manager that you can be is an essential part of that process.

May I wish you the very best of luck in your endeavours.

Appendices

Appendices

Appendix 1:
The standards mapped to the chapters

Part 1 – Managing yourself

- 1.1 Planning and managing your own professional development
  A1; A2

- 1.2 Clear communication
  A1; A2; A3; B5; B6; B7; D1; D2; D10; D12; E11

- 1.3 Managing your time
  A1; A2

- 1.4 Managing information and developing networks
  A1; A2; A3; D1; D2; D17; E11; E12; E13

Part 2 – Managing the business

- 2.1 Leadership, culture and vision
  B5; B6; B7; B9

- 2.2 Strategic management and business planning
  B1; B2; B3; B4; B10; D4; E8; F3

- 2.3 Operating within the law
  B1; B3; B4; B8; B11; B12; D3; D16; E5; E6; E7; E9

Part 3 – Managing change

- 3.1 Managing and implementing change
  C4; C5; C6

- 3.2 Innovation and opportunity
  C1; C2; C3

Part 4 – Managing people

- 4.1 Employing people
  D3; D4; D15

- 4.2 Establishing and managing relationships
  D1; D2; D10; D17

- 4.3 Building and leading the team
  B5; D5; D6; D8; D9; D14; E14

- 4.4 Developing and motivating others
  B5; B9; D5; D6; D7; D8; D13

- 4.5 Ensuring productive meetings
  D11; D12; E11

- 4.6 Effective negotiation
  D12; D17; E1; E15; F19

Part 5 – Managing resources

- 5.1 Financial planning, management and control
  E1; E2; E3

- 5.2 Setting and working with budgets
  E1; E2; E15; F1; F4

- 5.3 Managing resources
  D5; D6; E4; E8; E11; E12; E13

- 5.4 Working with suppliers
  D17; E15; E16; E17

Part 6 – Managing progress

- 6.1 Market research
  B1; B2; B3; F9; F16

- 6.2 Marketing and selling
  F4; F16; F18; F19

- 6.3 Customer service
  B3; F5; F6; F7; F8; F10; F11; F17

- 6.4 Project planning and management
  C4; C5; C6; D9; E1; F1; F2

- 6.5 Problem solving and decision-making
  B3; C4; E10; F1; F2; F5; F6

- 6.6 Implementing and managing quality systems and procedures
  F12; F13; F14; F15

Appendix 2:
The chapters mapped to the standards

Section A – Managing self and personal skills

- A1 Manage your own resources
  1.1; 1.2; 1.3; 1.4

- A2 Manage your own resources and professional development
  1.1; 1.2; 1.3; 1.4

- A3 Develop your personal networks
  1.2; 1.4

Section B – Providing direction

- B1 Develop and implement operational plans for your area of responsibility
  2.2; 2.3; 6.1

- B2 Map the environment in which your organisation operates
  2.2; 6.1

- B3 Develop a strategic business plan for your organisation
  2.2; 2.3; 6.1; 6.3; 6.5

- B4 Put the strategic business plan into action
  2.2; 2.3

- B5 Provide leadership for your team
  1.2; 2.1; 4.3; 4.4

- B6 Provide leadership in your area of responsibility
  1.2; 2.1

- B7 Provide leadership for your organisation
  1.2; 2.1

- B8 Ensure compliance with legal, regulatory, ethical and social requirements

  2.3

- B9 Develop the culture of your organisation

  2.1; 4.4

- B10 Manage risk

  2.2

- B11 Promote equality of opportunity, diversity and inclusion in your area of responsibility

  2.3

- B12 Promote equality of opportunity, diversity and inclusion in your organisation

  2.3

Section C – Facilitating change

- C1 Encourage innovation in your team

  3.2

- C2 Encourage innovation in your area of responsibility

  3.2

- C3 Encourage innovation in your organisation

  3.2

- C4 Lead change

  3.1; 6.4; 6.5

- C5 Plan change

  3.1; 6.4

- C6 Implement change

  3.1; 6.4

Section D – Working with people

- D1 Develop productive working relationships with colleagues

  1.2; 1.4; 4.2

- D2 Develop productive working relationships with colleagues and stakeholders

  1.2; 1.4; 4.2

- D3 Recruit, select and keep colleagues

  2.3; 4.1

- D4 Plan the workforce

  2.2; 4.1

- D5 Allocate and check work in your team

  4.3; 4.4; 5.3

- D6 Allocate and monitor the progress and quality of work in your area of responsibility

  4.3; 4.4; 5.3

- D7 Provide learning opportunities for colleagues

  4.4

- D8 Help team members address problems affecting their performance

  4.3; 4.4

- D9 Build and manage teams

  4.3; 6.4

- D10 Reduce and manage conflict in your team

  1.2; 4.2

- D11 Lead meetings

  4.5

- D12 Participate in meetings
  1.2; 4.5; 4.6

- D13 Support individuals to develop and maintain their performance
  4.4

- D14 Initiate and follow disciplinary procedure
  4.3

- D15 Initiate and follow grievance procedure
  4.1

- D16 Manage redundancies in your area of responsibility
  2.3

- D17 Build and sustain collaborative relationships with other organisations
  1.4; 4.2; 4.6; 5.4

Section E – Using resources

- E1 Manage a budget
  4.6; 5.1; 5.2; 6.4

- E2 Manage finance for your area of responsibility
  5.1; 5.2

- E3 Obtain additional finance for the organisation
  5.1

- E4 Promote the use of technology within your organisation
  5.3

- E5 Ensure your own actions reduce risks to health and safety
  2.3

- E6 Ensure health and safety requirements are met in your area of responsibility

  2.3

- E7 Ensure an effective organisational approach to health and safety

  2.3

- E8 Manage physical resources

  2.2; 5.3

- E9 Manage the environmental impact of your work

  2.3

- E10 Take effective decisions

  6.5

- E11 Communicate information and knowledge

  1.2; 1.4; 4.5; 5.3

- E12 Manage knowledge in your area of responsibility

  1.4; 5.3

- E13 Promote knowledge management in your organisation

  1.4; 5.3

- E14 Support team and virtual working

  4.3

- E15 Procure supplies

  4.6; 5.2; 5.4

- E16 Select suppliers through a tendering process

  5.4

- E17 Outsource business processes

  5.4

Section F – Achieving results

- F1 Manage a project

  5.2; 6.4; 6.5

- F2 Manage a programme of complementary projects

  6.4; 6.5

- F3 Manage business processes

  2.2

- F4 Develop and implement marketing plans for your area of responsibility

  5.2; 6.2

- F5 Resolve customer service problems

  6.3; 6.5

- F6 Monitor and solve customer service problems

  6.3; 6.5

- F7 Support customer service improvements

  6.3

- F8 Work with others to improve customer service

  6.3

- F9 Build your organisation's understanding of its market and customers

  6.1

- F10 Develop a customer focussed organisation

  6.3

- F11 Manage the achievement of customer satisfaction

  6.3

- F12 Improve organisational performance

  6.6

- F13 Manage quality systems

  6.6

- F14 Prepare for and participate in quality audits

  6.6

- F15 Carry out quality audits

  6.6

- F16 Manage the development and marketing of products/services in your area of responsibility

  6.1; 6.2

- F17 Manage the delivery of customer service in your area of responsibility

  6.3

- F18 Prepare sales proposals and deliver sales presentations

  6.2

- F19 Sell products/services to customers

  4.6; 6.2

Other titles from Thorogood

Managing People for the First Time

Julie Lewthwaite • ISBN: 9781854183323

Absolutely everybody in all types of organisation – business, professional, governmental, academic – has to make the critical leap to managing people for the first time. There are countless books on managing people but very little written from the perspective of the novice, someone faced with the daunting task of changing from following instructions to giving them.

'The value of this book is that it makes a worthwhile attempt to help the first-time manager. Combining training material with a storyline involving real people makes it a lot more digestible than a textbook. I was 39 before I became a director of a new business, with almost no experience of managing other people or relationships... Lewthwaite's book would have been extremely useful.' **PEOPLE MANAGEMENT, JUNE 2006**

Me Time: Lifecoach Yourself to Success

Barrie Pearson and Neil Thomas • ISBN: 9781854186072

Most coaching books are written – unsurprisingly – by coaches. This book has been written by two highly successful entrepreneurs who've actually followed and tested the advice they preach with very positive results.

We all spend most of our waking hours working for other people and even if we're self-employed we spend too little time thinking strategically and planning our own futures.

The authors show you how to put yourself first for a change, how to properly understand your strengths and weaknesses and how to build a blue-print for success in life that can become a reality.

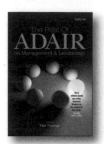

The Best of John Adair on Leadership and Management

Edited by Neil Thomas • ISBN: 9781854186089

This is a goldmine of ideas, advice and techniques from one of the world's leading writers on management and leadership. It brings together all of John Adair's thinking on leadership, teambuilding, creativity and innovation, problem-solving, motivation, communication and time-management.

Full of practical guidance, experience and insight, it's packed with a large number of charts, diagrams and forms. This is a repackaged and updated edition of the best-selling John Adair Handbook.

'A book for constant reference... A great achievement... ought to be found on every manager's bookshelf.'
JOURNAL OF THE INSTITUTE OF PUBLIC SECTOR MANAGEMENT

'[John Adair is] without doubt one of the foremost thinkers on the subject in the world.' **SIR JOHN HARVEY-JONES**

Janner's Complete Speechmaker

Greville Janner • ISBN: 9781854182173

The 'bible' – the definitive source of expertise for anyone who has to give a speech, make a presentation or chair a meeting. Fully updated, revised and expanded.

'Indispensable' **FINANCIAL TIMES**

'An excellent primer for those wishing to deal with the media.' **ADAM BOULTON, SKY NEWS**

Negotiate to Succeed

Julie Lewthwaite • ISBN: 9781854181534

Modern business relies on the ability to reach mutually beneficial agreements. You need the skills to plan, deliver and follow through on negotiations. This book provides accessible, practical guidance and techniques for negotiating, including:

- Useful skills for the negotiator
- Dealing with 'people issues'
- Negotiation in practice.

Written in a straightforward, non-academic manner, this book provides tips and techniques in a clear, easy-to-use checklist format designed for the busy manager.

The World's Business Cultures

Barry Tomalin and Mike Nicks • ISBN: 9781854186850

With the aid of a specially developed model – The 5 C's Model – expert authors demonstrate how to get your communications right internationally and ensure that meetings, both face-to-face and virtual, go according to plan.

Barry Tomalin and Mike Nicks offer strategies and tactics for getting people from different countries on your side, and detailing the knowledge you need to make the right impression and avoid giving offence. The authors provide a framework for understanding any culture in the world, but include specific chapters on the top 14 economies in the world in 2050, according to Morgan Grenfell bank: China, USA, Germany, UK, Russia, India, Brazil, France, Italy, Spain, The Gulf, Korea, Australia and Japan

'Tomalin and Nicks show how understanding culture can improve performance. Sprinkled with colourful anecdotes, The World's Business Cultures offers sound advice on meetings and negotiations, as well as decision-making, gift-giving and writing e-mails. Although it has chapters on countries forecast to the world's leading economies in 2050, such as India, China and Brazil, the book also warns that we can get it wrong even when dealing with our neighbours.' CLAIRE BARRON – FINANCIAL TIMES

Thorogood also has an extensive range of reports and special briefings which are written specifically for professionals wanting expert information.

For a full listing of all Thorogood publications, or to order any title, please call Thorogood Customer Services on 020 7749 4748 or fax on 020 7729 6110. Alternatively view our website at **www.thorogoodpublishing.co.uk**.

Focused on developing your potential

Falconbury, the sister company to Thorogood publishing, brings together the leading experts from all areas of management and strategic development to provide you with a comprehensive portfolio of action-centred training and learning.

We understand everything managers and leaders need to be, know and do to succeed in today's commercial environment. Each product addresses a different technical or personal development need that will encourage growth and increase your potential for success.

- Practical public training programmes
- Tailored in-company training
- Coaching
- Mentoring
- Topical business seminars
- Trainer bureau/bank
- Adair Leadership Foundation

The most valuable resource in any organisation is its people; it is essential that you invest in the development of your management and leadership skills to ensure your team fulfil their potential. Investment into both personal and professional development has been proven to provide an outstanding ROI through increased productivity in both you and your team. Ultimately leading to a dramatic impact on the bottom line.

With this in mind Falconbury have developed a comprehensive portfolio of training programmes to enable managers of all levels to develop their skills in leadership, communications, finance, people management, change management and all areas vital to achieving success in today's commercial environment.

What Falconbury can offer you?

- Practical applied methodology with a proven results
- Extensive bank of experienced trainers
- Limited attendees to ensure one-to-one guidance
- Up to the minute thinking on management and leadership techniques
- Interactive training
- Balanced mix of theoretical and practical learning
- Learner-centred training
- Excellent cost/quality ratio

Falconbury In-Company Training

Falconbury are aware that a public programme may not be the solution to leadership and management issues arising in your firm. Involving only attendees from your organisation and tailoring the programme to focus on the current challenges you face individually and as a business may be more appropriate. With this in mind we have brought together our most motivated and forward thinking trainers to deliver tailored in-company programmes developed specifically around the needs within your organisation.

All our trainers have a practical commercial background and highly refined people skills. During the course of the programme they act as facilitator, trainer and mentor, adapting their style to ensure that each individual benefits equally from their knowledge to develop new skills.

Falconbury works with each organisation to develop a programme of training that fits your needs.

Mentoring and coaching

Developing and achieving your personal objectives in the workplace is becoming increasingly difficult in today's constantly changing environment. Additionally, as a manager or leader, you are responsible for guiding colleagues towards the realisation of their goals. Sometimes it is easy to lose focus on your short and long-term aims.

Falconbury's one-to-one coaching draws out individual potential by raising self-awareness and understanding, facilitating the learning and performance development that creates excellent managers and leaders. It builds renewed self-confidence and a strong sense of 'can-do' competence, contributing significant benefit to the organisation. Enabling you to focus your energy on developing your potential and that of your colleagues.

Mentoring involves formulating winning strategies, setting goals, monitoring achievements and motivating the whole team whilst achieving a much improved work life balance.

Falconbury – Business Legal Seminars

Falconbury Business Legal Seminars specialises in the provision of high quality training for legal professionals from both in-house and private practice internationally.

The focus of these events is to provide comprehensive and practical training on current international legal thinking and practice in a clear and informative format.

Event subjects include, drafting commercial agreements, employment law, competition law, intellectual property, managing an in-house legal department and international acquisitions.

For more information on all our services please contact Falconbury on +44 (0) 20 7729 6677 or visit the website at: www.falconbury.co.uk.